Teachers are influencers. The faculty are t[...]
into teaching-learning encounters in our [...]
influence leads to equipping and forming Christian leaders for the church
in our world. Along with leading the academic program, a key area of
academic leadership is developing the faculty. To transform theological
education for transformed leaders, the academic leaders must walk with
faculty through their own development as teachers, as scholars, and as
servants of the Lord Jesus Christ.

Drawing on years of investing in leaders around the world, this
final volume from the IPAL training is filled with encouragement and
instruction on this work of faculty development. It will become a much-
referred-to manual for academic leaders in theological schools around the
world. I look forward to seeing theological schools and training programs
renewed as faculty develop through the processes outlined in this volume.
May the Lord transform us, so we can transform others.

Paul Allan Clark, PhD
Director of Education, Overseas Council,
United World Mission

Leadership can be a solitary art. This book not only provides a rich palette
of resources for those involved in leadership positions in theological
education, but also gives a sense of global companionship in the task.

Marvin Oxenham, PhD
Director, ICETE Academy
General Secretary, European Council for Theological Education

Faculty development is directly proportional to the growth of theological
schools. This book contributes to the healthy development of recruitment
and training of faculty. All the contributors are theological experts and
practitioners. Gone are the days when we measure the success of faculty
recruitment by the number of good recruits with excellent grades.
Leaders are not only readers, but mentors who dare to spend more time
in integrating theories with practical matters.

Joseph Shao, PhD
4th General Secretary of Asia Theological Association
President, Biblical Seminary of the Philippines

An integral part of achieving the mission and vision of theological higher education, rests on the ministry of our faculty. This book emphasizes their critical role and brings to our attention the need for a holistic approach to their professional development. The biblical models of Jesus and Paul provide the foundation to a well-rounded analysis of elements that must be considered in order to help our faculty grow, not only in their craft as teachers and educators, but also in their capacity of becoming academic leaders and mentors to others. One excellent component of this book is how it goes from the big picture to very practical tools that can be promptly applied in our schools. A must-read for current and future academic leaders.

Jenniffer Contreras Flores, PhD
Academic Dean, SEMISUD, Ecuador

ICETE Series

Leadership in Theological Education

VOLUME 3

ICETE International Council for Evangelical Theological Education
strengthening evangelical theological education through international cooperation

Langham

GLOBAL LIBRARY

Leadership in Theological Education

VOLUME 3

Foundations for Faculty Development

Edited by

Fritz Deininger and Orbelina Eguizabal

Series Editor

Riad Kassis

ICETE International Council for Evangelical Theological Education
strengthening evangelical theological education through international cooperation

Langham
GLOBAL LIBRARY

© 2018 Fritz Deininger and Orbelina Eguizabal

Published 2018 by Langham Global Library
An imprint of Langham Publishing
www.langhampublishing.org

Langham Publishing and its imprints are a ministry of Langham Partnership

Langham Partnership
PO Box 296, Carlisle, Cumbria, CA3 9WZ, UK
www.langham.org

ISBNs:
978-1-78368-477-9 Print
978-1-78368-478-6 ePub
978-1-78368-479-3 Mobi
978-1-78368-480-9 PDF

British Library Cataloguing-in-Publication Data

A catalogue record for this book is available from the British Library

ISBN: 978-1-78368-477-9

Cover & Book Design: projectluz.com

Contents

Introduction

*F*oundations for Faculty Development is the third volume of the ICETE three-volume series on *Leadership in Theological Education*. It builds upon Volume 1 that establishes the *Foundations for Academic Leadership*, and Volume 2 that provides the *Foundations for Curriculum Design*. The first volume discusses the foundations for theological education, highlights the characteristics and responsibilities of academic leaders, and provides insights into the administrative and leadership practices of academic leaders. The second volume addresses the foundations for curriculum design and development, facilitating the teaching and learning processes involved in curriculum development, and aspects of curriculum development that contribute to the creation of learning communities.

The concept of faculty development has taken different focuses and forms since its beginning in the US, which dates back to 1810 with the institution of sabbatical leave by Harvard University.[1] However, it is only in the last six decades that it has really grown, starting in the late 1950s with the student rights movement, followed by the 1960s and 1970s when the concept as we understand it today started to gain more attention. It evolved from exclusively rewarding research and publication success to a "more holistic focus on, and concomitant reward for, excellence in teaching and serving. . . . Faculty members increasingly advocated that institutional and career rewards, particularly tenure and promotion standards, should reflect a broad understanding of the nature of their work."[2] From the mid-1960s to the 1970s, the shift from research and publishing required the inclusion of instructional and organizational components for improving teaching effectiveness, which led to the emerging of faculty development units in a number of campuses in the 1980s. As faculty developers and faculty development became more

---

1. Matthew L. Ouellett, "Overview of Faculty Development," in *A Guide to Faculty Development*, ed. Kay J. Gillespie, Douglas L. Robertson, and Associates (San Francisco: Jossey-Bass, 2010), 4.
2. Ouellett, "Overview of Faculty Development," 4.

institutionalized, a dramatic paradigm shift took place in the 1990s: "the focus of instructional development moved from what had been a singular focus on the development of the pedagogical expertise and platform skills of teachers (the 'sage' on the 'stage') to include a focus on student learning (teachers as the 'guide on the side')."[3] In the previous and current decades a new approach to faculty development has emerged, which Ouellett, based on Sorcinelli et al. (2006)'s stages of faculty development, refers to as the "Age of the Networker."[4] This stage is characterized by an increasing number of practitioners who "bring specific expertise, such as instructional technology, to educational development."[5] This phenomenon is "strengthening the dialogue between seasoned faculty development practitioners and relative newcomers, with the idea that there is much to learn from each other."[6] Nowadays, faculty development offers "a wide array of programs and involves a growing body of highly professional, deeply dedicated professionals."[7]

Currently, faculty roles in academic institutions include, among many other functions, developing and teaching courses, developing curricular programs, advising students, mentoring students and fellow faculty members, being committed to the achievement of student outcomes, participation on examination committees, writing grant proposals for research funding, serving on a variety of committees, conducting research, writing for publishing, and participating in scholarly activities. In addition to this, a significant number of faculty serve their institutions at different levels of academic leadership, which requires intentional ongoing faculty development programs.

This volume is organized in three sections which focus on foundational and practical aspects of faculty development. In each chapter, the authors develop the roles and functions of faculty, as well as key components of faculty development.

---

3. Ouellett, 6.

4. Ouellett, 7. See M. D. Sorcinelli, A. E. Austin, P. L. Eddy, and A. L. Beach, *Creating the Future of Faculty Development: Learning from the Past, Understanding the Present* (Boston, MA: Anker, 2006).

5. Ouellett, 7.

6. Ouellett, 7.

7. Ann E. Austin and Mary Deane Sorcinelli, "The Future of Faculty Development: Where Are We Going?," *New Directions for Teaching and Learning* 133 (Spring 2013): 85, accessed 9 April 2018, http://wileyonlinelibrarycom, DOI 10.1002/tl.20048.

Part I addresses "Foundational Considerations in Faculty Development." In the *first chapter*, the author discusses the important role of faculty in theological education. He highlights the several factors that determine quality in theological education, including leadership, administration, facilities, academics, teachers, curriculum, students, and resources. However, he argues that teachers play an important role in theological education, related to the institution and the expectations of the students. Understanding the role of faculty is crucial because faculty members are part of the culture of the educational institution. He examines the models of Jesus and Paul as outstanding teachers and draws implications for teachers serving in theological institutions worldwide. As a teacher, Jesus "made an impact in his training of the disciples because of his mature personality, his authority as teacher, and the quality of his life." Similarly, Paul's ambition to know Jesus and live like him made him a teacher with many qualities that allowed him to make an impact on people in his teaching, making disciples, and his writings. In order to help faculty members succeed, academic leaders need to have a good understanding of the institutional environment and expectations of the faculty, in particular faculty expectations concerning their role in the institution. The author highlights the educational expectations of the teachers, including credibility, professional expertise, and the impact that teachers can have on their students as they teach them and prepare them to serve the church.

Due to the critical role of faculty in theological institutions, academic leaders committed to faculty success need to consider how to keep them effective in their teaching. *Chapter 2* provides some definitions and concepts which underline the philosophical foundation for a faculty development model. The author highlights the importance of looking at some key issues in the construction of the model, "so faculty formation has a clarity of target and intention." He argues that the aim of faculty development is to create a model of the excellent teacher, which, considering the biblical perspective of teaching using the models of Jesus and Paul, requires examining the nature and purpose of theological education, paying attention to the re-emphasis on spiritual formation, searching for integration, and considering the relational aspect of theological education. Faculty development includes key areas in which the development of a teacher needs to take place. The objectives of faculty development focus on academic development, professional competence, personal spiritual/discipleship, and calling and ministry development. According to the author, effective faculty development needs to take place in the context of the faculty team, where faculty members can thrive based on a common calling to theological education and a safe space or environment. That space needs to be one of mutual acceptance, respect, accountability to the team, spirituality, love, intellectual and interdisciplinary support, and "an enabling and prophetic space for the churches and society in which the college or seminary is placed."

Another foundational aspect in the development of faculty is the institutional culture. *Chapter 3* addresses the need to understand the institutional culture, which generally is influenced by external and internal factors. Consequently, academic leaders who want their institutions to be effective need to envision and shape an ideal culture, one that is established on a foundation of biblical and academic values. In order to attain such a culture, the school's various levels of leadership need to get on board with its establishment and development, starting with the board of directors (trustees) and the school's top leadership. Faculty and staff, too, can contribute to the planning and implementation of the institution's culture, committing to and living out the mission, vision, and institutional values. A hypothetical case at the end of the chapter helps the reader to see how the institutional culture works. The author concludes, "A healthy institutional culture creates a positive learning environment, projects a model for the students in their ministries, and brings glory to the One for whom the school ultimately exists."

Part II focuses on "Practical Ways in Faculty Development." Each chapter addresses key aspects that determine the success of educational institutions' ongoing efforts toward the development of their faculties. In *Chapter 4* the author suggests various practical steps for designing and implementing a faculty development plan. The first step consists of clarifying the school's goals by defining what is God's calling for each school. He suggests that the school's goals need to include three critical components toward faculty development: a culture of humble service and professional excellence, a culture of collaboration and mutual care, and a culture of growth. The second step has to do with assessing faculty development needs. Learning from faculty members about their areas of interest, expertise, frustrations, and desired growth is critical to a successful faculty development program which also takes into account the institutional culture. Third, determining the resources of time and money is critical in designing a plan, especially for institutions that possess limited resources. Fourth, a review of the available strategies at the outset is key to a successful ongoing development plan. Academic leaders are not limited to strategies that require funds; there are strategies that use resources that already exist in the institution. Fifth, prioritization of strategies and resources is very important. Identifying the highest-priority faculty need and accessibility will help in determining where to start "to move beyond intentions to a plan for the professional development of the faculty." Finally, after a careful process and consideration of the previous steps, implementing the faculty development plan is critical, because faculty are the "greatest resource" and they are "the curriculum of the school," and because as faculty we serve in a world that is constantly changing. The chapter is followed by some sample forms that can guide the reader to perform a class observation and report, annual performance reviews, and student course evaluation.

Among the many day-to-day administrative responsibilities that academic leaders carry out is dealing with faculty as part of building a body of those committed to the institution's educational tasks. The author of *Chapter 5* begins by establishing two premises regarding faculty in theological education. The first is that "theological institutions are first and foremost spiritual entities. Therefore, their faculties must, above all else, be spiritually alive." Second, "faculty members are first and foremost fellow Christians and human beings (1 Cor 12:12–26). Therefore, they must be treated as members of the Christian community." With this in mind, the author highlights some of the complex and challenging administrative responsibilities of academic leaders when it comes to dealing with faculty in the spiritual environment of institutions of theological education. Academic leaders are responsible for recruiting, retaining, and releasing faculty. To maintain the quality of the institution it is essential to hire well-qualified faculty who fit with the faculty and the culture of the institution. In addition, academic leaders can insure the success and retention of newly hired faculty by providing induction, orientation, and support, and by protecting them from overload or unnecessary committee assignments. A more delicate task has to do with releasing some faculty, which may be necessary for different reasons. Resolving conflict among and with faculty also requires immediate attention to preserve unity and harmonious relationships at all levels of the institution. Another challenging demand on the academic leader pointed out by the author is dealing with difficult faculty behavior. Enhancing a relational culture can contribute to a genuine spiritual community. Leaders can lead the faculty using a variety of meetings to enhance communication and a collaborative environment among the faculty community.

Evaluation is another important resource in the development of faculty. *Chapter 6* focuses on how evaluation can help teachers grow. Academic leaders can discover if faculty are competent in their fields, if they have the pedagogical (or andragogical) skills of teaching, if they are positively influencing students through their relationships with them, and if they are responsible in doing what they are supposed to do – and this requires clear expectations. Effective evaluation, according to the author, requires a reference point with clear definitions of the standards that faculty need to achieve through teaching to students. It also requires an adequate perspective to interpret the evaluations that come from students. In order to benefit from any evaluation it must be part of an ongoing evaluation system in the institution. Types of evaluation include self-evaluation, evaluation by students, and evaluation by colleagues. The author identifies the last as the most powerful tool to shape what teachers do, "in affirming their good habits, and in pushing them to change." Faculty can grow in confidence in the teaching team, in understanding how things fit together in the curriculum, and in awareness of the role that they play in shaping a healthy learning community. The author argues for the need for institutional assessment to understand how the faculty are doing, and whether the institution has the right faculty members for the programs it offers.

Part III discusses "Strategic Processes in Faculty Development." Building a faculty team is a strategic process in institutions of theological education due to the role of faculty in the formation of church ministers. *Chapter 7* establishes the foundations for faculty to function as a learning community that "continuously learns to improve and enhance its members' capacities to achieve their shared vision . . . [and] continuously grows together in Christlikeness." Therefore, academic leaders are called to build a faculty team. The foundations for team building highlighted by the author include disciplines such as a shared vision, trust, mental models, and dialogue. Acknowledging that trust is the underlying discipline for team building, the author focuses on and integrates the last two disciplines as critical for team building. The contribution of mental models resides in their influence on "how we act and react, behave, and interpret and view reality, people and experiences." Dialogue, on the other hand, builds upon skills such as listening, respecting, suspending, and voicing. It is enabled by trust. The author discusses several sources which all highlight "the importance of open discussions, constructive communication, conversation, or dialogue as a key practice in developing trust and building teams."

Developing the faculty as mentors is the focus of *Chapter 8* in which the author establishes the premise that "mentoring provides the missing element needed within institutions and beyond them to become more successful in helping fulfill the Great Commission as Christ envisioned it." Effective mentoring requires that faculty members know how to mentor the students and possess a personal commitment to doing so. Educational institutions need to sufficiently value the mentoring of students "to include it as a crucial element in their philosophy of education, and the job descriptions of the faculty and staff." Building upon the biblical foundation by highlighting the examples of teachers such as Jesus and Paul who served as mentors, the author argues for a commitment to mentoring among educational institutions. Academic institutions that want to be effective in mentoring students being trained to serve the Christian community need to include mentoring in the key components of the institution, such as (1) their guiding principles, balancing mentoring with academic rigor; (2) the school's curricula, to ensure it will take place, will be effective, and will be reinforced as part of the institution's DNA; (3) the institution's resource allocations, such as time, facilities, personnel, and funding; and (4) the faculty development plan, providing the picture of an effective mentor, and securing mentors who resemble that picture. The author concludes, "Training effective mentors is not an option for evangelical academic institutions; it is the essence of their calling in helping make Christlike, multiplying disciples."

Similarly, coaching is another concept that has gained attention in recent decades, especially in the business world. However, it has entered other spheres, such as academic circles. Thus, *Chapter 9* discusses how coaching is being used to help faculty members in their career development. The author makes a clear distinction between coaching and training, arguing that the primary objective of training is "meeting the needs and advancing the purposes of the *institution*," while coaching focuses on the individual needs. Another distinction has to do with the means of coaching; thus, while training takes place through instruction, coaching uses the means of inquiry, assessment, and modeling. Helping the faculty to allocate resources, including resources of time, funds, and connections, is also an important part of coaching. The purpose of coaching is to help individual faculty members in their career development, which includes two perspectives: moving from the individual to the collective, and from uniformity to uniqueness. Moving from an individual to a collective view of faculty allows the identification of different faculty profiles, in which the *academic profile* gets more attention. Moving from uniformity to a uniqueness perspective reflects the categories of development needed, including self-understanding, interdisciplinary conversations and contributions, teaching and learning, and biblical integration, which the author suggests should be high priorities in the coaching conversations. Coaching thus cultivates the "individual potential rather than the imposition of conformity to a uniform ideal."

Finally, as I (Orbelina) teach students pursuing their doctorates, I get to interact with them while they are studying and after they graduate. While some have come on our programs to pursue doctoral education specifically because they were already in academic leadership positions or needed the credentials to opt for an academic leadership position, others were not in an academic leadership position nor thinking they would get into academic administration, but have since been appointed as president, dean or academic director, associate dean, department chair, or director of programs. The latter group connect well to the topic that I explore in *Chapter 10* on developing academic leaders among the faculty. In the chapter, I discuss various aspects that can help encourage current academic leaders to consider how to develop their own faculty members and help them to be ready to undertake academic leadership positions in their institutions. First, due to the complexity of academic administration, faculty moving into such positions need to be clear that God is calling them to it. Knowing that they are responding to God's calling and their having a strong desire to support the mission and vision of the institution will help them navigate the challenges of their positions. I also argue that in order to develop academic leaders from among the faculty, it is important to understand the academic leadership structure. Understanding who should develop the emerging leaders or those who are already in position, as well as the challenges of developing academic leaders internally, is critical due to factors such as institutional and faculty culture, decision-making structures, the phenomenon of the influx of outsiders, and sometimes the institution's limited resources. Building leadership capacity will aid in developing the specific skills needed for each leadership level in the institution, and this requires being intentional in using strategies for training and preparing leaders. Some of those strategies are committee assignments, getting faculty and current leaders to participate in formal and informal training programs, mentoring, and personal career development plans, among many others that institutions can identify as effective strategies in their own contexts. In my chapter, I also argue for more opportunities to include female faculty in academic leadership, since women keep proving that they are qualified and can make a great contribution to the institution and therefore to higher education in general.

To conclude, we would like to reiterate the words of Austin and Sorcinelli in the conclusion of their article "The Future of Faculty Development: Where Are We Going?"

> Today, faculty development constitutes a strategic lever for institutional excellence and quality, and a critically important tool for fostering institutional readiness and change in response to the array of complex demands facing universities and colleges. Those working within the faculty development profession can be assured of work that is strategically important, intellectually demanding, and professionally rewarding in its contribution to fostering institutional and individual excellence.[8]

Fritz Deininger and Orbelina Eguizabal
Editors

---

8. Austin and Sorcinelli, "Future of Faculty Development," 95–96.

Part I

Foundational
Considerations in
Faculty Development

1

The Role of Faculty in Theological Education

Fritz Deininger

A chieving excellence in theological education is a challenging objective. It means preparing men and women well for ministry in the church and the world. Giving them the tools they need to manage their own lives and to minister effectively is the task of the seminary and the training programs. Even though academic leaders and faculty play a prominent role in facilitating quality education, it should not be overlooked that other factors contribute to excellence in theological education as well. This is shown in figure 1.1.

Figure 1.1: Factors Contributing to Excellence

As academic leaders develop excellence in theological education, they need to pay attention to all areas in order to discern what needs to be improved. Their task is to define what role each area is playing in the overall achievement of the objectives of the seminary. Facilitating a working relationship among the faculty and staff and an understanding of their important roles in the success and effectiveness of the training programs creates an atmosphere conducive to teaching and learning. This needs to be highlighted because faculty members cannot fulfill their roles in the seminary unless they relate well to other areas of the institution. They do not just teach in the classroom; they are part of the institutional culture.

Before proceeding to the role of the faculty in theological education, it is important to clarify the use of the term "faculty" because it does not convey the same meaning in all educational contexts. The term "faculty" can refer to a department of study in a university setting – for example, the "Faculty of Theology" or the "Faculty of Missiology." In other contexts, the term "faculty" refers to the teachers or professors in an institution, whether it is a university or seminary. This second meaning is the one adopted in this chapter.

In this study, the role of faculty in theological education will be explored, first of all, from a biblical perspective. This is mandatory because teaching theology requires that biblical standards of life are applied to the teacher. The roles of Jesus and Paul as teachers provide valuable insights for teachers today. Then, second, institutional aspects related to the role of the faculty will be considered. Academic leaders and the institution are instrumental in enabling the role of the teacher to be effective in teaching and learning. At the same time, there are expectations on the part of the faculty member that academic leaders need to be aware of. Teachers should fulfill their role within a supportive atmosphere in the institution. In a third part, the focus will be on expectations of the role of teachers from an educational point of view. Their impact as educators on the students, the church, and the world depends on their personal lives as well as on their professional expertise.

Role of Teachers: Biblical Reflections

The Bible is not explicitly a handbook for theological education or faculty development, but it contains much evidence that teaching plays an important part in firmly establishing believers in their faith in Christ and in preparing them for service in the church and the world. Jesus told his disciples to teach believers "to obey everything I have commanded you" (Matt 28:20). The early church adopted the practice of teaching the Word of God regularly (for example, in Acts 2:42). The apostles were aware that teaching, and preaching the Word of God focused on different objectives: "Preaching is for evangelization, to bring sinners to the Savior. Teaching, however, is for edification, to instruct and thereby spiritually nurture believers in Christ. One calls for repentance; the other for discipleship. One is to bring spiritual birth; the other is for spiritual growth."[1]

Many teachers played an important role throughout the Old and New Testaments. However, only two outstanding teachers shall be considered as examples here, namely, Jesus and Paul. Both were servants of God who preached and taught the Word of God. They had an impact on the lives of people who became leaders of the church without formal seminary training.

The Role of Jesus as Teacher

Teaching was certainly an important part of the ministry of Jesus. In his book *Teaching as Jesus Taught*, Roy Zuck provides an interesting statistic: "Of the ninety-five occurrences of the verb *didasko* in the New Testament, more than half (fifty-seven) are in the Gospels, with forty-seven of them referring to Jesus' teaching. The Gospel writers thus reveal that teaching was one of Jesus' most prominent activities. Clearly he was recognized as an eminent Teacher."[2] The statistical evidence indicates that Jesus fulfilled his calling and role as teacher while he was in this world. What made Jesus an effective teacher? How did he fulfill his role as teacher? What impact did his teaching ministry have on people? Some of the characteristics that made Jesus an outstanding teacher will challenge us today as theological educators.

His Maturity as Teacher

Jesus was the Son of God and yet, from a human point of view, he needed to develop like any other person. Luke tells us that Jesus "grew and became strong;

---

1. Roy B. Zuck, *Teaching as Paul Taught* (Grand Rapids, MI: Baker, 1998), 39.
2. Roy B. Zuck, *Teaching as Jesus Taught* (Grand Rapids, MI: Baker, 1995), 29.

he was filled with wisdom, and the grace of God was on him" (Luke 2:40). Luke also records that "Jesus grew in wisdom and stature, and in favor with God and man" (Luke 2:52). Both references suggest that Jesus matured in his life and grew physically (in stature), mentally (in wisdom), spiritually (in favor with God), and socially (in favor with people). Jesus developed into a perfect and mature person. His balanced personality made him a teacher who was loved by the people, such that Luke was able to report: "All spoke well of him and were amazed at the gracious words that came from his lips" (Luke 4:22).

Teachers today certainly can learn from Jesus that "Leading others to accept the things of God calls for teachers today to have balanced personalities – to be growing mentally, spiritually, and socially."[3] The role of teacher starts with a person who has developed to maturity or is open to being developed in the various aspects of life. Effective teaching that impacts the lives of students flows from a mature personality that has been developed in the school of the grace of God.

His Authority as Teacher

After Jesus finished teaching the Sermon on the Mount, people "were amazed at his teaching, because he taught as one who had authority, and not as their teachers of the law" (Matt 7:28–29). The people who listened to the teaching recognized a difference between Jesus and the teachers of the law. Jesus made an impression on the listeners because his teaching was inspired by God. The Jews could not comprehend how Jesus taught with such authority because he had not studied the Scriptures as they had (John 7:15). Jesus told them: "My teaching is not my own. It comes from the one who sent me" (John 7:16).

What made Jesus an authoritative teacher? Two kinds of authority can be distinguished. One is derived authority, which means that the authority has been given by others to someone who is elected or appointed to a position or role, and who exercises authority on the basis of this appointment. This applies to teachers today. Teachers do not appoint themselves to a teaching position; they are called or appointed by God, and also by the theological institution, to teach (the calling will be dealt with in the third section of this chapter). The second kind is inherent authority, which means that the authority is based on

---

3. Zuck, *Teaching as Jesus Taught*, 63.

who the person is or on the inherent position. This kind of authority belonged to Jesus because of his position as the Son of God. "Jesus had authority as a Teacher – not because someone appointed or elected him to that role, but because of who he is. His authority is inherent in his Person, as the eternal Son of God."[4]

Teaching with authority in theological education is an important part of the role of teacher. The authority of the teacher comes from God's Word. "It is not what we say that is authoritative; it is what God says in his written Word. Authoritative teaching lies in what we say *he* says!"[5] Teachers in theological education today need to have a firm biblical foundation to what they pass on to their students.

His Qualities as Teacher

In his extensive and profound study on Jesus as teacher, Roy Zuck, who served as professor of Bible exposition at Dallas Theological Seminary, provides a summary of the qualities of the life and personality of Jesus that made him an outstanding teacher: "The world's most masterful Teacher was the world's most popular Teacher! Why? Because he taught with authority, mastery, certainty, humility, consistency, spontaneity, clarity, urgency, variety, quantity, empathy, intimacy, sensitivity, and relevancy."[6] These characteristics of Jesus's teaching ministry can be seen in the way he taught individuals (e.g. the rich young man, Matt 19:16–22), groups of people (Luke 5:3), and the disciples (Matt 5:1–2), and answered the questions of religious people (the Sadducees, Matt 22:23–32).

As theological educators, it is essential to study the qualities that made Jesus an outstanding teacher. What qualities are needed or expected of a teacher today in a particular context or study program in order for the teaching to be effective? Individual teachers are challenged to reflect on the qualities and to create a personal development plan to help make their role more effective. It also could be an edifying exercise for the faculty to study together Jesus's qualities and learn from them for their roles as teachers. Academic leaders

---

4. Zuck, 45.
5. Zuck, 57.
6. Zuck, 90.

are instrumental in facilitating discussion on the qualities of teachers in theological education.

His Impact as Teacher

Jesus certainly left an impression on many people, including his opponents, through his preaching, teaching, and healing ministry. In this study, the focus is on his impact on the disciples as Jesus prepared them for ministry. What impact did Jesus have on his disciples as a teacher? Why was his teaching so effective in their lives that they became the founding pillars of the church? To what extent did their responsiveness to the teaching and training of Jesus contribute to their spiritual and professional growth? We shall look at just a few areas to illustrate Jesus's lasting impact on those whom he had chosen to carry on the ministry he had begun.

First of all, the impact on the disciples is related to the fact that Jesus had selected the twelve men to be with him, to be trained by him, and to be sent out to serve him (Mark 3:13–19). Their calling was the beginning of a journey in their life development. They were willing to follow Jesus and they committed themselves totally to him. Jesus became their teacher, mentor, and trainer. The two sides of their relationship with Jesus – the calling by Jesus and their commitment – provided the basis for the impact.

Second, the relationship between Jesus and the disciples was based not just on their formal roles as teacher and students; John tells us that Jesus loved his disciples: "Having loved his own who were in the world, he now showed them the full extent of his love" (John 13:1 NIV 1990). This love was expressed in his concern for the disciples. He had confidence in their abilities and he enabled them to carry out the ministry (Matt 10:1). As a teacher, Jesus cared for the disciples and for their holistic development, which certainly prepared them well for the time when Jesus left them.

Third, Jesus made an impact on the lives of the disciples by the way he trained them. Their preparation for ministry did not take place in the formal setting of a seminary; rather, the training they received was the impact of Jesus through his teaching and their practical involvement in many aspects of ministry. Roy Zuck tells us that "Jesus trained them by example, by verbal instruction by his miracles, by personal association, and by involvement. As a result, they were changed individuals, men who, because they believed him and were committed to him, were transformed by him."[7] As a role model, Jesus inspired the disciples so that, for example, when they saw how he communicated with the Father, they came to him to ask, "Lord, teach us to pray" (Luke 11:1).

Fourth, the disciples (except Judas) were remarkably open to the teaching and training of Jesus. This certainly contributed to the impact that Jesus had as teacher. They were open to being taught, corrected, and challenged by Jesus. The lives of the disciples were touched and transformed, and therefore they also became leaders who touched the lives of many others, starting a movement of people coming to faith in Christ. The disciples also taught the believers what they had experienced when they were with their teacher Jesus. When Peter and John were told that they should not speak or teach in the name of Jesus, they affirmed: "We cannot help speaking about what we have seen and heard" (Acts 4:20). What a remarkable testimony to what they had received from Jesus while they were with him!

Jesus was an outstanding teacher. He made an impact in his training of the disciples because of his mature personality, his authority as teacher, and the quality of his life. Even though theological educators today cannot be like Jesus, they can learn from him in order to be effective teachers who impact the lives of their students.

The Role of Paul as Teacher

Besides Jesus as one of the greatest teachers in history, we have the example of the apostle Paul, who was dedicated to God and served in a multifaceted ministry, as Roy Zuck describes in his exposition on Paul's teaching ministry: "He served God as pioneer missionary, a commissioned apostle, a zealous evangelist, an energetic church planter, a prolific writer, an insightful theologian, a vigorous apologist, a dynamic preacher, a warmhearted pastor, and a stimulating teacher."[8]

Paul had an extensive teaching ministry. He reminded the leaders of the church in Ephesus that he had spent much time and energy in teaching the believers: "You know that I have not hesitated to preach anything that would

---

7. Zuck, 121.
8. Zuck, *Teaching as Paul Taught*, 11.

be helpful to you but have taught you publicly and from house to house" (Acts 20:20). Paul's teaching ministry is also shown clearly in his first letter to the Thessalonians, where he describes how he cared for the Christians. For example, he says: "For you know that we dealt with each of you as a father deals with his own children, encouraging, comforting and urging you to live lives worthy of God" (1 Thess 2:11). Roy Zuck accurately describes the teaching ministry: "Teaching requires a heart of concern, comforting and guiding those taught, which in turn calls for careful instruction in biblical truths, the 'food' needed for spiritual growth."[9] Paul's personality was unique, and what he accomplished in his ministry is remarkable. His dedication to teaching and as a teacher can be inspiring for theological educators today. Out of his many qualities, we shall consider three areas that made him an effective teacher.

His Ambition as Teacher

His personal ambition is expressed in the words "I want to know Christ and the power of his resurrection and the fellowship of sharing in his sufferings, becoming like him in his death" (Phil 3:10 NIV 1990). Paul had an excellent theological training under his teacher Gamaliel (Acts 22:3). His profound theological knowledge and understanding can be seen in the way he referred to the Old Testament and in his interpretation of events in the history of Israel (e.g. 1 Cor 10:1–13). After Christ had revealed himself to Paul (Acts 9:1–19), Paul made it his ambition to preach Christ (1 Cor 2:1–5) and to develop his relationship with him.

On the basis of his personal ambition he included the value of true knowledge in his teaching, but he also aimed at the spiritual growth and maturity of those who studied with him. Paul longed to see "Christ . . . formed" in the believers (Gal 4:19). Their lives should evidence maturity in their relationship with God, in their relationships with Christians and those who did not believe in Christ, and in the way they expressed their faith in the circumstances of daily life. For Paul, spiritual maturity was expressed in the ambition to live for Christ (2 Cor 5:15). For him, spiritual development was a matter of "learning" that was related to both content and experience (Rom 6:17; Eph 4:20; 2 Tim 3:14).

---

9. Zuck, 34.

Theological educators need to reflect on their personal ambition as teachers. Is their knowledge of Christ and their relationship with him as important as it was to Paul? Personal ambition is certainly expressed in the teaching and learning objectives. The concern for academic knowledge must be accompanied by the objective to lead the students to spiritual growth and maturity.

His Qualities as Teacher

Roy Zuck provides an impressive list of Paul's qualities as a teacher. The focus is clearly on his character, and only the last quality listed emphasizes his knowledge and teaching skill as part of his exemplary life as a teacher, which tells us something about his commitment to God and his genuine interest in people: "The New Testament information on the church's outstanding apostle repeatedly manifests his godly devotion; his God-given authority and confidence; his personal integrity, honesty, and consistency; genuine humility; thoughtful courtesy; compassionate sensitivity to God and others; bold severity against his and God's opponents; unquenching fervency; dauntless tenacity when beset with numerous adversities and difficulties; deep-seated serenity; heartfelt felicity; and comprehensive mastery of doctrinal and ethical subjects."[10]

Can Paul function as a role model for teachers today? His life qualities are certainly desirable for those who are involved in theological education, according to Roy Zuck's summary: "These twelve characteristics – piety, authority, humility, integrity, courtesy, sensitivity, fervency, tenacity, severity, serenity, felicity, mastery – marked the apostle Paul as a truly outstanding teacher, one who stands as a supreme model for all teachers today."[11]

What qualities are expected of teachers in theological education today? When inviting or hiring faculty, the academic leader faces the challenge to find teachers who have the academic qualifications and the life qualities to be a role model for the students. In my experience in the Asian context, I know that students desire a teacher who knows the subject of teaching well and at the same time is an example who demonstrates biblical values through his or her life. Therefore, Paul would have been an excellent teacher in the Asian context.

---

10. Zuck, 61.
11. Zuck, 108.

His Impact as Teacher

The achievement of the teaching objectives can be measured by the outcome in the lives of the students. As a teacher, Paul was used to impact people in his time and beyond. We highlight two areas where Paul made an impact: he was effective in building the lives of people, and he left a legacy of written documents.

His Impact on People

Paul related to diverse audiences in his teaching and preaching ministry. It is remarkable how he adapted to people from different walks of life or religious backgrounds: "Paul's amazing evangelistic and pedagogical abilities are seen in the varied audiences and individuals he taught. He debated with religious leaders and spoke boldly to political rulers. He talked with an intelligent government administrator, uncultured pagans, well-to-do craftsmen, sophisticated philosophers, prominent women, prisoners, and Roman soldiers. He addressed huge crowds, religiously oriented groups, families, and individuals in private."[12]

An outstanding example of how Paul impacted the lives of individuals is Timothy. The two spent much time together, such that Paul became a mentor, model, and teacher to Timothy (2 Tim 3:10–17). Paul testifies: "You . . . know all about my teaching, my way of life" (2 Tim 3:10). He goes on to exhort Timothy: "But as for you, continue in what you have learned and have become convinced of, because you know those from whom you learned it" (2 Tim 3:14). Timothy absorbed the teaching and example of Paul, such that he became a church leader who in turn impacted other people.

Paul's teaching intentionally focused on multiplication, as he reminds Timothy: "And the things you have heard me say in the presence of many witnesses entrust to reliable people who will also be qualified to teach others" (2 Tim 2:2). The principle of multiplication became an important factor in the church and in evangelistic ministry. Those who believed in Christ spread the gospel (Acts 13:49; 16:5; 1 Thess 1:8). It must have been encouraging for Paul that his teaching motivated the learners to pass on what they had been taught.

---

12. Zuck, 128.

Another aspect, the time he spent in different locations, seems also to have contributed to his impact on people. This gave him the opportunity to teach the Word of God in depth and to instruct the believers in the will of God. The time Paul and Barnabas spent in Antioch certainly contributed to the fact that the church became the center of missions, because they had an extensive teaching ministry there (Acts 14:28; 15:35; 18:23).

The impact Paul had on people is beyond imagination and comprehension. His commitment to lead people to maturity in faith and to train individuals for ministry made him an outstanding teacher: "The number of people who heard the gospel from Paul, the thousands who became believers through his ministry, the many groups of Christians who received instruction from him over extended periods of times, and the scores of individuals who worked with him or were associated with him in some other way – these all evidence the remarkably widespread and deep impact of this man whose life was given totally to Christ and his cause."[13]

Paul's example is a challenge to theological educators today. Like Paul, teachers need to adjust to their audiences of students. Each class is different and might require adaptations in the presentation of the course material, the interaction in the classroom, or in the assignments. The role of the teacher is to foster multiplication. This can start with the course assignments helping the students to understand that the papers they write can be used in teaching others. It is obvious that the role of the teacher is closely related to the development of the individual student.

His Impact through His Writings

Paul's letters have had an impact on the churches and the lives of individuals from his time to the present day. Through his writings he laid the foundations for the Christian life and for theology. His written legacy had a lasting impact because as a theologian he established biblical principles that were valid for generations to come. Paul responded to questions in the churches or in the lives of individuals (1 Cor 7:1). He warned against false teaching and corrected errors (Col 2:8, 16–19). Paul was concerned about the unity of the church and

---

13. Zuck, 141.

the Christian life (Eph 4:1–3). Many other examples could be added, but what is important is that Paul used his writings to teach Christians the way of the Lord. His role as teacher was not limited to the classroom and to the development of individuals for ministry; it was extended to the Christian community.

The role of teachers in theological education today should also be seen as an opportunity to provide solid biblical foundations for the Christian community. Theological educators are in the best position to teach and write about contemporary issues, how to live the Christian life in modern society, or how the church should deal with heresy or false teaching. The legacy of a teacher can be of great value.

Role of Teachers: Institutional Considerations

Teachers are at the heart of the seminary or training program. The responsibility of the academic leader is to create an institutional environment that enables the faculty to be free for their relevant work of teaching. Therefore, it is essential that the academic leader invests time and energy into the relationship with teachers and in faculty development. Two aspects from the institutional point of view need to be considered: the institutional environment of the faculty and the expectations of the faculty concerning their role in the institution.

Institutional Environment for the Faculty

The successful role of the faculty in the institution and in theological education depends on their integration into the institutional culture. This certainly starts with the selection of teachers who fit into the purpose and mission of the school, and the introduction to the institutional culture. Gordon Smith is right when he says that "integration with the culture, mission, ethos, and values of the school is a profoundly significant indicator of likely success as faculty member."[14] Academic leaders should adopt the principle that they want to make the faculty feel committed to the institution right from the beginning when they join the teaching staff: "The success of individual faculty members and the strength of

---

14. Gordon T. Smith, "Attending to the Collective Vocation," in *The Scope of Our Art: The Vocation of the Theological Teacher*, ed. L. G. Jones and Stephanie Paulsell (Grand Rapids, MI: Eerdmans, 2002), 241.

a school's faculty long-term depend on advanced planning for the shape and composition of the faculty, initiative in the cultivation and recruitment of able candidates, care in their selection, and active concern for the integration of new faculty into the academic community. The dean's leadership and pastoral care for faculty are critical at each stage of this process."[15]

It is essential for the institution to communicate clearly to teachers, including part-time teachers, the expectations besides the role in teaching and learning. Are the teachers expected to attend chapel and worship times? Are they expected to be part of seminary activities? What is their role as mentor? It is the task of the academic leader to introduce the faculty to what is expected of them.

Academic leaders need to facilitate the work of the faculty and assist them so that they succeed in their role as teachers, because they are the heart of the school. Students benefit from teachers who are satisfied in their teaching ministry. Jeanne McLean concludes from her research about the relationship between academic leaders and faculty: "Through their teaching, scholarship, and service, faculty carry out the mission, establish the school's reputation, and, through curricular and hiring decisions, determine its future. If the faculty succeed, 'the rest of it works.' When chief academic officers facilitate the faculty's essential work, they also serve the students, the seminary, and the church in the process."[16]

The institution needs to assist teachers in their career development and also show appreciation and care. "A smart institution can help faculty navigate the ebb and flow of a teaching career, because teaching is what suffers when we are too busy with other obligations."[17] This is a call to academic leaders to make it a priority to attend to faculty and to the holistic development of teachers. It includes a pastoral role that strengthens the role of the faculty and honors achievement. "An implication of the new and complex demands on our time is

---

15. Jeanne P. McLean, *Leading from the Center: The Emerging Role of the Chief Academic Officer in Theological Schools*, Scholars Press Studies in Theological Education (Atlanta: Scholars Press, 1999), 126.

16. McLean, *Leading from the Center*, 109.

17. Gretchen E. Ziegenhals, "Faculty Life and Seminary Culture: It's about Time and Money," in *Practical Wisdom: On Theological Teaching and Learning*, ed. Malcolm L. Warford (New York: Peter Lang, 2004), 65.

that *institutions have to work harder to help faculty feel valued and honored in their vocation as teachers.*"[18] Therefore, the relationship between the academic leader and the faculty impacts the role of teacher and facilitator: "Caring for faculty takes many forms, including knowing them, communicating openly and honestly, involving them in projects by consulting and delegating, dealing with them fairly and with understanding of their difficulties and differences."[19]

A powerful tool to develop the role of the faculty and make teaching and learning more effective is the ongoing assessment of the teacher's performance in general and the evaluation of the outcome of a particular course of study. The academic dean can assist the teacher to reflect on the teaching and also to develop an action plan for improvement. "One of the most powerful tools for a faculty developer is cultivating a commitment to reflective practice on the part of faculty members, helping them to adopt a 'scholarship of teaching and learning' strategy to assess systematically the effectiveness of their instructional design. Systematic assessment logically follows systematic design, and it is the action that leads to improvement."[20]

The individual teacher is able to fulfill the expected role in the institution when the academic leader establishes a trusting relationship, cares for the development of the teacher, and creates the institutional environment for faculty to be satisfied in their multifaceted task. The atmosphere of the institution depends to a large extent on the satisfaction of the teachers with their clearly defined roles and expectations.

Institutional Expectations of the Faculty

The institutional expectations include both what the faculty expect and what the institution expects. Looking at the amount of work teachers need to cope with, Gretchen Ziegenhals suggests that faculty might find more time if they learned to trust the administrators to do their share of the work. She adds a further consideration for teachers with regard to their attitude toward the

18. Ziegenhals, "Faculty Life and Seminary Culture," 65. Italics original.

19. McLean, *Leading from the Center*, 123.

20. Michael Theall and Jennifer L. Franklin, "Assessing Teaching Practices and Effectiveness for Formative Purposes," in *A Guide to Faculty Development*, ed. Kay J. Gillespie, Douglas L. Robertson, and Associates, Jossey-Bass Higher and Adult Education Series, 2nd ed. (San Francisco: Jossey-Bass, 2010), 158.

administration of the institution: "The faculty preference for group or consensus decision making, while democratic and honoring of diverse opinions, often eats up hours of time and energy. As we educate students for the church's ministries, perhaps doing less, better – by trusting others to do their work – would help us see the myriad ways in which God moves and works in our history. Our vocation as theological teachers needs to affect the quantity of what we do."[21]

The effective working relationship between faculty and academic leadership depends on the mutual understanding of their respective roles and their expectations of each other. The academic leader needs to know the expectations of the faculty. "Faculty expect deans not only to be competent academic administrators and to possess the infinite list of attributes and skills the work entails, but they also expect deans to know and understand them, to advocate for their interests, to protect them from administrative busy-work, and to focus their attention on important issues informed by broad institutional and theological education perspectives."[22]

The institutional expectations certainly vary in different contexts. Often, they include a variety of tasks that demand much time and energy. Is it possible to fulfill all responsibilities adequately? Teachers need to have a disciplined life in order to manage all tasks assigned by the institution. "Faculty are expected to stay current with their guilds, publish, teach, serve on multiple committees, lead worship, be multilingual, provide online courses, deliver PowerPoint lectures, be available to students for counseling and formation, grade effectively, tutor, support students through the transitions and crises of seminary life, and keep the scattered community from falling to pieces."[23]

Teachers can be expected to develop personally and professionally. The academic leader can assist the teacher in a self-reflection exercise about his or her personal and professional development. "Professional development is not exclusively a matter of acquiring job-related competencies and skills (although this is critical), but it also must support activities that foster the growth and

---

21. Ziegenhals, "Faculty Life and Seminary Culture," 63.
22. McLean, *Leading from the Center*, 113.
23. Ziegenhals, "Faculty Life and Seminary Culture," 53.

renewal of the whole person."[24] The academic leader should motivate the teachers to rest, research, and write.

Role of Teachers: Educational Expectations

Teachers are a gift from God to the church for all believers (Eph 4:11). Their teaching is used for spiritual growth in faith, so that Christians can understand the truth and apply it to their daily lives. The church carries the responsibility of teaching believers "to obey everything" Jesus has commanded (Matt 28:20). The task also includes the teaching and preparation of students for ministry in the church, in society, and in the world. The training for ministry has been delegated to the seminary or study program that has been designed for that purpose. Theological educators are therefore called to an important ministry, and high expectations are placed on their performance as teachers. The following is an attempt at a definition of an excellent teacher:

> An excellent teacher is an educator whose quality of life, teaching skills, ministry experience, and academic knowledge are blended together to be effective in teaching and learning and in personal interaction with students inside and outside the classroom. The personal, spiritual, academic, and professional qualities of the person match the role of teacher, mentor, and facilitator in theological education.

Some institutions may have specific expectations of the role of teacher for their context. It could be a valuable exercise for the faculty to write a definition that encapsulates those expectations. The definition could also be made known to the students, and serve in the assessment of the faculty.

There are many expectations concerning the role of teachers. Here we highlight three which are especially relevant in theological education. First, teachers need to be credible. What they teach should flow from their lives. Second, their professional expertise as teachers should build trust in the students as they explore areas of knowledge for themselves. They should know that they can rely on the teacher who will guide them in their studies. And,

---

24. McLean, *Leading from the Center*, 223.

finally, the impact of the teacher shows that the role in teaching and learning has been effective.

The Credibility of Teachers

In theological education credibility belongs to the role of the teacher because the personal walk of life and academic teaching in the classroom cannot be separated. From my own experience in academic leadership, I can testify that students observe the life of the teacher and notice whether it conforms to what is being taught. In their assessments, they sometimes express disappointment when teachers do not live up to their own standards. Therefore, it must be expected of teachers that they are credible; they should be examples of how to integrate the praxis of faith into their lives and relate it to teaching and learning. This can be a powerful role model for students that they want to follow when they are in ministry.

An outstanding example of how to integrate personal study and the praxis of faith and teaching is Ezra, who "devoted himself to the study and observance of the Law of the LORD, and to teaching its decrees and laws in Israel" (Ezra 7:10). As a teacher in Israel he had great influence, and he made an impact on the people.

In his book *Knowing God*, James Packer wrote a chapter entitled "The People Who Know Their God" where he points out the possibility that "one can know a great deal about God without knowledge of Him." This certainly is an important and challenging statement for theological educators. Is it possible to teach biblical subjects, to teach theology, to teach about God, without knowing him personally and intimately? Packer goes on to say something that theological educators should reflect on regarding their own role as teachers of the Word of God:

> We read books of theological exposition and apologetics. We dip into Christian history, and study the Christian creed. We learn to find our way around in the Scriptures. Others appreciate our interest in these things, and we find ourselves asked to give our opinion in public on this or that Christian question, to lead study groups, to give papers, to write articles, and generally to accept

responsibility, informal if not formal, for acting as teachers and arbiters of orthodoxy in our own Christian circle.[25]

James Packer uses Daniel 11:32, "the people who know their God shall stand firm and take action" (RSV), as the basis for four characteristics of people who know their God. I mention them here without any comment, but teachers (and, of course, all Christians) need to reflect on the meaning and implications for their lives and teaching role: "1) Those who know God have great energy for God. 2) Those who know God have great thoughts of God. 3) Those who know God show great boldness for God. 4) Those who know God have great contentment in God."[26] These certainly are challenging statements. The credibility of a teacher depends on his or her relationship with God.

Another example that highlights credibility as an important part of the role of the teacher comes from Asia. Ken Gnanakan and Sunand Sumithra emphasize the importance of the personal experience of the theologian that relates to what is being taught: "Relevant theology for Asia must come from men and women who have personally experienced the power of Christ and who possess a passion to make this power known."[27] The role of the teacher in theological education is to demonstrate the power of Christ and the gospel to the students: "Theologisation in Asia has to do with credibility and creativity that will show from the courage of the theologian who is bold enough to release all of the potential of Christ for our context. But this can only be done when the living power of the Gospel is demonstrated in our lives."[28] What is here described as relevant for theologians in Asia is certainly applicable to and true for other parts of the world. Those who teach theology need to demonstrate not only that they approach God on an intellectual level, but also that they live out what they teach. It is true that "the appropriate approach to God is the doxological approach."[29]

25. J. I. Packer, *Knowing God* (Downers Grove, IL: InterVarsity Press, 1973), 21.
26. Packer, *Knowing God*, 23–26.
27. Ken Gnanakan and Sunand Sumithra, "Theology, Theologization and the Theologian," in *Biblical Theology in Asia*, ed. Ken Gnanakan (Bangalore: Theological Book Trust, 1995), 45.
28. Gnanakan and Sumithra, "Theology, Theologization and the Theologian," 45.
29. Gnanakan and Sumithra, 41.

The credibility of the teacher contributes to his or her trusted role as educator. It is part of the hidden curriculum in teaching and learning. The impact on the students should not be underestimated. I have listened to many students who testified about the exemplary lives of teachers. They also benefited much from the teaching because of the credibility of the teachers.

The Professional Expertise of Teachers

According to Paul, teaching is a gift from God (Rom 12:7). Some assume that this means that good teachers are born with the gift of teaching. Others maintain that completing a degree in higher theological education automatically makes someone a good teacher. Do teachers still need to develop their teaching skills? It certainly is true that God enables the teacher and provides his gift of teaching beyond expectation. At the same time, teachers need the expertise of teaching and to develop their skills, as Maryellen Weimer points out: "Being a good teacher entails more than a decision to be enthusiastic, organized, clear, stimulating, and knowledgeable. It involves translating those abstract ingredients into tangible behaviors, policies and practices and then assembling from that wide repertoire of possibilities a set of instructional nuts and bolts that fit the requirements of our own style proclivities, the configuration of our content, the learning needs of our students, and the instructional context in which they will occur."[30]

Effective instruction in teaching and learning fits first of all the person of the teacher and, second, the content and the needs of the students. The teacher is challenged to develop his or her personal capacity in teaching that fits the personality. Teachers can learn from others, but they cannot copy the way others fulfill their role in teaching and learning. Therefore, it needs to be taken into account that "Effective instruction 'fits' the individual – it is a suitable, comfortable set of activities, policies, and practices for the teacher involved, but that is not the only relevant 'fit.' Effective instruction *fits the configuration of the content, the learning needs of students, and the instructional setting*."[31]

---

30. Maryellen Weimer, *Improving Your Classroom Teaching*, Survival Skills for Scholars 1 (Newbury Park, CA: Sage, 1993), 16.
31. Weimer, *Improving Your Classroom Teaching*, 13. Italics original.

Lee Wanak asserts that the Holy Spirit makes us teachers and also is active in our development as teachers. However, it is our responsibility to nurture and develop the gift. The educator functions as someone who makes the Bible relevant in the contemporary context, as well as applying the text to the personal life. Wanak concludes that "The task of the theological educator is to bridge the ancient text and the contemporary context, ancient pedagogy and the modern approaches to academic, spiritual and ministerial formation. The Holy Spirit is our guide in this process (1 Cor 2:9–16), not only in the relationship of text and context, but also in our personal outworking of being both theologian and educator."[32]

Even though in our time information is easily available through the Internet, the professional expertise of teachers is still important in theological education. The information available needs to be processed and evaluated under the guidance of an expert. The role of the teacher can be compared to that of a guide who points in the right direction and assists in sorting the pieces of information so that they fit together. At the same time, teachers share from their own experience and academic knowledge. They know that their role is defined as preparing "[God's] people for works of service" (Eph 4:12). How can teachers remain relevant, even after many years of teaching? Maryellen Weimer suggests, "One way to keep your teaching fresh and invigorated across a career is to change always to new things: new textbooks, new strategies, new assignments, new questions. Sometimes you can recycle, bring something back after a break, but you always need to be on the lookout for new ideas, new approaches, and new challenges."[33]

Assessment of teaching and learning practices can be a powerful tool to develop the role of the teacher in theological education. To teach effectively involves both the teacher and the learner, but here we are concerned only with the experience of the teacher. His or her willingness to improve the processes and practices in areas such as teaching methods, teaching techniques, evaluation of teaching outcomes or skills, and ability to engage the students in

---

32. Lee C. Wanak, "Theological Education and the Role of Teachers in the Twenty-First Century: A Look at the Asia Pacific Region," in *Educating for Tomorrow: Theological Leadership for the Asian Context*, ed. Manfred W. Kohl and A. N. L. Senanayake (Bangalore: SAIACS; Indianapolis: Overseas Council International, 2002), 171.

33. Weimer, *Improving Your Classroom Teaching*, 27.

the learning process contributes to the effectiveness in achieving the learning outcomes. Teachers need to have knowledge of the content they are teaching, pedagogical knowledge about teaching and learning strategies, and curricular knowledge related to teaching the required course of study. Michael Theall and Jennifer Franklin sum up the requirements of the three areas of knowledge:

> Curricular knowledge also involves the ability to identify important principles and to translate complex concepts and ideas into understandable and usable form. Curricular knowledge embodies instructional strategic thinking since teachers with curricular knowledge are able to assess student learning and to respond to and remedy issues and problems impeding learning. Assessing teaching involves examining the extent to which a teacher possesses these three kinds of knowledge, and assisting teachers involves helping them to move from being primarily content experts to enhancing the connections between content and effective pedagogy.[34]

The professional expertise of the teacher that can be expected is related to the development of teaching skills that suit the person of the educator. Good teachers know their subject well and are able to relate the content to the lives of the students and to the context in society and in ministry.

The Impact of Teachers

Paul uses the image of the body (Rom 12:3–8; 1 Cor 12:12–30) to convey the idea that we do our work and fulfill our vocations with a high degree of interdependence, as Gordon Smith points out: "We cannot speak of the individual vocation except in the context of the community. All vocations are fulfilled in solidarity with others; each person fulfills an individual vocation in partnership with another."[35] He also is convinced that "Our individual potential is achieved in collaboration and partnership with others, whether it is our potential of personal transformation or the potential of making a difference

---

34. Theall and Franklin, "Assessing Teaching Practices," 155.
35. Smith, "Attending to the Collective Vocation," 241–242.

in the world."[36] The impact of the individual teacher depends on the vocation and his or her part in the community.

Teachers play an important role in the lives of students. They teach important knowledge; they stimulate quality learning experiences; they challenge students in critical thinking, so that they are able to integrate knowledge and experience. Good students value teachers who have high ethical and academic standards and expectations. One day a student told me that he had taken a course with a certain professor who was very demanding in terms of assignments. He had high standards for his own life and applied these to the students. The student admitted that he decided not to study another course with this professor. However, after some time of reflection, he came to the conclusion that he should enroll on another course with him. He realized that he gained much in studying with this professor, even though the work was demanding.

The impact on the students also comes from a teacher who is enthusiastic about the subject and material being taught. I personally realized this when I taught introduction to Greek and Greek exegesis at the seminary in Bangkok. Naturally, students found it difficult to study the ancient language because of the grammar which was so different from that of their own language. To motivate the students and to be enthusiastic about the importance of knowing the language was a challenge, but it was rewarding. The students were eager to learn. I can echo what Maryellen Weimer writes: "Enthusiasm is the component students regularly identify as the most important ingredient of effective instruction. It has such priority for them because it stimulates, motivates, and involves them. The instructor becomes the plug that connects students with the power source. Our enthusiasm energizes them. They come to care because we have shown them how much we care."[37]

Another role of the teacher is to build the capacity of the students so that they discover God's calling for effective ministry. The teacher entrusts students with knowledge to pass on to others, as we have seen from the example of Paul (2 Tim 2:2). Teachers are not only lecturers, but they are involved in the lives of the students. Joy Oyco-Bunyi was involved in accreditation visits to many

---

36. Smith, 242.
37. Weimer, *Improving Your Classroom Teaching*, 23.

seminaries. From her experience in meeting students she was encouraged that many testified to the value of the faculty in their lives: "Student after student interviewed during accreditation expressed the impact of faculty on their lives. Because of the faculty's singular impact on theological education, schools cannot be lax in faculty recruitment and development. Investing in the personal and professional growth of faculty is worth every effort."[38]

The impact of the faculty is not limited to classroom teaching. Teachers should make a contribution in the areas or fields of expertise related to theology or to contemporary issues. As theological educators, their voices will be heard and they can impact the church and society. This fact was highlighted earlier when looking at the teaching ministry of Paul.

Teachers have unique opportunities to impact the lives of the future leaders and teachers of the church. Therefore, to be a theological educator is a high calling with challenging expectations. Teachers need to remember that "whatever you do, whether in word or deed, do it all in the name of the Lord Jesus, giving thanks to God the Father through him" (Col 3:17).

Conclusion

Teachers play an important role in theological education related to the institution and the expectations of the students. They should follow the examples of Jesus and Paul and learn from them how to be effective in building people up, so that they can have a fruitful ministry. I conclude with the words of Steven Hardy and his description of excellent teachers:

> Good teachers are the greatest resource that any school or training program has. We are blessed if we have teachers who know how to pastorally care for and equip students so that they will be ready to take on the ministries to which God has called them. We need those who know their subject matter well and who model what they know. We also want them to know the techniques of teaching

---

38. Joy Oyco-Bunyi, *Beyond Accreditation: Value Commitments and Asian Seminaries* (Bangalore: Theological Book Trust, 2001), 79.

so that they can creatively help their students explore the real world, as well as the world of ideas and books.[39]

Reflection and Action Points

1. Faculty should study together the lives of Jesus and Paul as teachers. What made their teaching ministries effective? What are the lessons for the personal development of a teacher?

2. Discuss the following statement among the faculty: "The school is only as strong as its faculty."[40] Do you agree? Why? Do you disagree? Why?

3. How conducive is the environment of your institution to the faculty's effectiveness? What adjustments are needed? What are the expectations of the faculty?

4. In what ways can the academic leader support the role of the faculty in your institution? Develop an action plan that could realistically be implemented.

5. How can teachers support each other in fulfilling their multiple tasks in teaching and learning? This question could be discussed in a workshop organized by the academic leader.

Resources for Further Study

Gnanakan, Ken, and Sunand Sumithra. "Theology, Theologization and the Theologian." In *Biblical Theology in Asia*, edited by Ken Gnanakan, 39–46. Bangalore: Theological Book Trust, 1995.

Hardy, Steven A. *Excellence in Theological Education: Effective Training for Church Leaders*. Peradeniya, Sri Lanka/Edenvale, South Africa: The Publishing Unit, Lanka Bible College and Seminary; Distributed by SIM, 2007.

---

39. Steven A. Hardy, *Excellence in Theological Education: Effective Training for Church Leaders* (Peradeniya, Sri Lanka/Edenvale, South Africa: The Publishing Unit, Lanka Bible College and Seminary; distributed by SIM, 2007), 183.
40. Oyco-Bunyi, *Beyond Accreditation*, 79.

McLean, Jeanne P. *Leading from the Center: The Emerging Role of the Chief Academic Officer in Theological Schools*. Scholars Press Studies in Theological Education. Atlanta: Scholars Press, 1999.

Oyco-Bunyi, Joy. *Beyond Accreditation: Value Commitments and Asian Seminaries*. Bangalore: Theological Book Trust, 2001.

Smith, Gordon T. "Attending to the Collective Vocation." In *The Scope of Our Art: The Vocation of the Theological Teacher*, edited by L. G. Jones and Stephanie Paulsell, 240–261. Grand Rapids, MI: Eerdmans, 2002.

Wanak, Lee C. "Theological Education and the Role of Teachers in the Twenty-First Century: A Look at the Asia Pacific Region." In *Educating for Tomorrow: Theological Leadership for the Asian Context*, edited by Manfred W. Kohl and A. N. L. Senanayake, 160–180. Bangalore: SAIACS; Indianapolis: Overseas Council International, 2002.

Warford, Malcolm L., ed. *Practical Wisdom: On Theological Teaching and Learning*. New York: Peter Lang, 2004.

Weimer, Maryellen. *Improving Your Classroom Teaching*. Survival Skills for Scholars 1. Newbury Park, CA: Sage, 1993.

Ziegenhals, Gretchen E. "Faculty Life and Seminary Culture: It's about Time and Money." In *Practical Wisdom*, edited by Malcolm Warford, 49–66. New York: Peter Lang, 2004.

Zuck, Roy B. *Teaching as Jesus Taught*. Grand Rapids, MI: Baker, 1995.

———. *Teaching as Paul Taught*. Grand Rapids, MI: Baker, 1998.

2

Definitions and Concepts of Faculty Development

Graham Cheesman

The tendency in discussions of faculty development, in the literature and in colleges and seminaries, is to move almost immediately to practical arrangements and plans. This chapter takes an initial step back from the practice and asks the question: On what theological and educational basis do we engage in, and design programs for, faculty development?

There are two main usages of the phrase "faculty development." It is used first for the development of teachers as effective individuals, and then also for the development of an effective faculty – the team of teachers.[1] This chapter will mainly concentrate on the first, but toward the end, as a natural development, say some important things about the second.

We should not progress before underlining the vital nature of the concept and practice. Ultimately, theological education takes place when a teacher is face to face, or otherwise in contact, with students. Good theological education can take place in a mud-built classroom in a Majority World situation, or not take place in a multimillion-dollar campus in the West. It all hangs in the end

---

1. For a useful survey and interpretation of faculty development from the secular higher education perspective, see Graham Webb, *Understanding Staff Development* (Buckingham: Society for Research into Higher Education/Open University Press, 1996). See also Andy Armitage et. al., "The Post Compulsory Teacher: Learning and Developing," in *Teaching and Training in Post-Compulsory Education* (Maidenhead: McGraw-Hill, 2003), 33–60.

on the quality of the teacher. Understanding and working for the development of the teacher and his or her faculty group is, therefore, of fundamental importance and a vital task for all theological schools and their leadership.

There are a number of sources from which we can draw help and inspiration for this task of thinking the matter through. The subject is a live one within higher education today, although it also generally suffers from a precipitate jump to the practice before the theory is enunciated. There have been a number of important debates in theological education in the last fifty years as to nature and purpose, its emphasis, its integration, and the relationships involved. We can draw on these for guidance. There is, also, key biblical material, not least the example of Christ in the training of the Twelve, and the writings of the apostle Paul about the gift of teacher to the church and the development of his or her spiritual life, emotions, and attitudes.

As is often pointed out in the literature, all faculty development assumes a model of a good teacher. This is certainly true in theological education, which itself assumes a number of things about the intentions and aims of this calling. Our first section, therefore, will briefly visit a number of key issues in the construction of that model, so faculty formation has a clarity of target and intention. Our second task will be to set out the key areas in which the development of a teacher needs to take place, or, to put it another way, the objectives of faculty development. Third, we will turn to ideas behind the development of the faculty as a team of teachers, and discuss such things as the concept of common calling and the creation of a rich space for faculty development.[2]

The Aim of Faculty Development: Creating a Model of the Excellent Teacher

Most colleges and seminaries operate practically with a standard threefold model of objectives in theological education: the training of the head, heart, and hands; or the formation of the student academically, spiritually, and

---

2. A useful list of issues can be found in Steven A. Hardy, "Factors in Developing the Faculty That We Need," in *Excellence in Theological Education: Effective Training for Church Leaders* (Peradeniya, Sri Lanka: Lanka Bible College, 2007), 150–169.

ministerially.[3] Behind the catalogues and brochures of the schools, however, lies a whole biblical and historical set of ideas and practices as to the nature and delivery of theological education by a faculty – and, therefore, the development of its members.

Biblical Perspectives

Cultural and situational difference makes the hermeneutical task of applying Scripture to discern a model of excellence for theological educators a difficult one.

Jesus himself is the perfect example of grace, love, dedication, and a life that pleases God. And, as many have pointed out, he taught a "class" of future ministers and missionaries for a three-year course. However, he asked them to be his own disciples, something no other theological educator should ever do; he was perfect, while all other teachers can and should make use of their weaknesses and mistakes for their own humility and the profit of their students, although we must note the role of humility in Christ's ministry. Yet there are patterns of excellence to follow.

Jesus taught with a natural and deliberate contextualization. He used the local culture, history, and situation as a communication tool; he spoke into the needs of the people and answered the practical and theological issues of the day from the Scriptures; he used the educational patterns of the place and time – the role of the rabbi – as his mode of teaching. Yet he was also counter-cultural. In adopting the rabbi role, he modified it as necessary, and he confronted current cultural and religious attitudes.

Jesus clearly saw as important the need to teach in relationship and community. He called the Twelve and formed them into an intimate, almost family community, where teacher and students shared life and became close. In that environment, he taught them as those he knew, and he was an example as

---

3. For an interesting exposition of this threefold model applied to the academic theological educator, see David Adams, "Putting Heart and Soul into Research: An Inquiry into Becoming 'Scholar-Practitioner-Saint,'" *Transformation* 25, no. 2–3 (April/July 2008): 144–157. Increasingly popular is a fourfold model speaking of character formation separately from spiritual formation. There was a progression in this direction between Vatican II's Decree on the Training of Priests, which adopted a threefold model in October 1965, and *Pastores Dabo Vobis* which adopted a fourfold model in March 1992. Similar developments have taken place in some evangelical literature.

one they knew. He saw the need of modeling ministry and then "sending out" in the learning process.[4] Above all, Jesus had a paramount spiritual intention in his teaching. Certainly, he taught – on the mount, beside the fire in the evening, deeply in the upper room – but he also taught them to pray,[5] the great aim was the growth of the disciples' faith, and the last examination question for Peter was "Do you love me?"[6]

We see in the life of Paul a good example of how the ministry of Jesus can be interpreted into the situation of a fallible sinful human seeking to bless the church by the exercise of his ministry – something reassuringly close to home. Once we see that theological education is fundamentally a form of ministry to God's church, and that Paul is a good example of that ministry, whole new vistas open up to us. So how did Paul understand and exercise that ministry?

We see a shift from the language of discipleship with Jesus to the language of collegiality with Paul. Paul traveled with colleagues, worked with colleagues, and wrote letters jointly with colleagues.[7] These "co-workers" were treated with respect, even when, as in the case of Timothy, Paul was a sort of father figure to them. If the calling to and ministry of teaching was a theme in Paul's writings, his own example in practicing the teaching office shows how he regarded it. He was surprisingly and unashamedly emotional in his relationships with those he taught. He spoke of tears and groans, and joy – and occasional anger. He was a passionate man and he made no secret of his passions, relating his feelings about those he nurtured, and about those who would harm them. And that emotion was returned. When he finally said goodbye to the Ephesian elders on the shore at Miletus, they wept.[8] Such a relationship also caused a remarkable degree of sharing his own spiritual life and struggles, such as when he described his "thorn in the flesh" and his ecstatic experiences.[9] He speaks of his struggles

---

4. Matt 10:1–16.

5. Matt 6:5–15.

6. John 21:15.

7. Robert Banks, *Reenvisioning Theological Education: Exploring a Missional Alternative to Current Models* (Grand Rapids, MI: Eerdmans, 1999), 113–117.

8. Acts 20:13–37.

9. 2 Cor 12:1–10.

with sin.[10] He followed his Lord in giving not just truths, but his "very self" to those he taught in Thessalonica.[11] His pastoral care was deep and real.

Although teaching from a position of intellectual strength, Paul ministered from a *sense of weakness*. His view expressed to the Corinthians was that God tended to use the weak rather than the strong,[12] and Paul had personal experience of this, believing that God had sent him the thorn in the flesh to weaken him so he might understand that "[God's] power is made perfect in weakness. . . . Therefore I will boast all the more gladly about my weaknesses, . . . For when I am weak, then I am strong."[13] Not that this stopped him offering himself as an example.

Fundamental themes of excellence as a teacher emerge with clarity from this very brief biblical survey. An excellent theological educator works for understanding with spiritual intent, is concerned with the practice of ministry, gives him- or herself to those taught, manages critical contextualization, works within relationship and community, and thinks and lives humbly.

A Significant Debate

The nature and purpose of theological education, and therefore of the theological educator, has been the subject of a sustained discussion for some time. This was triggered by Farley's seminal book *Theologia: The Fragmentation and Unity of Theological Education* in 1983.[14] This has been well set out elsewhere,[15] but a key moment came when Kelsey published his books *To Understand God Truly* in 1992 and *Between Athens and Berlin* in 1993.[16] Kelsey saw current theological education in tension between the *Wissenschaft*, or scientific theology, approach typified by Schleiermacher's University of Berlin – a body of theoretical knowledge with practical import for society leading to a

---

10. Rom 7:7–25.

11. 1 Thess 2:8.

12. 1 Cor 1:26–31.

13. 2 Cor 12:9–10.

14. Edward Farley, *Theologia: The Fragmentation and Unity of Theological Education* (Philadelphia: Fortress, 1983).

15. For instance, in Banks, *Reenvisioning*, 16–69.

16. David Kelsey, *Between Athens and Berlin: The Theological Education Debate* (Grand Rapids, MI: Eerdmans, 1993); *To Understand God Truly: What's Theological about a Theological School?* (Louisville, KY: Westminster/John Knox, 1992).

professional model of ministry – and *paideia*, the Greek or classical concept of pre-Enlightenment personal development based on classical texts. He tried to gather these together to form a model for theological education.

Banks, in his book *Reenvisioning Theological Education* in 1999,[17] saw this as stimulating but inadequate, and proposed a third location, that of Jerusalem, as a way of proposing a missional model, requiring a radical realigning of the task to the mission of God that demanded a more practically connected curriculum for the whole lives of the whole people of God. Edgar, in a well-received article "The Theology of Theological Education" in 2005,[18] considered the three poles of Athens, Berlin, and Jerusalem as inadequate modeling, and added a fourth, Geneva, an affirmation that theological is also confessional. We teach in order that we might know God better through the creeds, confessions, and traditions of a particular faith community. Other writers have jumped on the bandwagon of concepts by locations.

The debate is wider than this sketch, involving significantly more scholars, and is often carefully nuanced. However, taking the four locations proposed, we can see in theological education today a state of tension existing between the academic (or scientific), spiritual (or personal), and ministerial (or missional) objectives, that task in tension being carried out within a confessional community.[19] It is within this descriptive understanding that faculty development takes place. All schools and teachers feel this tension, but different schools tend to combine the poles in different ways with different priorities, thus creating a diversity of approaches to faculty development. We could even go so far as to say that faculty development occurs mainly in the area circumscribed by these four poles, and partakes of this tension. Academic, personal, and ministerial formation must apply to faculty if they are to apply to students, and all need to understand and develop their relationship with their confessional community.

---

17. Banks, *Reenvisioning*.

18. Brian Edgar, "The Theology of Theological Education," *Evangelical Review of Theology* 29, no. 3 (2005): 208–217.

19. We should note that the models mentioned cross the simple boundaries put forward in this statement. For instance, Schleiermacher's model used by Kelsey includes a professional approach to ministry based on *Wissenschaft*, which in some aspects overlaps with Banks's missional model, but is in tension with it in a number of key aspects.

A Re-emphasis

Perhaps the most significant issue affecting theological faculty development in recent years has been the re-emphasis placed on spiritual formation. The growing post-Second World War emphasis on academic excellence began to be widely seen as relatively sterile spiritually, and prompted a reconsideration of the role of spiritual formation. A wide-ranging set of conferences sponsored by the Association of Theological Schools, from the Task Force on Spiritual Development set up to report in 1972 to the Denver conference in 1980,[20] the Iona Declaration and process begun in April 1987 with the workshop in Iona, and culminating in the conference in 1989 in Indonesia,[21] the growing body of articles and books, and the "Manifesto for Theological Education" produced by the ICETE (then ICAA),[22] all testify to a reassessment of the vital importance of spiritual formation in theological education. This had a significant effect on the ground in the schools, although there are studies that suggest the effect was not as deep or wide-ranging as it should have been.[23] Again, this has been chronicled elsewhere.[24]

This has proved to be a game-changer for faculty development in theological education. Whereas more traditionally, development was seen especially within the Berlin model and was tied mainly to professional academic development, now it is increasingly seen as also the development of the teacher as mentor. This has caused not a little anxiety among teachers who were hired years ago in order mainly to discharge their responsibility as academics, and who may not see themselves as gifted or able in this area.

---

20. "Report of the Task Force on Spiritual Formation," *Theological Education* (Spring 1972): 153–197; Tilden Edwards, "Spiritual Formation in Theological Schools: Ferment and Challenge," *Theological Education* 17, no. 1 (1980): 7–52.

21. Samuel Amirtham and Robin Pryor, *Invitation to the Feast of Life: Resources for Spiritual Formation in Theological Education* (Geneva: World Council of Churches, 1989).

22. ICETE, "Manifesto on the Renewal of Evangelical Theological Education," *Evangelical Review of Theology* 19, no. 3 (1995): 307–313. This is a re-issue of the original, first issued in 1983 in *Theological Education Today* 16, no. 2 (April–June 1983).

23. Robert Ferris, "Renewal of Theological Education: Commitments, Models and the ICAA Manifesto," *Evangelical Review of Theology* 14, no. 1 (Jan 1990): 64–75.

24. For instance, Graham Cheesman, "Spiritual Formation as a Goal of Theological Education," Theological Education.net, last modified 2011, accessed July 2015, http://www.theologicaleducation.net/articles/view.htm?id=106.

Searching for Integration

There has been increasing frustration in the literature with the fragmented nature of our understanding of theological education and its discussion. After all, we are not training heads, hands, and hearts; we are training students who need to integrate these things in order to become whole people.[25] The tendency of our schools is not to do this well: to see the lecture room as academic formation, the chapel as spiritual formation, and practical placements as ministerial formation, leaving the students to somehow put these things together (although, increasingly, schools are addressing this problem). The older approach was to seek for some sort of balance, so Warfield in the nineteenth century spoke about a soldier needing to stand on two legs (academic and spiritual),[26] and others have used the picture of balancing a three-legged stool.[27] But this is by no means satisfactory, nor is it easy to understand what balance actually means in a school. However, integration – where the elements of formation work together within each other, where lectures include spiritual application, chapel talks are academically solid and where ministry flows from both academic understanding and spiritual commitment – is a deeper concept. This is far more powerful, and it is a right reflection of scriptural norms.

The impact on faculty development here is immense when we realize that it is in the very life and person of the teacher as an integrated person that we find the most powerful tool for student integration of life.

Relational Teaching

There is one more area of discussion today in theological education that has important implications for faculty development, and that is to see the teaching task as fundamentally taking place on the basis of relationship. In line with movements in higher education theory and practice, there has been a shift

---

25. Just one example would be Gordon T. Smith, "Spiritual Formation in the Academy: A Unifying Model," *Theological Education* 33, no. 1 (1996): 83–91.

26. B. B. Warfield gave an address to students at the autumn conference at Princeton Theological Seminary on 4 October 1911.The most accessible version is that published as a booklet: Benjamin B. Warfield, *The Religious Life of Theological Students* (Phillipsburg, NJ: P & R, 1983); also in John E. Meeter, ed., *Benjamin B. Warfield: Selected Shorter Writings*, vol. 1 (Grand Rapids: P & R, 1970), 411–425.

27. For instance, Graham Cheesman, "Competing Paradigms in Theological Education Today," *Evangelical Review of Theology* 17, no. 4 (1993): 484–495.

away from models which do not require close personal engagement with the student toward those which see teaching as taking place within a real live, even reciprocal, relationship between teacher and student, rather than a "lecture and leave – and please note my example" approach.[28]

The seminal model for this in theological education has been Henri Nouwen's and Parker Palmer's pictures of the teacher as host who creates a safe, welcoming, and challenging space of learning for the student.[29] Margaret Guenther uses the model of the midwife, that is, someone who does not give birth herself but is the guide and helper to the student who gives birth to personal transformation.[30] Perry Shaw has used the model of paraclete, a helper who comes alongside to encourage and bless,[31] and Don Shepson developed this using the concept of helper throughout Scripture in his useful article "A Scriptural Model of Relational Spiritual Formation" in 2012.[32] Other relational models include that of friend and, lest this seem too close a relationship between teacher and student, we need to be reminded that Jesus described his disciples in this way. "Companion on the way" is a model used in conjunction with a journeying concept of spiritual formation which is increasingly used more than the older conception of "molding" students into a standard package spiritually.[33] The model of the lead climber who holds the rope for the student as he or she climbs toward better understanding is a development of this model, emphasizing pastoral care while academic development takes place.[34] John

28. "Good teachers exhibit a capacity for connectiveness." Parker Palmer, *The Courage to Teach: Exploring the Inner Landscape of a Teacher's Life* (San Francisco: Jossey-Bass, 1998), 11.

29. Henri Nouwen, *Reaching Out: The Three Movements of the Spiritual Life* (Glasgow: William Collins, 1976), 69; Parker Palmer, *To Know as We Are Known: Education as a Spiritual Journey* (New York: HarperCollins, 1993), 69–71.

30. Margaret Guenther, *Holy Listening: The Art of Spiritual Direction* (London: Darton, Longman & Todd, 1992), 84–112.

31. Personal correspondence with the author.

32. Don Shepson, "A Scriptural Model of Relational Christian Formation," *Christian Education Journal* 9, Series 3 (Spring 2012 supplement): 180–198.

33. Katarina Schuth, *Reason for the Hope: The Futures of Catholic Theologates* (Wilmington, DE: Michael Glazier, 1989).

34. Graham Cheesman, "The Lead Climber," *Teaching Theology* (blog), 30 September 2012, accessed July 2015, http://teachingtheology.org/2012/09/30/the-lead-climber/.

Hitchen has developed a model around the New Testament usage of *huperetes*, variously translated – for instance, as "steward."[35]

None of these models is impossible through distributed learning increasingly conducted through the Internet, but plenty of ingenuity and technical expertise is needed to achieve significant relationship between teacher and student. So we have the interesting developing scene of a growing realization of the importance of real and significant relationships while making more and more use of the Internet, which creates problems for that very emerging model. The key point for faculty development is that we are returning to a biblical modular set, exemplified in Jesus and Paul, which makes a much greater demand on the teacher than the old "lecture and leave" model that used to dominate our schools.

The Objectives of Faculty Development: Teacher Growth

The discussions above have clarified the aim of faculty development; we have come to a picture of the excellent teacher as a devout scholar practitioner, teaching via meaningful relationships with his or her students within a real and confessional community in context. What are the key areas and objectives for the development of such a teacher today?

Academic Development

Faculty members are scholars operating in a particular subject area as Christians, so it is this threefold requirement which concerns us here: development as a scholar, development in the subject area, and development of a spiritual relationship with study.

Development as a scholar often means attitude development. There are sets of good scholarly attitudes, partly Enlightenment-driven, partly much older, but which have a universality about them as the right way to use the mind. These would include such things as a carefulness with the evidence and truth. Christians, no less than other scholars, find it frighteningly easy to push evidence and arguments into the molds that support their previous convictions

---

35. John M. Hitchen, "Confirming the Christian Scholar and Theological Educator's Identity through New Testament Metaphor," *Evangelical Review of Theology* 35, no. 2 (2011): 276–287.

or their argument at the time. A carefulness in this respect is a matter of honesty, which is a Christian virtue. Such an attitude will appreciate the distinction between commitment and truth – in other words, an understanding that a passionate commitment to a cause does not in itself invest that cause with truth or rightness. It would include courtesy toward all other people, and a gentleness of spirit which comes out of humility when debating and even rejecting the views of others.

Development in any subject area in theological studies, in depth and breadth to the point of mastery, is increasingly difficult today. Subject areas are moving fast, and scholarship is discovering new tools and ways of looking at Scripture and doctrine. To do this, the teacher will participate in the life of academia in the subject, including the journals, the conferences, and the new books. One marker of subject area development in secular higher education is contributing to research, and this is increasingly demanded in theological education. A doctorate is usually seen as the beginning of a life of contribution to the development of the subject which shows itself in publication. Some will be especially gifted in this area, but all must be encouraged toward the primary calling not just to research, but also to teach.

It is in this area that the scholar has to pay particular attention to both contextualization and globalization.[36] The academic world is now intensely globalized, with subject areas developing via cohorts of scholars from different countries in touch via email, using internationally accessed journals, and Internet-based resources, working on issues together. Yet every scholar is also contextually embedded and must work within the classic fourfold parameters of contextual theological education: theological, structural, pedagogical, and missiological contextualization.[37] Interestingly, an increasing number of Internet-based courses possess cohorts of students from all over the world, and the diversity of their contexts provides a richness for all provided we uphold the imperative of contextualization over the pressure toward sameness coming from the global reach.

---

36. See Judith Lingenfelter and Sherwood Lingenfelter, *Teaching Cross-Culturally: An Incarnational Model for Learning and Teaching* (Grand Rapids: Baker, 2003), especially ch. 6, "The Role of the Teacher," 71–85.

37. C. Lienemann-Perrin, *Training for a Relevant Ministry: A Study of the Contribution of the Theological Education Fund* (Geneva: World Council of Churches, 1981), 174–176.

Developing a spiritual relationship to study is equally important for the scholar. The theological teacher in the present academic environment will need to construct a personal relationship with his or her academic work which goes beyond the Enlightenment attitude of disinterested or non-committed, assumption-free study still prevalent in many university and accreditation situations.[38] Academic work is a large part of our discipleship and should be done as an expression of our love for God and desire to serve him with our minds.[39] Theology in the New Testament was written by missionaries and pastors as part of their service, and only spiritual experience can ultimately put us in a position to understand both biblical text and theology. Study of the Hebrew words will get us some way to understanding the Psalms, but spiritual experience akin to that of the writer will be essential for us to understand them deeply.[40] If theology is a distillation of the experience of God in Christ, found in Scripture, and interpreted by the believing church, then it too needs spiritual life for full comprehension. All this will mean that the Christian scholar will cultivate a reading in two ways. He or she will read for truth's sake, and will also read for the student's sake, for the sake of ministry, for the sake of the kingdom of God in this world: reading for both truth and relevance.

Professional Competence Development

The tendency in theological education is to ask those who teach in our schools to do so on the basis of their knowledge of the subject rather than their ability to develop students academically, spiritually, and in ministry ability. A PhD is a narrow qualification. Our professional duty is to so teach with competence that we prepare men and women to love and serve God. This also has to be studied

---

38. N. Wolterstorff, "The Travail of Theology in the Modern Academy," in *The Future of Theology: Essays in Honor of Jürgen Moltmann*, ed. Miroslav Volf, Carmen Krieg, and Thomas Kucharz (Grand Rapids: Eerdmans, 1996), 35–46.

39. See also the interesting article by Michael Battle, "Teaching and Learning as Ceaseless Prayer," in *The Scope of Our Art: The Vocation of the Theological Teacher*, ed. L. Gregory Jones and Stephanie Paulsell (Grand Rapids: Eerdmans, 2002), 155–170.

40. Some exegesis can be described as akin to taking apart the piano to understand a Chopin nocturne.

and learnt, and teachers must develop in competence in their professional task.[41]

There are gifted teachers, but there are also attitudes, knowledge, and techniques which can be learned and applied in teaching. Theological educators are communicators; this task is studied today in depth, and there are plenty of good books and courses available expressing good practice in formal settings, small groups, and one-to-one counseling. We should not necessarily confuse good communication with the use of the latest technology, although often this helps. A good communicator is someone who can help the other person not only to see ideas, but to gain a passion for those ideas, to pass on an enthusiasm along with truth. Modeling good practice, properly learnt technique, and an emotional engagement with the truth as it is passed on will help students reproduce these attitudes in ministry. Importantly, higher education and adult education teaching theory and practice is a major area of enquiry today. We now know a great deal more about how students learn and how best to teach. This is the professional side of the job we must attend to as well as the subject content.

Courses exist to help. Generally, those offered in secular situations such as universities have real value but need discernment. A theologian or biblical studies scholar placed in a class or cohort with those who teach biology, history, or physics must not assume that teaching theology and Bible is done in the same way or with the same objectives as any other subject.[42] There is a great need for more good courses on the professional job of the theological

---

41. Please note that I am using the term "professional" not in the full sense in which it is debated today in theological education, but in the sense of having studied how to do a good and competent job in the calling and task of theological education. Jackson Carroll was funded by the ATS and released on sabbatical by the Hartford Seminary in 1984 to research the status of the model of "professional" as a motif in ministry and theological education. His paper was published in the spring of 1985. See Jackson Carroll, "The Professional Model of Ministry: Is It Worth Saving?," *Theological Education* 21, no. 2 (Spring 1985): 7–48. More recent discussion can be located in Linda Cannell, *Theological Education Matters: Leadership Education for the Church* (Charleston, SC: Booksurge, 2008); and Graham Cheesman, "A True Professional?," *Journal of Theological Education and Mission* 1, no. 1 (Feb 2010): 57–64.

42. Arun K. Sarkar, "Non-Formal Faculty Development in Theological Seminaries: An Adult Educational Approach," in *Tending the Seedbeds: Educational Perspectives on Theological Education in Asia*, ed. Allan Harkness (Quezon City: Asia Theological Association, 2010), 129–143.

educator today, and for schools to take the lead in seeing that their teachers are developed in this way.

Personal Spiritual/Discipleship Development

Thomas à Kempis once said – and I usually begin my theology lectures with this quote – "Of what use is it to be able to discourse learnedly on the Trinity if you lack humility and so displease the Trinity?"[43] It would be invidious to claim that this subject could be dealt with adequately in a few paragraphs. The area in question is the whole matter of the Christian life on which countless books have been written.

One area which must be mentioned, however, is the teacher's interior life with God. Each of us needs a discipline of being present to God in solitude on a daily basis, to worship, confess, share one's desires and emotions, and engage in intercession. Teaching theology is never a technical matter. It is always leading people for God and to God, so our relationship with God is a priority. Jesus, in commissioning Peter to leadership, asked simply, "Do you love me?"[44] It is easy to allow the busyness of leadership in theological education to squeeze out the desire for relationship with God. We can become busy people just like other busy people who are rewarded with a sense of identity and self-worth that seems to hang on our busyness. In particular, we are busy with words; we belong to one of the most "wordy" professions. It is solitude in the deliberate presence of God which counteracts these occupational diseases of theological education.[45]

Yet we cannot understand our spirituality solely in terms of interior devotion. It has been a standard criticism of Western spirituality, especially of the Pietist tradition (unfairly), that it is selfish. This critique was particularly represented in the Iona process.[46] Partially behind this historical criticism was the growth of liberation theology attitudes coming out of Latin America in the 1960s and 1970s. Such traditions rightly criticize theologians and theology teachers for an interiority which cares mostly for their own spiritual progress

---

43. Thomas à Kempis, *The Imitation of Christ* (Harmondsworth: Penguin, 1952), 27.
44. John 21:16.
45. Henri Nouwen, *The Way of the Heart* (New York: Ballentine, 1981), 39–40.
46. Amirtham and Pryor, *Invitation*, 148.

while neglecting the suffering of the marginalized and poor in the world. It is a reaffirmation of the second "great" commandment that we should love our neighbor as ourselves.[47] Such a love needs to show itself in a reflection of God's love for the world, but particularly it is to be directed by a teacher toward his or her students. Students are needy human beings. Outside the classroom, they wrestle with problems of relationships, family, finance, and self-esteem. Inside the classroom, they have fears of not keeping up or of being made to look foolish. Many look with trepidation to the future.[48] A recent study of first-year theological and religious studies students in North America highlighted the struggles they often go through in integrating their critical academic study with their personal faith.[49] Faculty are to develop in compassion for their students.

Calling and Ministry Development

The location of the role of a theological educator must be found in the gift of "teacher" to the church.[50] Paul lists this gift as third after apostles, and prophets.[51] James advises that not many should enter this role since those who do so will be judged with greater strictness.[52] It is, then, a form of ministry, and just as people were called to be apostles and prophets, so there is a personal calling to be a teacher of the church that is also a church calling. The concept of the teacher's calling to ministry implies three main things for development. First, the teacher needs to be helped to develop in his or her sense of calling – which is dealt with elsewhere in this book. Second, calling to ministry implies duty and stewardship. Third, calling to ministry implies pastoral care skills with students.

Calling to ministry implies duty. Concepts of duty, responsibility, and faithfulness are not used as widely as before, but they are fundamental Christian

---

47. Luke 10:26–27.

48. See a recent study, Graham Cheesman, "So What Are They Really Thinking?," *The Theological Educator* 5, no. 2 (Feb. 2013), accessed July 2015, http://thetheologicaleducator.net/2013/02/08/so-what-are-they-really-thinking/.

49. Barbara E. Walvoord, *Teaching and Learning in College Introductory Religion Courses* (Oxford: Blackwell, 2007), 25–34.

50. "*Didaskalos*," in Colin Brown, ed., *The New International Dictionary of New Testament Theology*, vol. 3 (Grand Rapids: Zondervan, 1986), 765–768.

51. 1 Cor 12:28.

52. Jas 3:1.

virtues and spoken of frequently by both Christ and the apostles. A number of parables are told by Christ to illustrate stewardship, which is a concept embracing these virtues. For theological educators, this implies that they have a responsibility to the truth. There is a certain aspect of our calling and charge given us by God to preserve and teach the truth of the Word of God. For all the right explorations and exercise of critical judgment, there remains a sense of "for what I received I passed on to you as of first importance" (1 Cor 15:3) about the teaching of the Word of God. And there is a duty to students. The best way to serve God as a teacher in theological education is to produce good servants out of students. This leads us to have an obligation to each student to fulfill all the aspects of formation we are set up to deliver in their lives while they are with us. The teacher needs to believe in the students and to draw out of each one of them the potential they have for serving God and living a happy life in God's presence in this world. Before all others, teachers have a deep responsibility to every student God has given them. Teachers are stewards who will one day give account for the truth and for the students God gave them on loan for a few years of their lives. Faithfulness in this stewardship is part of our development as teachers.

Calling to ministry also implies pastoral attitudes toward and skills with students. Ministry always has to be about people, not just ideas. Yet this has been a difficult area of development for many faculty members in recent years. There is a strong tradition of the teacher as spiritual guide for the students under his or her care,[53] but more recently, colleges and seminaries, often after a long struggle for academic excellence, have increasingly responded to the new understanding of the importance of spiritual development, creating pastoral-type tutor groups and asking faculty to oversee the spiritual development of students. As we have seen, teaching as ministry implies the building of relationships between the teacher and the taught, and this is fundamental in the area of spiritual guidance. Yet the legacy of the struggle for academic excellence often includes teachers hired almost exclusively for their knowledge and academic skills. Such need a gentle and reassuring process of development

---

53. Philip Jacob Spener, *Pia Desideria: or Heartfelt Desires for a God-Pleasing Improvement of the True Protestant Church* (1675), in *Pietists: Selected Writings*, ed. Peter C. Erb, Classics of Western Spirituality (New York: Paulist, 2003), 41–43.

toward calling to ministry, including the necessary care and help to link this with their expertise in their subject area. The reward of such development will be great, not only for the students in training but also for their students in ministry later in their lives. Far too many have gone out from our colleges and seminaries with a model of ministry imbibed from their lecturers involving well-prepared intellectual teaching that is seen to do the job of personal development by itself. They enter ministry and assume that a good, well-prepared sermon on Romans 8 will sort out their congregation's spiritual lives with minimal pastoral engagement.

The Context of Faculty Development: Team Formation

We must now take a brief look at the other standard usage of the term "faculty development," that of creating, sustaining, and above all developing the faculty team. This is a vast subject, involving leadership issues,[54] team concepts, subject, gifting balance in the group, and much more. We will have to be selective and so will look at just two fundamental background ideas which provide objectives for development: the concept of a common calling, and the vision of a rich space of continuing learning to fulfil that calling.

The importance of faculty team development is based on the truth that, while faculty are each members of the wider community of the institution, which includes students and administrative staff, they also compose their particular sub-frame within that community which has its own rules and culture and is powerful in influencing its members and also the wider community of the institution. This influence of the faculty culture is great. When negative patterns emerge within it, such as tension, anger, breaking of relationships, and emotional disagreement as to vision, curriculum, or working patterns, the resultant atmosphere makes the task of the individual faculty member not only unpleasant but also difficult. Furthermore, faculty as a whole are no longer able to model for the students how Christians engage in ministry together.

---

54. An excellent little book on leadership arising out of experience in a major theological institution is Walter C. Wright, *Relational Leadership: A Biblical Model for Influence and Service* (Exeter: Paternoster, 2000).

Development of the faculty as a happy, growing, working group therefore has to be high up on the list of priorities for leadership. It will involve communications, work on interpersonal relationships, and plenty of time spent both talking about the issues and relaxing together. We should note that the four main areas of personal development discussed above (academic development, professional competence development, spiritual/discipleship development, and calling/ministry development) all have their corporate elements. Faculty members can and do grow together. There are many mechanisms which promote this reality, such as peer review, mentoring, joint interdisciplinary study sessions, assessment, and guidance sessions by leadership, and these will be dealt with elsewhere in the book.

Developing Common Calling

The concept of common calling was usefully described in an article by Gordon Smith published in *The Scope of Our Art: The Vocation of the Theological Teacher* in 2002.[55] It is common, perhaps even inevitable, that tensions arise between our sense of individual calling and the corporate sense of vocation of a college or seminary, not least because faculty members generally grow up in a culture and church environment which emphasizes their responsibility to be called and guided by God as individuals. Our desires as to how to serve God are not always realized within a structure where a number of people must work and decide together. Clearly, there needs to be a high degree of congruence between the teacher's vocation and that of the school, but the myth of the peg being fashioned for many years by the experiences God sends us, and our growing vision for service, and it finally fitting exactly the hole of our faculty appointment is partly to blame. We will always struggle with elements of poor fit, otherwise how will we discern the need for God's strength, comfort, and help – especially in our weaknesses when faced with our responsibilities? This has a biblical base. We cannot theologically speak of individual vocation except in the context of community, fulfilled in solidarity with others, and this requires discussion, selflessness, and a certain level of compromise.

---

55. Gordon T. Smith, "Attending to the Collective Vocation," in Jones and Paulsell, *Scope of Our Art*, 240–261. For an older view of the vocation of the theological teacher, see H. Richard Niebuhr et al., *The Advancement of Theological Education* (New York: Harper, 1957), 55–59.

Understanding the college or seminary's vision, in line with that of its mission statement, its history, and its subsequent development, and acknowledging the necessary compromises needed for each to share in that vision as we fulfill our own, is often only the first step in faculty team development. In most colleges and seminaries, there is (and indeed should be) a large element of shared governance involving the faculty as a team applying and developing that vision. This requires spiritual maturity, communal discernment, clarity about how shared vocation works in each challenge, and agreed mechanisms and attitudes which allow the faculty team to take decisions together. Common calling and the concepts and processes involved in working as a faculty team do not undermine the individual responsibility of the faculty member before God to develop in his or her life and work and to take responsibility for actions and mistakes. However, it does involve discerning how, and specifically where, corporate and individual responsibilities, visions, and decisions affect each other.

One great task of faculty development, then, is the molding together of a disparate group of people, each with his or her own ministry and calling, so they can together contribute to the common calling of the theological education institution.

Developing the Faculty Space

What is of primary importance in creating a faculty which can live and thrive within a common vision is the creation and strengthening of a faculty space which encourages individual and joint development. I am not thinking here so much of a literal space, although a staff room is a good idea, but something closer to the concept of the space or deliberate atmosphere described by Parker Palmer and others[56] as the basis of student development. His work listed a number of characteristics of such a space for student development. What are the characteristics of such a space for staff development?

First, it will be a space of mutual acceptance and respect, not just as scholars, but also as believers. Whatever our differences of emphasis, desires, subject, abilities, weaknesses, and sins, we have been welcomed by God in

---

56. Palmer, *To Know as We Are Known*, 69–87.

Christ, and given a task to do together for his kingdom.[57] Second, it will be a safe space leading to openness. Faculty members need the freedom to make mistakes within the safety of the group, to voice their intellectual views and even struggles on difficult issues which divide Christians, and to disagree as to the outworking of the corporate vision, without penalty, but with an acknowledgment of accountability to the team. Third, it will be a spiritual space, including real *diakonia*, worship together and prayer for each other and for the common task. Faculty retreats, faculty days, as well as weekly times together all help, but even more important is the intention to grow spiritually together, helping each other grow closer to Christ.[58] Fourth, it will be a space where love rules the relationships. We have already seen that there is bound to be tension at times within a faculty team, and we are not required to agree with or even like each other all the time, but, as many of us have experienced, the basic rules of Christian love – preferring the other, self-sacrifice, acts of love – make a vast contribution to peace and effectiveness. Fifth, it will be a sharp intellectual space where each member challenges and sparks the others into deeper and wider thought. Interdisciplinary work is more and more necessary in our specialized faculty teams and, although friendly rivalry will always exist between Old Testament and New Testament scholars, and between theologians and missiologists, a desire to learn from each other and study issues together is enriching. Sixth, often this develops into an enabling and prophetic space for the churches and society in which the college or seminary is placed. Churches struggle to cope with the stream of new ideas and attitudes occurring in society, from postmodernity to debate over the latest medical procedures, legal decisions, films, and books. It is the faculty teams of the colleges and seminaries which are best placed to guide the churches' thinking and speak into society on these issues – and they should be encouraged to do so as a prophetic group, together fulfilling their mission. This, then, is a snapshot of the vision of a faculty space which makes delivery of a corporate vision possible, and drives the development and servanthood of the faculty team.

---

57. Dietrich Bonhoeffer, *Life Together* (London: SCM, 1954), 7–26.

58. This is often best realized in the wider group which includes non-teaching staff.

Conclusion

The ultimate aim of theological education is the formation of students. This, in turn, depends to a great extent on the formation of faculty. In this short essay, we have set out a model of just what we are aiming for – an excellent faculty member; discussed key objectives of development needed to achieve this; and shown how it is not just an individual task but one done in the community of the school and especially the faculty team. Further chapters will show how this becomes effective in practice.

Reflection and Action Points

1. Does your school have a written statement of the objectives of theological education to which it works? In the light of this chapter, are you satisfied with it? Is it in need of review by the faculty?

2. Look at this little playlet by Tokunboh Adeyemo:

> Student: I can't outline what you say.
> Teacher: Life, and thought, and conversation seldom conform to an outline.
> Student: But that makes it hard to prepare for the exam.
> Teacher: What exam?
> Student: The one at the end of your course.
> Teacher: You'll be taking my exams the rest of your life.
> Student: I don't understand a lot of what you're teaching us.
> Teacher: You won't for three years.
> Student: That's the whole course?
> Teacher: No, it's only the beginning of the course.
> Student: Do you have any idea what my class standing will be?
> Teacher: You'll fail the course, along with the rest. But then all of you except one will turn the world upside down.
> Student: When we've finished, will we know as much as the Pharisees?
> Teacher: No, you won't know as much, but you'll be changed. Do you want to be changed?
> Student: I think so. Is your teaching relevant?

Teacher: Is it true?

Student: You seem to throw questions back at me instead of answering them.

Teacher: That's because the answers are in you, not in me.

Student: Will we see you in class tomorrow?

Teacher: The class continues at supper and at the camp fire tonight. Do you think I only teach words?

Student: Is there an assignment?

Teacher: Yes, help me catch some fish for supper.[59]

What does it tell you about Jesus as teacher? How do you separate context and principle?

3. In your culture, how acceptable is it to show emotion, and to share your personal experiences as teacher (in the light of the example of the apostle Paul)?

4. How do you rate Edgar's fourfold pattern of "locations," set out in figure 2.1,[60] as a set of aims for faculty?

CLASSICAL	Transforming the individual	Knowing God	CONFESSIONAL
	ATHENS Academy		GENEVA Seminary
	THEOLOGIA	DOXOLOGY	
	MISSIOLOGY	SCIENTIA	
	JERUSALEM Community		BERLIN University
MISSIONAL	Converting the world	Strengthening the church	VOCATIONAL

Figure 2.1: Edgar's Fourfold Pattern of "Locations"

59. In Paul Bowers, ed., *Evangelical Theological Education Today* (Exeter: Paternoster, 1982), 7–8.
60. From Brian Edgar, "The Theology of Theological Education," last modified 2005, accessed July 2015, http://brian-edgar.com/wp-content/uploads/downloads/2010/05/Theology_of_Theological_Education.pdf.

5. To what extent and how does your school strive for an integrated approach to student formation, and what would a faculty member who exemplifies this look like?

6. A number of models were given for a relational attitude to being a theological teacher. Which of the ones listed below do you most empathize with, and why? Is there a contextual element in your choice? Are there dangers attached to this approach? Are there other models you would suggest?
- Host
- Midwife
- Paraclete
- Friend
- Companion on the journey

7. Is research an important element of academic development for faculty? What are the key connections between research and good teaching?

8. List the main elements in a spiritual relationship to academic study for faculty members, and say a little about how each of them functions.

9. What percentage of your faculty members has received professional training
- In teaching?
- In theological education specifically?
Are there ways in which these percentages could be increased?

10. In the light of the role of leadership and faculty in governing the community, what would "loving students" look like, and are there ways that this has to be limited in theological education
- for individual lecturers and
- for the leadership of the school?

11. Do you agree that fundamentally the role of the faculty is Christian ministry? If so, what are the key implications of this for your leadership?

12. Have there been tensions within your faculty team arising from a lack of ownership of a corporate calling and vision? How are such tensions best dealt with?

13. In your context are there opportunities and duties for your faculty to speak together prophetically to society and the church? How are you developing this function, and in what areas?

14. Sum up four main action points you intend to pursue as a result of reading and studying this chapter:

1.

2.

3.

4.

Resources for Further Study

There is little material produced directly on the subject of definitions and concepts of faculty development in the evangelical tradition. Here is a selection of sources with relevance to the subject. For more material, see the notes.

Amirtham, Samuel, and Robin Pryor. *Invitation to the Feast of Life: Resources for Spiritual Formation in Theological Education*. Geneva: World Council of Churches, 1989.

Banks, Robert J. *Reenvisioning Theological Education: Exploring a Missional Alternative to Current Models*. Grand Rapids, MI: Eerdmans, 1999.

Bonhoeffer, Dietrich. *Life Together*. London: SCM, 1954.

Edgar, Brian. "The Theology of Theological Education." *Evangelical Review of Theology* 29, no. 3 (2005): 208–217.

Farley, Edward. *Theologia: The Fragmentation and Unity of Theological Education*. Philadelphia: Fortress, 1983.

Jones, L. Gregory, and Stephanie Paulsell, eds. *The Scope of Our Art: The Vocation of the Theological Teacher*. Grand Rapids, MI: Eerdmans, 2002.

Kelsey, David. *Between Athens and Berlin: The Theological Education Debate*. Grand Rapids, MI: Eerdmans, 1993.

Nouwen, Henri. *Reaching Out: The Three Movements of the Spiritual Life*. Glasgow: William Collins, 1976.

Palmer, Parker. *To Know as We Are Known: Education as a Spiritual Journey*. New York: HarperCollins, 1993.

Webb, Graham. *Understanding Staff Development*. Buckingham: Society for Research into Higher Education and the Open University Press, 1996.

3

Establishing an Institutional Culture as a Foundation for Faculty Development

Pablo Sywulka

Introduction: A Case in Point

Justin had just completed his first month as president of Silver Tree Seminary. When he accepted the invitation from the board of directors, he knew there would be challenges. Stepping from the pastorate into the presidency was in itself a major change.

On the surface, things seemed to be going fairly well at Silver Tree. A recent building campaign had resulted in a new library building. A state-of-the-art software system had just been installed. Enrolment had held its own due in part to some major scholarship grants. The external auditor's report praised the school for its balanced budget. Under the surface, however, there were rumblings of discontent. There seemed to be little cohesion between the different departments. The academic dean's office complained that it had no access to financial information from the business office. The director of student affairs was frustrated with the quality of the students being accepted through the admissions office. Chapel attendance had dropped dramatically, and prayer times for faculty and staff were almost nonexistent. Students complained that the professors were often not available. Some of the donors were starting to ask questions, and a few had stopped giving.

As Justin reflected on his first month as president, he realized that his major challenge was not financial or academic. His priority had to be establishing a healthy institutional culture for the seminary.

Understanding Institutional Culture

While the recognition that institutions have a culture is not new,[1] the subject has received greater attention in recent years. Robert Birnbaum, in his book *How Colleges Work* (1988),[2] discusses four "Models of Organizational Functioning" (The Collegial, Bureaucratic, Political, and Anarchical Institutions). He then proposes integrating these models in what he calls "The Cybernetic Institution."[3] Although he does not stress the term "institutional culture," that is essentially what he is talking about.

William Bergquist and Kenneth Pawlak, in their book *Engaging the Six Cultures of the Academy* (2008),[4] describe six cultures (Collegial, Managerial, Developmental, Advocacy, Virtual, and Tangible). They conclude that while these cultures are "markedly different," "they 'live' together on each campus."[5] The challenge for leadership is not to create a uniform culture, but, ironically, to begin by helping members of the organization understand "the points of view of those with whom they are most likely to disagree before they attempt to overcome these disagreements."[6]

---

1. For example, H. B. London, *The Culture of a Community College* (New York: Praeger, 1978), cited in William Bergquist and Kenneth Pawlak, eds., *Engaging the Six Cultures of the Academy* (San Francisco: Jossey-Bass, 2008), 270.

2. Robert Birnbaum, *How Colleges Work: The Cybernetics of Academic Organization and Leadership* (San Francisco: Jossey-Bass, 1988).

3. For each institutional model, Birnbaum presents characteristics, points out what he calls "Loops of Interaction" and "Tight and Loose Coupling," and gives suggestions for effective leadership.

4. Bergquist and Pawlak, *Engaging the Six Cultures of the Academy*. This is a revised and expanded edition of Bergquist's *The Four Cultures of the Academy* (San Francisco: Jossey-Bass, 1992).

5. Bergquist and Pawlak, 248.

6. Bergquist and Pawlak, 248.

Obviously institutional culture is a complex matter. It is there whether we realize it or not, and it influences all aspects of the institution, whether or not we are aware of its effect. Juan Manuel Manes calls institutional culture "the phantom that governs."[7]

What is institutional culture? Manes describes it as "the combination of shared beliefs, values, and customs that establish the norms which regulate the life of an educational institution."[8]

Basic Premises Regarding Institutional Culture

Justin's conclusion about his major challenge as president was not unique. If leaders want their schools to be effective, they need to give attention to the institutional culture. The following premises can help to create a frame of reference for this important task.

To begin with, it is important to understand that *every school has a culture.* The culture is developed and influenced by multiple factors, including the vision of its founders, the setting in which it is located, the role of its leaders, and the varied backgrounds of its students.

Second, *the culture of any school normally includes positive and negative elements.* Even the worst cultures will have saving elements, and the best cultures will have areas that need attention.

Third, *the culture of a school can be continually developed and improved.* Areas of weakness can be shored up, and areas of strength can be made even stronger. Culture is dynamic, not static.

In the fourth place, *institutional culture should be built on the firm foundation of the school's values, vision, and mission.* The goal is to align every aspect of the school's life – procedures and programs, activities and ambience – with its stated vision and values.

Fifth, *the establishment of the school's culture requires a clear commitment at all levels of leadership,* from the board to the president and his team, to

---

7. Juan Manuel Manes, *Gestión Estratégica para Instituciones Educativas,* 2nd ed. (Buenos Aires: Granica, 2004), 53. The phrase in Spanish is "El fantasma que gobierna."

8. Manes, *Gestión Estratégica.*

leaders at the intermediate and lower levels. A concerted and united effort is essential to this effort.

Finally, *establishing an institutional culture involves the implementation of a plan*, with appropriate action steps and evaluation.

Understanding the Context of the Institution

The External Culture and Its Influence

In order to analyze the culture of an institution, it is helpful to understand the external factors that influence it. There will usually be a major influence from the surrounding society, even when the school is international in its composition. The students and staff, as well as the immediate communities which the school serves, cannot be properly understood apart from their culture.

Especially those who come from outside, but also even those on the inside, need to be aware of the external cultural elements that can influence the internal dynamics of the institution. It can be helpful to ask key questions such as the following: Are differences managed in a direct, confrontational way, or with an indirect, non-confrontational approach? How important is it to save face, either in the case of oneself or in the case of others? How strong are the bonds of loyalty to family and community?

A helpful resource on understanding cultures is the book by Geert Hofstede and others, *Cultures and Organizations: Software of the Mind.*[9] The authors analyze the culture of a number of countries on the basis of several factors. These include what they describe as Power Distance, Collectivism versus Individualism, Assertiveness versus Modesty, Avoidance of Uncertainty, Short- and Long-Term Orientation, and Indulgence versus Restraint.

There are usually certain religious or theological concepts that underlie the surrounding culture. Work can be viewed as a curse (something to be avoided when possible) or as a blessing (something to be embraced). Telling the truth can be considered an absolute moral obligation (it's always wrong to lie) or a relative moral obligation (it's OK to lie if there are reasons to do so).

---

9. Geert Hofstede, Gert Jan Hofstede, and Michael Minkov, *Cultures and Organizations: Software of the Mind* (New York: McGraw-Hill, 2010).

It is essential to understand these concepts and to reinforce or confront them as the case may be, in order to properly develop your institutional culture.

In addition to the major surrounding culture, there may be subcultures that need to be understood. Churches and evangelical communities often have their own ways of doing things and their own points of view on issues. Theological schools will do well to be aware of these and other subcultures as they seek to develop their own culture.

Internal Factors That Influence the Culture

The culture of an educational institution is influenced not only by the surrounding culture, but also by internal factors. Two of those factors are the purpose of the school and the impact of prominent leaders.

Most institutions were founded with a particular purpose or vision. The founding purpose may have been to train pastors for rural churches, to form expositors of the Scriptures, to provide upper-level leadership for the evangelical community, or to respond to some other felt need. Even when the purpose of the institution has evolved over time, the original reason for its founding normally continues to shape the culture to some degree.

Of course, the vision may be restated or recast as the school develops. The needs which the school proposes to meet may change as the church matures. The academic level may be raised as the educational opportunities in the country increase. But whether it be the founding vision or the current statement of the school's vision, the purpose for which an educational institution exists will influence its culture.

The contribution of important people in the life of the school is another internal factor influencing the culture. The founders often leave their mark on a school, whether in the way things are done or by the values they communicated to those who followed them. Current leaders and professors influence the culture in much the same way. Do they show a passion for knowing and serving Christ, or do they reflect other interests? Do they go out of their way to serve, or do they appear to be indifferent to the needs of others? Are they deeply committed to a life of holiness? How do they balance responsibility to the ministry with responsibility to their family? The qualities modeled by the leaders and teachers in a school can have a profound effect on its culture.

Envisioning the Ideal Culture

Envisioning the Ideal Culture: Biblical Values

In order to develop the culture of an institution, it is important for the leaders to know where they want to take it. They need to have as clear a view as possible of the ideal culture to which they are committed. Even while they recognize that they may not fully reach the ideal, they will continually strive to move toward it.

Above all, the ideal culture should be established and developed on a foundation of biblical values. If we identify ourselves as "theological," our understanding of God and his purposes represents the most important element in that process. Since God has revealed himself in the Scriptures, we must look there first of all for the principles which will undergird and shape our culture.

It is to be expected that the vision, mission, and values of the school will be biblical in their focus. However, that cannot necessarily be taken for granted. They should be examined in the light of Scripture. A clear understanding of the attitudes and relationships that God desires for his redeemed people will provide a frame of reference for the culture we envision for our institution.

Biblical values often represent a "counter-culture" to the society in which we live. For that reason, they need to be promoted and emphasized intentionally. They represent an ideal toward which we are called to strive. What follows is a brief reflection on some important aspects of God's ideal culture for his people.

First of all, *the ideal biblical culture is one that values and promotes dependence on God.* Proverbs 3:5 sums it up: "Trust in the LORD with all your heart and lean not on your own understanding." The Old Testament presents examples of leaders such as Jehoshaphat who chose to trust in the Lord and who led their people in that same attitude of dependence (2 Chr 20:1–30). It also relates situations in which God's people relied on their own wisdom and failed to consult him, with disastrous results (e.g. Josh 9:14). Jesus taught his disciples to depend on the Father (Matt 6:33; 7:7) and also modeled that dependence (Luke 6:12). Paul learned through difficult experiences to depend on God and not on himself (2 Cor 1:9). Because dependence on God is expressed and cultivated through prayer, the practice of prayer should be one of the main components in the culture of a theological school.

Second, *the ideal biblical culture is one that values and promotes servant leadership.* Jesus not only taught and modeled dependence on God; he also emphasized servant leadership. He taught the disciples that "Whoever wants to become great among you must be your servant, and whoever wants to be first must be slave of all" (Mark 10:43–44). Then he added, "For even the Son of Man did not come to be served, but to serve, and to give his life as a ransom for many" (Mark 10:45).

It is interesting that when Jesus presented himself as an example, he focused on humility and servanthood. He could have pointed out his expertise as a teacher, but he didn't. He said, "Take my yoke upon you and learn from me, for I am gentle and humble in heart" (Matt 11:29). When he said, "I have set you an example that you should do as I have done for you" (John 13:15), he was referring to the way he took the place of a servant and washed his disciples' feet. When Peter speaks of Jesus's "leaving you an example, that you should follow in his steps" (1 Pet 2:21), he is referring to the way Jesus humbly accepted suffering, without protest or retaliation.

The apostle Paul also presents Jesus as an example of humility and service. He exhorts the Philippians to "do nothing out of selfish ambition or vain conceit. Rather, in humility value others above yourselves" (Phil 2:3), imitating the example of Christ who "made himself nothing by taking the very nature of a servant" (v. 7). Peter underlines this value at the end of his first letter. After exhorting the leaders to serve the flock with a humble, caring attitude, he adds: "All of you, clothe yourselves with humility toward one another" (1 Pet 5:5).

Servant leadership is extremely important. Especially in cultures where the position of a servant is looked down upon, but also in any culture, humble service to others needs to be put at the top of the values we seek to teach and model.

Third, *the ideal biblical culture is one that values and promotes a Christlike character.* God's goal is that we should "be conformed to the image of his Son" (Rom 8:29), reflecting the character of Jesus in our relationships. One of the outstanding characteristics of Christ's life was his humility. Another was his love – his unqualified, unconditional, unselfish love. Jesus put the good of his disciples above his own comfort or convenience. He "showed them the full extent of his love" (John 13:1 NIV 1990) as he washed their feet, gave them his final instructions, and then laid down his life for them on the cross. The ideal school is one where the love of Christ is lived out: where professors put aside their personal pursuits to listen to a student, where students rally around a worker in his or her moment of need, where leaders communicate a genuine concern for the welfare of each member of the community.

Jesus extended his love to the unlovely. He spent time with people who were looked down on by the "righteous" members of society. He was accused of being "a friend of tax collectors and sinners" (Luke 7:34). He openly related to despised people, such as the woman of questionable reputation who anointed his feet (Luke 7:39). An institutional culture which reflects the love of Jesus will include a component of compassionate outreach to those in need.

Another quality seen in Jesus was his holiness. He exemplified a life wholly given over to God and fully separated from sin. He provided a perfect example of someone who "committed no sin, and no deceit was found in his mouth" (1 Pet 2:22). We are called to be holy, even as he is holy (1 Pet 1:15–16). While we look forward to the experience of full holiness at Christ's coming (1 Thess 5:23), we are called to "make every effort to . . . be holy," because "without holiness no one will see the Lord" (Heb 12:14). Confession of sin (both corporate and individual), along with promotion of holy living, should be part of our institutional DNA.

Jesus also exemplified justice. He severely condemned those leaders who took advantage of vulnerable people, such as widows (Luke 20:47). He took the side of those who were looked down on by society at large because they were viewed as poor or as sinners. In our institutions, we are called to imitate the justice of our Lord – to treat people without preferences, and to take a stand against prejudice based on race, culture, gender, or social and economic standing.

Many other qualities of Jesus's character could be mentioned, such as his patience with the disciples in their learning process, and his willingness to forgive. How do we handle students in our institution who have difficulty learning or who learn slowly? To what extent is full, genuine, and spontaneous forgiveness practiced in our community?

It is by the way that Jesus's character – especially his love – is shown in our community that the world will know we are his followers (John 13:35). Christlikeness is the goal of discipleship. It is what our graduates will hope to see in those to whom they minister. When they learn this as part of our institutional culture, they will be able to say like Paul to the Galatians: "My dear children . . . I am again in the pains of childbirth until Christ is formed in you" (Gal 4:19).

Envisioning the Ideal Culture: Academic Values

A theological school needs to have a clear focus not only on biblical values, but also on education. After all, it is a place where students come to learn. And they will learn in the context of the institution's culture. Therefore, the academic values of that culture, and the way the teaching–learning process is viewed, need to be adequately understood.

Paul's instructions in 2 Timothy 2:2 illustrate some of the key academic values for a theological school: "The things you have heard me say in the presence of many witnesses entrust to reliable people who will also be qualified to teach others." These values include a learning environment, ethical responsibility, and missional outreach.

Paul the missionary was also a teacher. He realized that the continuation of his ministry depended on the training and empowering of others. He apparently did some of his teaching in a formal setting; Acts 19:9 states that during his two-year stay in Ephesus he "had discussions daily in the lecture hall of Tyrannus." However, much of his teaching was carried out in a non-formal environment, in the process of ministry and in the course of travel. Paul taught through words, but also through his life. He was able to say to his followers, "Whatever you have learned or received or heard from me, or seen in me – put it into practice" (Phil 4:9).

Paul developed *a learning environment* in his missionary team and in the churches where he ministered. He taught in a community setting; he mentions to Timothy "the things you have heard me say in the presence of many witnesses." The importance of a learning environment is amply discussed in the book *Schools That Learn*.[10] The authors underscore "the connection between living and learning," pointing out that "learning is at once deeply personal and inherently social; it connects us not just to knowledge in the abstract, but to each other."[11]

---

10. Peter Senge et al., *Schools That Learn: A Fifth Discipline Fieldbook for Educators, Parents, and Everyone Who Cares about Education* (New York: Crown Business, 2012).

11. Senge et al., *Schools That Learn*, 4.

A learning environment implies that we learn together, in interrelationships. This factor should be taken into account for the traditional classroom setting as well as for online classes. But a learning environment also implies that we encourage the members of our community to develop the ongoing habit of inquiring, of exploring, of participating in academic debate. If a learning environment is important for our institutional culture, it ought to be intentionally promoted.

Academic values include *ethical responsibility*. Going back to Paul's instructions, those who are taught need to be "reliable," or "faithful" (ESV). The root of the Greek word translated "reliable" in 2 Timothy 2:2 carries the idea of "trust"; a good translation would be "trustworthy."[12] Proven reliability should be a prerequisite for training, and it should also be evidenced through the training process.

Reliable people can be counted on to faithfully carry out an assignment or fulfill a responsibility. The academic value of reliability implies that students will be responsible to turn in their assignments on time; it also implies that teachers will be responsible to grade those assignments in a timely fashion. Administrators will be responsible to turn in their required reports. If there are assigned office hours or meetings to attend, faculty members will fulfill those responsibilities.

Reliable people can also be counted on to tell the truth. The academic value of truthfulness implies that what students turn in as their own work will indeed be their own work. The temptation to include in a written project what others have said without recognizing the source should be resisted by both students and professors. The ethical basis for truthfulness in academic pursuits needs to be explained from biblical and professional perspectives. Proper procedures for giving credit need to be emphasized from the beginning. Teachers need to know how to recognize plagiarism, and appropriate sanctions need to be clearly defined and strictly applied.

The academic values of a school's culture not only include a learning environment and ethical responsibility; they also include *missional outreach*.

---

12. The Greek phrase is *pistois anthropois*. The word *pistos* is derived from *pistis*, "faith," which can also mean "faithfulness." The word *anthropos* is the generic term for human beings; it is better rendered "people."

Those who are taught should be "qualified to teach others." The Greek term translated "qualified" in the NIV is rendered "able" in several other versions; the idea is that of being fit or sufficiently prepared.[13] The ultimate goal is not just that those who are taught will be qualified to teach, but that as a result they will actually "teach others."

Paul passed on to Timothy the truth he had received; Timothy was to pass that truth on to trustworthy people; and they in turn were to pass it on to others. The implication is that the chain goes on and on; those who are taught teach others, who will teach others, who will teach others. Trustworthy recipients of God's truth can be counted on to continue the transmission of that truth.

Theological education should never be simply an academic exercise. Those who receive training in our schools should come with the goal of passing on what they will learn, and they should leave with that same commitment.

The Great Commission in Matthew 28:19–20 provides an important frame of reference for our educational task. We should never lose sight of the global extent of that task; we are to go to "all nations." Ideally, a commitment to cross-cultural, global missions should be part of our institutional culture. At the same time, we should not lose sight of the communities and groups around us that need the Lord.

We are called to "make disciples," or followers of Jesus. The first element in the process is conversion, represented here by baptism. The second element is ongoing instruction: we are to "teach them to obey everything I have commanded you." We should model a style of teaching in our institution that not only communicates theoretical truth, but also calls to a life of obedience.

It is one thing to talk about the characteristics of an ideal institutional culture; it can be quite another thing to implement that kind of culture. But this is the challenge we face. In order to establish an institutional culture, certain basic elements need to be present. They include a commitment on the part of leadership, a plan of action, and an awareness of key factors for implementing the culture. These elements will be considered next.

---

13. The Greek word is *hikanos*, which can mean "worthy, fit; sufficient, able" (Barclay M. Newman, ed., *A Concise Greek–English Dictionary of the New Testament* [London: United Bible Societies, 1971]).

Establishing Institutional Culture

The Role of Leadership

In order to establish an institutional culture, the various levels of leadership have an important role to fulfill. Clearly the board of directors needs to be brought into the process. A visionary board might want to actively participate in defining what the culture should look like. Other boards may prefer to respond to the initiative of the school's president and his or her team. In any case, the board of directors should feel a sense of ownership. After all, if they are responsible for the institution, they are responsible for its culture. They need to understand what that culture should look like, and take an active interest in its development.

It goes almost without saying that a major role in establishing an institutional culture corresponds to the school's top leadership. They are the ones who need to clarify and communicate the vision for that culture, as well as implement it. The president will be the main spokesperson, but he or she will need the enthusiastic support of the academic dean and other top leaders. The president will also need the backing of the board and its chairperson.

The school's intermediate leadership and the faculty also need to be involved in the process. They should be actively teaching, modeling, and promoting the biblical and academic values of the school's culture. All levels of leadership should understand the vision for the institution's culture, and participate actively in establishing it.

The Importance of a Plan

Every school has its culture. However, the question should be asked: Is it going to be an unplanned culture, or a planned culture? Without intentional planning, the culture can slide into a "default" mode, shaped unconsciously by the external and internal factors that influence it. On the other hand, a planned culture requires clarifying the goal, getting your people on board, defining actions to be taken, and evaluating progress.

The first step in a plan for establishing institutional culture is to *clarify the goal*. The culture envisioned for the school should be characterized by specific biblical and academic values. Those listed earlier in this chapter can provide a starting point for discussion; but ideally each institution should work out its own list of the values that ought to characterize its culture. One question that can be asked is: What do we really want our school to look like?

The second step is to *get your people on board.* As was mentioned above, the different levels of leadership will need to actively support efforts to implement the cultural values of the school. The more they are involved in the process of defining the goals, the more likely they are to participate in reaching them. Eventually, all the members of the institution need to be brought into the process, but it has to start with the school's leaders and faculty.

The third step is to *define actions to be taken.* What can be done in a practical way to help establish the institutional culture which you envision? A good starting place might be to make sure that the board of directors supports the vision. Perhaps the key will be a board retreat to address the topic. The president will want to discuss at length the envisioned institutional culture with his or her leadership team and make sure that they are fully supportive of it. The faculty will need to be brought in, possibly through an extended workshop or a series of meetings.

In the process of defining actions to be taken, questions like the following can be addressed: How can we express the vision for our institutional culture in writing? How can we communicate it to our stakeholders and our students? How can we keep it in front of us all, so that we are continually reminded of its importance?

The fourth step in the process is to *evaluate progress.* The calendar for evaluation will be set up from the beginning. When it is time to evaluate, questions such as these can be asked: To what extent do the board and the school's leadership remain committed to the envisioned institutional culture? How well have we communicated it on the different levels? Are there ways we can improve on that communication? How have we modeled, or failed to model, the ideal values for our culture? What can we do to better model those values?

Establishing an institutional culture requires intentionality and dedication. Developing and implementing a plan for this takes work. But it is certainly worthwhile. We would do well, borrowing the words of the apostle Peter, to "make every effort" (2 Pet 1:5) to develop the best institutional culture possible.

Key Factors for Implementation

While the factors that will be discussed here have already been mentioned, they deserve special attention. The process to effectively establish an institutional culture requires effective communication, visible modeling, and constructive relationships.

In order to move forward in establishing an envisioned institutional culture, there needs to be *effective communication*. You might be able to push people in a certain direction, and they might comply, but the process is likely to be much easier if they understand why you are moving them. Establishing an institutional culture is much easier when those who participate in that process understand what is involved and why it is important.

The school's leadership will want to be sure that every member of the community is adequately informed regarding the desired institutional culture – its theological basis, its values, and its implementation. The board should be informed, as should the school's leadership, faculty, staff, students, and even friends.

Communication can be verbal, written, and/or pictorial. Workshops for the different groups in the institution can help to get the message across. Sermons and lectures in chapel times or conferences are another way to communicate. Bulletins, letters, posters, and banners can keep the message in front of people. The school's website on the Internet and the use of social media have become essential ways of communicating. If establishing the institutional culture is important, every means of communication should be used to reinforce the message.

Another essential factor for establishing an institutional culture is *modeling the values* of that culture. We may communicate broadly about the culture we envision for our school, but the ideals we talk about will not get very far unless they are modeled by the leadership and the staff. On the other hand, the modeling of those ideals can be a powerful force to help implement them. For example, one of the values might be dependence on God. If the leadership actively promotes times of prayer and visibly participates in them, and if you can see people praying for each other on the campus, those visual examples can do more to create a culture of dependence on God than a statement in the list of institutional values.

A third key factor for establishing an institutional culture is *constructive relationships*. When people feel that their leaders genuinely care for them, when they sense that their leaders are open and approachable, and when trust has been developed, it is much easier to establish a positive institutional culture.

Scott Barfoot, who has studied in depth the topic of trust in leadership, states his conviction that every leader "*must* more intentionally consider the pressing issue of trust."[14] He mentions four basic elements that help to build trust: integrity, development of skills, communication, and presence. This last element deserves particular attention.

Barfoot defines presence as "the manifestation of a leader's genuine care, compassion and benevolence toward another."[15] He points out the importance of receptivity, stating that "a receptive leader is one who makes himself or herself available and diligently employs active, empathetic listening, seeking to understand what followers say." He adds that "personal presence incorporates supportive encouragement to others." Finally, he mentions that "prayer centers both receptivity and encouragement in ultimate trust and dependence on the Lord."[16]

When people become aware of the personal presence of their leaders, when they feel they are genuinely cared for, and when an atmosphere of trust has been developed, the establishment of the institutional culture will flow more easily. Without this, the process will be more difficult. The personal presence factor requires intentionality and the investment of time on the part of the leader, but it is well worth the effort.

Doug Booker, an independent leadership consultant, makes the following comment on the basis of his experience: "When you create comfort, trust, respect, great communication and a desire for people to want to be there with YOU and the others . . . great things can and will happen."[17] Perry Shaw, a leader in international theological education, sums up the importance of modeling and relationships in a school's culture with these words: "The

---

14. Scott Barfoot, "The Trust Factor," in *Crisis Leadership*, ed. Scott Barfoot and David Fletcher (Austin: XPastor, 2014), 97.

15. Barfoot, "The Trust Factor," 109.

16. Barfoot, 109.

17. Doug Booker, *Triangles, Compasses and God* (Milwaukee, WI: Drambert, 2015), 37.

relationship between the administration, the faculty, the staff and the students communicates potent messages about the nature of Christian leadership and community. Where administrators are distant and authoritarian, students will follow this model, ignoring any classroom instruction about the importance of team leadership. If unresolved interpersonal conflicts exist within the school, students will not take seriously lessons that urge the centrality of reconciliation and peacemaking in the leadership of Christian faith communities."[18]

Where an envisioned institutional culture is effectively established, it will be in large part due to effective communication, modeling of the values, and constructive relationships.

Conclusion: A Case in Point

As Justin reflected on the challenge ahead of him, he decided to begin by trying to understand the culture of Silver Tree Seminary. He had several conversations with people who knew the school's history or who understood the dynamics of the surrounding society. He then began to form a list of the ideal characteristics he envisioned for the school.

He shared his conclusions with the chairman of the board, who agreed that a retreat to discuss the culture of the school would be a great idea. Many of the board members had not been aware of the concept before, and they all took part enthusiastically in the discussion. With the support of the board, Justin met with his leadership team to talk about the issues, and to map out a strategy for involving the whole school in the process.

The leadership team planned and then led a retreat for the faculty. The first presentation was on institutional culture – what it is, what factors help to form it, and how it can be understood. The initial lecture was followed by a group discussion time. Each group wrote up a list of characteristics of the institution's culture as they saw it, and the results were compared in a general discussion.

After a break, the academic dean led a Bible study on values that should characterize a Christian community. Again, there was group interaction followed by general discussion. A commission was named to prepare a list of the values seen as most important, along with a brief description of each one.

---

18. Perry Shaw, *Transforming Theological Education* (Carlisle: Langham Global Library, 2014), 87.

Next there was a brainstorming session on how to implement the ideal culture, followed by a time of prayer.

The leadership team took the results of the retreat and wrote up a description of the culture that was being envisioned. Then they began to draw up a plan of action. It began with communication. They considered several options for a key phrase, topics for messages in chapel, posters and banners, information on the website, bulletins, and flyers. They even talked about ideas such as using T-shirts, bracelets, and bumper stickers to help convey the message.

They set apart one full day in each quarter for a faculty seminar where topics such as modeling the school's values and constructive relationships would be developed. They decided on a schedule for evaluating progress, involving both internal and external assessment. The leaders put themselves at the top of the list for evaluation. And they committed themselves to consistent, focused prayer for progress toward the ideal institutional culture which they had made their own.

The story of Justin and Silver Tree Seminary is hypothetical, but it can help to illustrate the process of establishing an institutional culture. Every school will need to envision its own ideal culture and then work on the process of implementing it. The process may not always be smooth, and obstacles will likely appear. But, with the commitment of the whole school community and confidence in the Lord, significant progress can be made toward the goal. A healthy institutional culture creates a positive learning environment, projects a model for the students in their ministries, and brings glory to the One for whom the school ultimately exists.

Reflection and Action Points

The following exercises are designed for group discussion, particularly in response to the presentation of this topic in an IPAL seminar. If the topic is presented in another setting, such as a faculty workshop, the questions can also be used there.

1. *Understanding the culture of your institution.* Begin by discussing the following points:
(a) What do you consider to be the major strengths of your institution's culture?

(b) What do you consider to be the major weaknesses of your institution's culture?

(c) In what ways does the culture of the surrounding society influence your institution's culture? Try to be specific, taking into account both positive and negative factors.

(d) In what ways has the history of your school shaped its culture? Think of factors such as its founding purpose and key events in its development.

(e) How has your institution's culture been shaped by people who have had a major influence on it? Who are they, and in what way have they shaped it?

2. *Envisioning the ideal culture for your institution.*

(a) The biblical values mentioned in this chapter as part of an ideal culture are dependence on God, servant leadership, and a Christlike character. If you were asked to make a list of biblical values for your school, what would they be, and why do you think it is important to include them?

(b) The academic values mentioned in this chapter as part of an ideal culture are a learning environment, ethical responsibility, and missional outreach. If you were asked to make a list of academic values for your school, what would they be, and why do you think it is important to include them?

3. *Establishing the ideal culture for your institution: The role of leadership.*

(a) What role has the leadership of the institution played in the development of its culture in the past? What is its present role?

(b) If you are a leader, how can you participate more effectively in the establishment of your institution's culture?

(c) If you are not a leader, how can you encourage your leaders in their efforts to establish a positive institutional culture?

4. *Establishing the ideal culture for your institution: The place of planning.*

(a) The first step in the planning process is to define the goal. Imagine that you have been asked to prepare an initial draft to that effect. Describe in a brief paragraph the institutional culture you would like to see envisioned for your school.

(b) The second step is to get people on board. Mention three ways that you think would be effective to bring key groups in your institution to support the goals you envision.

(c) The third step is to define a plan of action. Make a preliminary list of recommended actions that you feel would be helpful in establishing the culture you envision.

(d) The fourth step is to evaluate progress. Write out a plan for evaluating the progress that has been made. When and how often would the evaluation be done, and by whom?

5. *Establishing the ideal culture for your institution: Key factors for implementation:*
(a) *Effective communication.* Make a list, in order of importance, of the means of communication you would recommend to promote the message about your envisioned institutional culture.

(b) *Modeling the values.* Using the list of values from question 2, give an example of how each value is being modeled, along with a recommendation of how it can be better modeled.

(c) *Constructive relationships.* In light of the comments by Barfoot and Shaw, evaluate the relationship dynamics in your institution, providing some positive examples and suggesting how they might be improved.

Resources for Further Study

Ayers, Edward. "The Academic Culture and the IT Culture: Their Effect on Teaching and Scholarship." EducauseReview. 1 January 2004. http://www.educause.edu/ero/article/academic-culture-and-it-culture-their-effect-teaching-and-scholarship.

Barfoot, Scott, and David Fletcher, eds. *Crisis Leadership.* Austin: XPastor Press, 2014.

Bergquist, William, and Kenneth Pawlak. *Engaging the Six Cultures of the Academy.* San Francisco: Jossey-Bass, 2008.

Birnbaum, Robert. *How Colleges Work: The Cybernetics of Academic Organization and Leadership.* San Francisco: Jossey-Bass, 1988.

Booker, Doug. *Triangles, Compasses and God.* Milwaukee, WI: Drambert, 2015.

Calian, Carnegie Samuel. *The Ideal Seminary: Pursuing Excellence in Theological Education.* Louisville, KY: Westminster John Knox, 2002.

Freed, Jann E., et al. "A Culture for Academic Excellence: Implementing the Quality Principles in Higher Education." *Eric Digest.* Published 1997. http://www.ericdigests.org/1997-4/quality.htm.

Hofstede, Geert, Gert Jan Hofstede, and Michael Minkov. *Cultures and Organizations: Software of the Mind.* New York: McGraw-Hill, 2010.

Kezer, Adriana, and Peter D. Eckel. "The Effect of Institutional Culture on Change Strategies in Higher Education." *The Journal of Higher Education* 73, no. 4 (July–Aug 2002): 435–460.

Manes, Juan Manuel. *Gestión Estratégica para Instituciones Educativas*. 2nd ed. Buenos Aires: Granica, 2004.

The New York Times online. "Campus Culture or Climate." http://www.nytimes.com/ref/college/collegespecial2/coll_aascu_ecculture.html.

Senge, Peter, Nelda Cambron-McCabe, Timothy Lucas, Bryan Smith, Janis Dutton, and Art Kleiner. *Schools That Learn: A Fifth Discipline Fieldbook for Educators, Parents, and Everyone Who Cares about Education*. New York: Crown Business, 2012.

Shaw, Perry. *Transforming Theological Education*. Carlisle: Langham Global Library, 2014.

Part II

Practical Ways in
Faculty Development

4

Designing and Implementing a Faculty Development Plan: Strategies for Faculty Development

Robert W. Ferris

If you have read this far, you may have concluded that faculty development is an important concept. You may even have decided that it is the key to more effective graduates and enhanced service to the church in your region. What does it take, however, to give legs to these ideas? This chapter suggests a six-step procedure for launching a faculty development program in your school.

Step One: Clarify Your Goals

As leader of the faculty, the dean holds both the authority and the responsibility to establish the standard toward which faculty members – individually and collectively – will strive. Paul reminds us, "It is required of stewards that they be found trustworthy" (1 Cor 4:2 RSV). With authority and responsibility comes accountability. The writer of Hebrews reminds us that leaders "will have to give an account" (Heb 13:17 RSV). Stewardship requires our best as we lead our faculty colleagues to greater fulfillment of their stewardship in their classroom, in their family, in the community, and in Christ's church.

How do you pray for the members of your faculty? What would you like to see God do through your school? What do you ask him to do in the lives of the men and women of your faculty? What would you like to see God do through you, as you lead this faculty?

The first step is to clarify our goals. Each school is distinct, just as the churches we serve and the ministries to which God has called us are distinct. The goals you adopt will be of little value (and may prove counterproductive) if they do not fit the calling God has given your school. Let me suggest three areas to consider as you formulate your own list of faculty development goals.

A Culture of Humble Service and Professional Excellence

Schooling is biased toward elitism and relational hierarchy,[1] but Jesus modeled servanthood, and called his disciples to reject elitist pursuits and to embrace the role of servant (Matt 20:25–28). In this, Jesus challenges us to examine our motives. Servanthood does not mean assuming the menial (although at times it may require that – see John 13:3–17). It does mean, however, that the interests of the other – a faculty colleague, a student, the church, or the lost of our community – are privileged over my own.

It is a mistake, however, to assume that a culture of servanthood precludes commitment to excellence. Both Christ and those we serve, as teachers and as leaders in our homes, churches, and communities, deserve our best. Furthermore, God has given us the capacity to learn, to grow, and to improve. Cultivating a campus culture that combines pursuit of excellence in all things with commitment to humble service may be a goal you choose to claim.

A faculty that embraces and models humble service and professional excellence is an invaluable asset to any ministry training program, since these are values that we teach and that we desire in our graduates. Although we may emphasize these values in the classroom, students will embrace them only when they see those values lived out in our work, our families, and our

---

1. Robert W. Ferris, "Leadership Development in Mission Settings," in *Missiology: An Introduction*, ed. J. Mark Terry, 2nd ed. (Nashville: Broadman & Holman, 2015), 457–470.

relationships on and off campus. Ultimately, the faculty *is* the curriculum.[2] Cultivating commitment to servanthood and excellence within the faculty is the most effective way for a dean to ensure that graduates of his or her school will model those values in the church and community.

A Culture of Collaboration and Mutual Care

The structures and processes of Western schooling reflect their roots in Hellenic individualism,[3] but this should trouble us as Christian teachers and equippers of those who will lead Christ's church. Whereas Jesus taught that love (i.e. caring for the other) is the mark of the Christian, and prayed for oneness among his followers, Western schooling insists that each student work alone, and brands collaboration as "cheating." Too often, competition is rife on our campuses, among both faculty members and students – there can be only one "top-notcher" in each class.

In contrast to schooling's promotion of individualism and competition, the Bible affirms the importance of relationship and community. God created humans like himself in order to invite us into a circle of personal relationships that has existed among members of the Trinity from eternity past. The "one another" passages in the New Testament assume and enjoin relationships of community and mutual care.

Unless community and mutual care are experienced on our campuses, students will carry into their ministries the orientation toward individualism and competition that is endemic in schooling. Given our training model, why should it surprise or disappoint us that so many graduates aspire to be "the big man" in their community, or tend to view other churches and their leaders as competitors? Teaching community and mutual care has little positive effect in schools where individualism and competitive values are modeled. The implicit curriculum always trumps the explicit curriculum. Despite the biblical truth taught, students will follow the example of their teachers rather than their words. With this in mind, among your faculty development goals you may

---

2. Robert W. Ferris, "Ministry Education for the Global Church," *Evangelical Missions Quarterly* 52, no. 1 (Jan 2016): 6–13.

3. Cory J. Nederman, "Individualism," in *New Dictionary of the History of Ideas*, vol. 3, ed. Maryanne Cline Horowitz (Detroit: Charles Scribner's Sons, 2005), 1114.

want to adopt promoting a culture that values community, collaboration, and mutual care.

A Culture of Growth

Professional development is about growth – as persons, as teachers, as ministers, and as a community. Cariaga-Lo and her colleagues note, "While funding is an important requirement, developing an infrastructure that fosters dialogue and collaboration among faculty members from across the disciplines is equally important and highly valued by the faculty participants."[4] Values and expectations regarding growth must be negotiated and articulated if they are to be shared. Only shared values regarding growth and development – those broadly owned by the school's leadership and faculty – are likely to be realized.

Among the faculty, it is the dean's privilege and responsibility to model commitment to growth – relationally connected, personally growing, challenging others, and helping them to grow. Just as it is unrealistic to expect students to own values that are not modeled by their teachers, so it is unrealistic to expect members of the faculty to exhibit greater commitment to personal and professional growth than is seen in their leaders. As you consider professional development goals for your faculty, you may decide it is important to foster a culture of growth.

Personnel development models a kingdom responsibility to nurture others.[5] This is the reason why faculty development is important and clear goals are essential. Setting goals and determining the path for your faculty development efforts is part of your spiritual ministry. Pursue it prayerfully.

Step Two: Assess Faculty Development Needs

Needs assessment need not be difficult or complicated. Much can be learned simply by talking to faculty members, individually, about their areas of interest, expertise, frustrations, and desired growth. Unless a dean is new to the school, she or he probably has observed areas of strength and weakness

---

4. L. Cariaga-Lo, P. W. Dawkins, R. Enger, A. Schotter, and C. Spence, "Supporting the Development of the Professoriate," *Peer Review* 12, no. 3 (Summer 2010): 19–22.
5. Eph 4:11–16.

among members of the faculty. Reports from students and alumni also can provide insight into areas where the personal and professional growth of faculty members would enable the school to serve the church more effectively. Collection of student and alumni observations and recommendations should be systematic, however, since anecdotal reports can be biased and unfair.

The professional development needs of individual faculty members are not the only focus of needs assessment, however. The school's culture also must be assessed. If relationships among the school's faculty and leadership are open, with high levels of trust, this is positive and a cause for praise. When the campus community is not healthy, however, addressing the culture of cliques, criticism, or conflict may be the most urgent agendum among professional development initiatives.

With these data in hand – that is, data from faculty self-assessments, the dean's own observations, surveys of students and alumni, and assessment of intra-faculty cultural dynamics – it is a good discipline to list the growth areas identified and to prioritize that list in light of one's goals for professional development.

Step Three: Determine Resources

The first resource to be measured is the commitment of leaders and the faculty to the task of faculty development. If faculty members are overloaded with teaching assignments, and burdened by personal and family concerns, a thoughtfully designed faculty development program may be rejected or ignored. Similarly, any approach to faculty development will falter if it lacks strong support from the school's leadership. Efforts toward faculty development that are viewed by others as one person's crusade will face strong headwinds in any school. It is essential, therefore, that the school's leadership team is united in its commitment to promoting truly Christian community and professional excellence within the faculty. It is equally important that leadership should recognize that this commitment entails cost.

Faculty development takes time and may require funding. Planning that fails to consider time or funds available has little hope of success. Much can be done with a little time and minimal or no funding, but greater resource allocation can expect more dramatic outcomes. If needs are clearly identified, and a definitive plan to address those needs exists, the school should consider requesting a grant from sponsoring churches or Christian foundations to underwrite the plan. Caution is required, however. Donors expect an account of the use and effectiveness of donated funds. If an aggressive plan is funded but the plan lacks administrative support, or faculty members lack time and interest in the project, the effect can damage the school's reputation and drain trust from both the faculty and the donors.

Step Four: Review Possible Strategies

With goals clarified, needs prioritized, and resources identified, the time has come to review and select specific professional development strategies for implementation. There is a broad menu from which to choose. Some strategies are very expensive, while others require no budget at all.

Strategies That Do Not Require Special Funding

While specific strategies will be more appropriate for pursuit of some goals than for others, many things can be done to develop the faculty without burdening the school's budget.

Small Groups That Nurture Relationship and Trust

When the goal is to strengthen community and a culture of mutual care within the faculty, the dean may opt to place faculty members in small groups with an assignment to share their stories and get to know one another better. Any faculty can benefit from strengthened bonds; this strategy need not be limited to schools where relationships are strained.

I have some experience with this strategy. The first semester I served as dean of Columbia Biblical Seminary and School of Missions, I requested faculty members to identify others on the faculty they felt they knew best. I then assigned them to triads, with a request to meet (with their spouses, if married) at least three times during the semester. I suggested that they meet in one another's homes simply to share their stories, perhaps over a meal, and to get to know one another better. My only restriction was that they avoid talking about the school, their courses, or their discipline fields.

The following semester I increased the level of risk; I asked faculty members to list others on the faculty they would like to know better. Again, I assigned them to triads with the same requests and restrictions. The project was very helpful in building a sense of community across the faculty.

Collaborative Ministry or Work Projects

Another strategy that is useful for building community is a faculty ministry or work project. A faculty may plan an evangelistic outreach to a nearby village or neighborhood, preferably in partnership with a local congregation. As they minister together in a context very different from the classroom, they have opportunity to observe one another's gifts and heart for ministry. This experience can radically alter relationships when the faculty returns to the campus, reflected in new areas of appreciation and trust.

A work project may have a similar effect. It may involve minor repairs, or painting a church's worship center, cleaning streets and empty lots in the neighborhood of the school, or assisting a new member of the faculty with the task of settling into a new home. As we leave our offices and the campus, we come to see one another in new ways that open doors to deeper relationships upon return to campus.

Professional Development as Part of Each Faculty Meeting

The observation often is made that our budgets and our calendars reveal our true priorities. If something is important to us, we will do what is necessary to fund it or to find time for it. One way that deans can demonstrate the importance of professional development of their faculties is to allocate time for faculty development activities in regular faculty meetings. Time allocated to faculty development, however, should be designed primarily to promote collective growth rather than to celebrate scholarly achievement.

A simple activity is to request members of the faculty to read an article that addresses a social or missional issue facing the church as preparation for a discussion led by one of their faculty colleagues. The article may be taken from a local newspaper or magazine, or may be downloaded from the Internet. Whether the article purports to represent a Christian or alternative perspective, the task of the faculty is to bring their various disciplines to bear on the issues raised with the purpose of stimulating thoughtful discussion that can benefit the church and the school – and that can benefit faculty members, individually and collectively.

A variation on that strategy (which does entail some expense) is to select a book for the faculty to read together. I have done this, as dean, in two different faculties. At the beginning of the school year I announced the book that we would read together, and assigned different members of the faculty to lead our discussion of each of the chapters. Then, at faculty meetings throughout the year, I allocated thirty minutes for discussion of the chapter assigned for that meeting. The books I selected dealt with pedagogical issues and strategies on which all could contribute and from which all could benefit. Depending on one's faculty development goals, however, a book on a cultural or missional issue may be most appropriate. Again, the goal is to engage an issue together in order to stimulate discussion and encourage growth.

Yet another approach to using faculty meeting time for professional development is to highlight a member of the faculty who is especially effective in some aspect of teaching, whether that is designing effective learning activities, lecturing, leading discussions, incorporating media clips or Skype interviews into classroom interactions, combining in-class and out-of-class learning activities, providing constructive feedback to students, in-context mentoring or assessing student work. The faculty member may be asked to provide examples of his or her approach, to explain the process by which this approach was developed, and to speak candidly about the benefits and challenges inherent in the process. Time for questions and answers is an important aspect of any such presentation. The dean would do well to collaborate with the faculty member in preparation for the faculty meeting, since brilliance is not always self-aware.

Whatever the topic or approach, the point is to stimulate professional growth through disciplined interaction. Mallard suggests, "In order to discover the soul of scholarship, professors need a community that encourages the kind of productivity that comes from formal and informal faculty interaction. I envision a community where dialogue is prevalent, energizing and productive."[6]

---

6. Kina S. Mallard, "The Soul of Scholarship," in *Scholarship in the Postmodern Era: New Venues, New Values, New Visions*, ed. Kenneth J. Zahorski (San Francisco: Jossey-Bass, 2002), 67–68.

Faculty Lunch Discussions

A variation on the use of faculty meeting time for professional development is the faculty luncheon.[7] It rarely is desirable to schedule faculty luncheons daily, but a faculty lunch once or twice a month may work well. In the informality of eating together, a topic for discussion should be introduced, perhaps based on an article shared in advance. Allowance for forethought by faculty participants is important; while free-ranging discussions on topics of current interest may be interesting and enjoyable, without opportunity for disciplined preparation they rarely have developmental benefit.

Another use of the faculty luncheon is to invite a member of the faculty to share a project in which she or he is engaged. That may be an article for a church publication or a professional journal, a contribution to a biblical commentary, or an apologetic or missional project. The purpose of the session is not to honor the presenter but, as a community of professionals, collectively to examine the work to see what each can learn and contribute. This requires humility on the part of the presenter, and constructive engagement by her or his colleagues, but the benefits for both the presenter and others can be significant.

Peer Coaching

A faculty that has developed a culture of growth is open to learning from one another. When approached intentionally and structured, this may be described as peer mentoring, or peer coaching. Huston and Weaver suggest, "Peer coaching is defined as a collegial process whereby two faculty members voluntarily work together to improve or expand their approaches to teaching. Peer coaching may be reciprocal, with each partner serving as coach to the other, or it may be one-way with one partner serving as the coach and the other as the recipient of the coaching."[8]

Two elements in this definition merit emphasis. First, peer coaching is voluntary; the dean may outline the potential benefits and the methods of peer coaching, and may encourage members of the faculty to consider initiating

---

7. Donna E. Ellis and Leslie Ortquist-Ahrens, "Practical Suggestions for Programs and Activities," in *A Guide to Faculty Development*, ed. Kay J. Gillespie, Douglas L. Robertson, and Associates, 2nd ed. (San Francisco: Jossey-Bass, 2010), 120.

8. Therese Huston and Carol L. Weaver, "Peer Coaching: Professional Development for Experienced Faculty," *Innovation in Higher Education* 33, no. 1 (June 2008): 5–6.

a peer coaching relationship, but faculty members should be free to elect a coaching partner. Second, faculty members, rather than an administrative leader, should establish the purpose of the peer coaching relationship, whether to address recognized areas for improvement or to extend their repertoire of teaching methods. (There may be occasions when the dean recognizes that a faculty member needs help to avoid failure and assigns a colleague as coach, but that is not a peer coaching relationship.)

Peer coaching typically works best when entered for a specified time (e.g. one term) and when faculty peers employ a prescribed process. At an initial meeting for a reciprocal coaching relationship, each peer should specify his or her goal in the relationship – that is, the area or areas of desired growth. Then each peer observes the work of the other, including observing one or more classes taught. Each observation is followed by a meeting for sharing observations and suggestions related to the goals stated for the coaching relationship.[9] These may include personal advice or recommendation of resources related to the area of desired growth. This process may be repeated through several cycles, especially if the peers find the relationship beneficial and the relationship is extended.

A high level of trust is required for faculty members to discuss with candor their fears and failures as a basis for positive growth. For this reason, the peer coaching relationship should be protected as confidential, free from fear of embarrassment or discipline by an administrator.[10] Nevertheless, when peer coaching is done well, with tangible professional benefit, the peers may be asked to report on the process and benefits of their experience at a faculty meeting or luncheon. When done discreetly, this can be an encouragement for others to initiate peer coaching relationships.

The Syllabus Review

There are also ways that the dean can engage with individual members of his or her faculty in order to promote professional growth. The first of these is the syllabus review.

---

9. Huston and Weaver, "Peer Coaching," 8.
10. Huston and Weaver, 15.

In order to assure and improve the integrity of the school's curriculum, it is common for the dean to require members of the faculty to submit their syllabi for review. Few deans can afford to review every syllabus every term, but good practice suggests that syllabi reviewed should include (1) every new course introduced into the curriculum, (2) every course taught for the first time by a different instructor, and (3) one course (not recently reviewed) taught by each instructor.

The purpose of the syllabus review is to ensure (1) that the course goals defined in the school's curriculum are appropriately addressed, (2) that the school's mission and core values are appropriately reflected in the design of the course, (3) that the subject matter is current and contextually appropriate, (4) that the course is designed to promote student learning, rather than simply "to cover the subject," and (5) that the course assignments and requirements represent an appropriate workload for both students and (with respect to marking or assessments) the instructor.

The syllabus review may be approached as an assessment of the instructor's competence, but this is not necessary. When approached that way, a valuable opportunity for faculty development is missed. Rather, the syllabus review should be seen as an opportunity for the dean to strengthen the members of her or his faculty – to commend the creative and effective teacher, to mentor those who need help, and to challenge all to a higher standard.

Class Observation with Debriefing

A second way that a dean can engage with faculty members to promote their professional development is by observing instructors as they teach. Although some faculty members may be stressed by the thought of the dean observing their class, this is minimized when all understand that the purpose is to promote development rather than to assess. Class visits should always be prearranged, and it is a courtesy to schedule a visit with the faculty member to ensure that the class visited is both typical and demonstrative of the teacher's skills.

A class observation guide (see appendix A) is a useful tool. This guide should be reviewed with the whole faculty when introducing the plan for class observation visits, so faculty members are aware of the areas to be observed.

Following the class observation visit, it is important for the dean to debrief the visit with the faculty member whose class was observed. "Providing feedback to teachers about the results of their observations and helping them reflect on this feedback in productive ways provides the bridge between knowledge about what matters for students and changes in teachers' actual practice."[11] Ideally, this should be done immediately following the class, while memories are fresh. If an immediate debrief is impossible, an early appointment should be scheduled. When debriefing the class observation visit, the observation guide and report should be shared with the faculty member as a context for commending good practice and for addressing areas worthy of attention or needing improvement. Goals should be set, resources reviewed, and a plan for growth established. It is important that the debrief appointment is marked by constructive and supportive affirmation of the faculty member. This is an opportunity for the dean to demonstrate friendship and commitment to the professional development of her or his faculty members.

Annual Performance Review

The annual performance review affords a third opportunity for the dean to engage members of the faculty to promote personal and professional development. If trust is weak, the annual performance review can be threatening for faculty members. It is critically important, therefore, that the dean clearly communicates his or her collegial and developmental intent. The purpose of the annual performance review is to help *foster improvement and growth*, not to judge. If areas of weakness are identified, and experience demonstrates that the faculty member is unwilling or unable to resolve those weaknesses, the time may come when a more difficult conversation is needed. That more difficult conversation should not occur, however, in the context of the annual performance review. The performance review should be a friendly and helpful conversation that highlights excellence and sets goals for personal and professional growth.

The focus of the annual performance review should be twofold: (1) the faculty member's commitment to and demonstration of the school's mission and core values, and (2) the faculty member's professionalism in teaching and

---

11. Megan W. Stuhlman, Bridget K. Hamre, Jason T. Downer, and Robert C. Pianta, "How Classroom Observations Can Support Systematic Improvement in Teacher Effectiveness" (University of Virginia), accessed 3 April 2015, http://curry.virginia.edu/uploads/resourceLibrary/CASTL_practioner_Part5_single.pdf.

mentoring. In both areas, the dean's commitment is to help this faculty member recognize areas of excellence, areas where growth has been observed, and areas still needing disciplined attention. This supportive and constructive approach is critical to the success of the annual performance review.

Three sources should inform the annual performance review. First, the faculty member himself or herself should provide a self-assessment. It is most helpful if this is done using the form for the annual performance review. (A sample form is provided in appendix B.) This affords the faculty member an opportunity to assess her or his performance, and to identify areas for growth using the categories addressed in the performance review. It also gives her or him an opportunity to report on growth goals achieved during the past year, and to propose growth goals and strategies for the year ahead.

A second source that can inform the annual performance review is student reports. Student reports should be collected in one or more courses taught by all faculty members at or near the end of each term. Some schools may implement a policy of student course evaluations in every course. (A sample student course evaluation form is provided in appendix C.) In other schools, the dean may invite selected students to a guided focus group discussion of individual courses. Whatever the procedure, the issues addressed should be the teacher's demonstrated commitment to the school's mission and core values, and his or her professionalism as teacher and mentor.

The third source that informs the annual performance review is the dean's own observations, both formal and informal, regarding the faculty member's performance during the year under review. The dean should not be sensitive about bringing personal observations into the annual review process; the purpose is to be as helpful as possible. The dean's observations will inform review of data from the other two sources when preparing for the annual review appointment. At this time, the dean will complete an annual performance review form that includes evidence from all three sources. (Caution: Don't underestimate the time required to do this thoughtfully. You may need up to two hours per instructor.) This form will be the primary focus of the annual review appointment.

The annual review appointment should be scheduled well in advance, perhaps at the time the self-assessment is requested. At the appointment, the annual performance review form should be reviewed and discussed, with special attention given to areas of excellence. Areas for improvement also should be discussed, and goals, resources, and support negotiated for addressing those areas in the coming year. If the faculty member does not believe the annual review process has fairly represented his or her performance, opportunity should be given to provide additional evidence. Thus every effort is made to assure that the atmosphere of the annual performance review is open, constructive, collegial, and fair. By assisting faculty members to recognize their areas of excellence and needed development, and by helping faculty members frame realistic goals and strategies for personal and professional growth, the dean fosters a culture of growth in the school.

Strategies That Require Special Funding

While there is much that can be done to promote the development of the faculty without special funding, opportunities for personal and professional development expand when special funding is available. Faculty development need not be a large budget item; a great deal can be accomplished with a small investment.

An Annual Faculty Retreat

If an annual faculty retreat is held on campus, costs may be minimal. An off-site retreat, however, affords a change of venue that can be conducive to discussions that may not occur on campus. Furthermore, an off-site retreat neutralizes any temptation for faculty members to attend to issues in their offices or to entertain interruptions by staff or students. A day-long retreat at a modest conference center within an hour's travel from campus will entail limited costs. If the retreat is scheduled for more than one day (entailing overnight accommodation), or at a more distant conference or retreat center, the costs are more substantial.

If the faculty retreat is held at the beginning of the school year, there will be administrative information to share. The dean should ensure, however, that a significant amount of time is given to promoting faculty development. Among other things, this could include review and discussion of the school's mission and core values, alignment of curricular and course goals with the school's mission, interactive instruction on methods of teaching, creative strategies for assessing student learning, or interaction with theological or practical issues arising from the cultural context or the constituent church. Of course, the faculty retreat should also nurture the spiritual life of the faculty, so the retreat schedule should include time for the faculty to study the Scriptures together, to share how God is growing their personal relationships with himself, and to pray together – in a large group, in small groups, and individually. An effective faculty retreat will require careful advance planning, but the effect on community and personal growth can be significant.

Professional Growth Book Shelf

Good books are expensive, so one way a school can promote the professional growth of faculty members is to invest in a faculty development library. A basic library of even twenty to thirty books can provide a significant stimulus for faculty growth. (For an English language basic faculty development bibliography, see "Resources for Further Study" at the end of the chapter.) Adding even three or four good books a year to the school's faculty development library can cost US$100 or more, and five or six books a year can cost US$200 or more, so the administration should approach the faculty development library as a long-term commitment. On the other hand, to collect a few books then discontinue acquisitions sends the wrong message regarding the administration's commitment to faculty development.

When books are added to the faculty development collection, it is helpful if the dean provides a scholarly, yet practical, review of the book at a faculty meeting, or requests another member of the faculty to do so. When the dean or a member of the faculty points out the helpfulness of a book, others are more likely to read it.

Book and Media Allowances

If resources permit, providing each member of the faculty with a cash allowance to spend on professional books and journals or on audio or video media for use in the classroom can be a significant statement of the school's commitment to the professional development of its faculty. An oversight procedure should be provided to ensure that the allowance is spent for the purposes given. An alternative is to provide reimbursement up to a specified limit to ensure that book and media expenses are justified. When the school is investing in their growth, faculty members can be expected to stay abreast of scholarship in their field, and to model commitment to growth before their students.

Growth Contracting

A growth contract is an agreement between the school and a faculty member in which the faculty member describes a project designed to address an area of needed growth and the school agrees to fund the project. The project may be a program of reading, research to support an article for publication, enrollment in a specialized course, workshop, or seminar, or any other appropriate activity that requires resource support. Project expenses may include the cost of books, course tuition, workshop or seminar registration, travel, and other costs directly incurred by the project.

Typically, the growth contract application demands a rigorous rationale to support the professional development benefit of the proposed project, and includes an expectation that benefits of the project will be shared with the rest of the faculty. Schools that budget for growth contracting typically appoint a committee of administrators and faculty members, sometimes including external stakeholders, to review growth contract applications and to award contracts. A vigorous program of growth contracting can provide a wonderful stimulus and support for the professional development of faculty members, but it also requires significant commitment on the part of the school's board and administration to assure substantial funding over time. A growth contracting program that is abandoned after only a year or two may be viewed as a boon to selected individuals while undermining a broader culture of growth.

Faculty Study Leave

A faculty study leave also should be approached as a contractual agreement between the school and a member of its faculty. Typically, the school's board will adopt a faculty study leave policy that stipulates (1) who is eligible to apply for a faculty study leave, (2) standards for a faculty study leave proposal, (3) the length of the faculty study leave, and (4) who is responsible for awarding faculty study leaves.

Most schools will restrict faculty study leaves to those who have served on the faculty for a minimum number of years (e.g. five or six years) and who have not recently had a faculty study leave (e.g. not within the past six years).

Although a faculty study leave may be referred to as a "sabbatical leave" (and "sabbatical" implies rest), a faculty study leave is not a vacation; it is a time for concentrated academic work or ministry engagement that will develop the faculty member professionally and benefit the school and its students. The study leave proposal should be negotiated with the dean and should describe the benefits anticipated. Furthermore, the study leave contract should require a formal report to the dean and to faculty colleagues, at the end of the study leave, on work accomplished and benefits realized during the study leave.

Since a one-year study leave may prove disruptive, it often is wisest for policy to limit the leave to a single term. If a one-term leave is granted, the study leave policy may allow more frequent study leaves (e.g. after three or four years). It also is common to obligate those awarded a faculty study leave to remain with the school for a stated period (e.g. three times the length of the leave) following the study leave. During the study leave, the school will pay the faculty member's salary, but the contract should state that salary received during the study leave must be repaid if the faculty member leaves the school before the contract expires. The period of the contract, then, is the time of the leave plus the faculty member's contractual obligation following the leave.

The school's study leave policy should provide for proposals to be submitted to the dean, but awarding a faculty study leave should require action by the school's leadership, including the principal and the chief financial officer. In some cases, the school's leadership may seek advice from a committee of the faculty. It is not uncommon for the dean to have more applications on file than the school's budget can sustain. Difficult decisions are required. It is important to consider the needs of the whole faculty, and to ensure that study leaves are granted fairly, without any hint of favoritism.

The award of a faculty study leave may prove to be the most expensive investment in faculty development, or it may cost the school almost nothing at all. When a study leave is awarded, the subjects normally taught by the faculty member on leave must be taught by someone else. If this means the school must hire adjunct instructors, the impact on budget can be significant.

There is an alternative, however, for schools with larger faculties. If faculty members will agree in advance to accept an overload, it may be possible for others on the faculty to teach subjects normally taught by the instructor on leave. Then, when others are awarded a faculty study leave, those who have benefited in the past are expected to step forward to teach on behalf of their colleagues. When the study leave is limited to a single term, most instructors can handle an overload for one term. Teaching an overload for consecutive terms is more problematic, both for faculty colleagues and for the school.

This review of faculty development strategies is intended to be suggestive rather than exhaustive. The goal is development of the professional effectiveness of members of the school's faculty in ways that promote the school's mission. In any context, there may be ways to grow the awareness, the skills, and the missional effectiveness of faculty members that are not included in this list. There is no substitute for creative engagement with the school's context and the development needs and aspirations of the faculty.

Step Five: Prioritize Strategies and Resources

Having clarified the school's goals, assessed its needs, determined the resources available, and surveyed possible faculty development strategies, a decision must be taken on what to do. It may be helpful to begin by identifying those strategies (or that strategy) that most directly address the highest-priority faculty development need. This may be considered the school's most strategic approach to faculty development. It also is prudent to identify those strategies that are most accessible, that is, that can be implemented with the least demand on the faculty and on the school's resources. Whenever feasible, the strategic approach should be pursued. If the strategic approach is not immediately feasible, it may become feasible in the future. In the meantime, leaders should not permit difficulties in launching the most strategic approach to deter them from doing what they can. Even small beginnings can be an encouragement to faculty members and can lead to significant faculty development. The point is to move beyond intentions to a plan for the professional development of the faculty.

Step Six: Implement the Faculty Development Plan

Any plan is only as good as its implementation; if the plan is not implemented, good intentions will benefit nothing. Faculty development is important because the personnel of a college are its greatest resource; the dean and the school's leadership team has a stewardship obligation to foster the growth of each member of the faculty for the benefit of the school's mission, of the churches it serves, and of its students. An extensive study of faculty development at United States and Canadian colleges and universities "validate[d] our belief that faculty development is a critically important lever for ensuring institutional excellence."[12]

Faculty development is also important because the faculty *is* the curriculum of the school. The lives of faculty members in and out of class, how they pursue their disciplines, how they relate to students, how they handle God's Word, how they relate to the church, and how they relate to the non-Christian society around them will shape the lives and ministries of students and graduates. If the campus is shaped by a culture of growth, if faculty members are committed to personal and professional growth, and if faculty members are supported by a leadership team and a board that is committed to fostering the professional growth of the faculty, students will develop similar aspirations and life patterns. This is the missional incentive for strong initiatives in faculty development.

Finally, faculty development is important because the world in which we live is changing. The world in which the faculty members were trained for their present roles is past. The world in which our students will minister does not yet exist. In the meantime, our cultures are changing, and the challenges facing the church in our cultures are changing. It is not responsible to offer our students yesterday's answers for tomorrow's challenges. God's Word does not change, but cultures and contexts change, and therefore growth is essential. This is the curricular incentive for a strong program of faculty development.

There are many excuses for opting not to consider a faculty development initiative. Some excuses are simply myopic. "We don't have time for faculty development" is a common excuse. The fable of two woodsmen applies. Which woodsman will chop more wood in a day: the one who stops to sharpen his axe, or the one who works harder with a dull axe? A better prepared, more accomplished faculty is best able to realize the goals of the school. If we find

---

12. Mary Deane Sorcinelli, Ann E. Austin, Pamela L. Eddy, and Andrea L. Beach, *Creating the Future of Faculty Development: Learning from the Past, Understanding the Present* (Boston, MA: Anker, 2006), 175.

that we don't have time to sharpen our skills, we probably need to reassess our priorities.

A second myopic excuse suggests that "We can't afford faculty development." The previous section includes several faculty development strategies that require no funding. Usually, "That's not in the budget" is a coded message to be translated "That's not important to me." At home and on our campuses, we find funding for the things we consider important. Any school that dismisses appeals for faculty development on the basis of budget has not considered the stewardship, missional, and curricular importance of faculty development.

Another common excuse suggests that it is unnecessary for the school to adopt a faculty development program because faculty members will pursue growth on their own initiative. This often is a gratuitous assumption. Faculty members may desire growth, but without the support of leaders and colleagues who are growing, a personal growth plan is difficult to sustain. Even more worrisome, when a school's leadership does not value growth, faculty members soon come to adopt the same mentality.

Conclusion

This chapter has described a six-step approach to planning and implementing a program of faculty development. Faculty development is "strategically important, intellectually demanding, and professionally rewarding in its contribution to fostering institutional and individual excellence."[13] Primary responsibility for initiating a faculty development program rests with the dean, although the support and participation of both the school's leadership team and the faculty will make the task easier. Any program of faculty development should align with the school's mission and core values, should be oriented to the development needs of the faculty, and should make wise use of all available resources. There are many strategies that may be considered, so priorities must be established and a plan developed. Only when that plan is implemented, however, are benefits derived.

---

13. Ann E. Austin and Mary Deane Sorcinelli, "The Future of Faculty Development: Where Are We Going?" *New Directions for Teaching and Learning* 133 (Spring 2013): 85–97.

Faculty development is an investment in the future of your school; *it should not be viewed as an expense!* The initial budget need not be large; even a small allocation (among many pressing demands!) will communicate that the leadership recognizes this is important. *Fund it!* Furthermore, if faculty development is not intentional, it rarely will happen. *Plan it, commit to it, and do it!*

Resources for Further Study

Banks, Robert. *Reenvisioning Theological Education: Exploring a Missional Alternative to Current Models.* Grand Rapids, MI: Eerdmans, 1999.

Brookfield, Stephen D. *Becoming a Critically Reflective Teacher.* San Francisco: Jossey-Bass, 1995.

———. *The Skillful Teacher: On Technique, Trust, and Responsiveness in the Classroom.* 3rd ed. San Francisco: Jossey-Bass, 2015.

Cranton, Patricia. *Understanding and Promoting Transformative Learning: A Guide for Educators of Adults.* 2nd ed. San Francisco: Jossey-Bass, 2006.

Davis, Barbara Gross. *Tools for Teaching.* 2nd ed. San Francisco: Jossey-Bass, 2009.

Elmer, Duane. *Cross-Cultural Servanthood: Serving the World in Christlike Humility.* Downers Grove, IL: InterVarsity Press, 2006.

Ferris, Robert W. *Establishing Ministry Training: A Manual for Programme Developers.* Pasadena, CA: William Carey Library, 1995.

Fink, L. Dee. *Creating Significant Learning Experiences: An Integrated Approach to Designing College Courses.* San Francisco: Jossey-Bass, 2003.

Horne, Herman. *Jesus the Teacher: Examining His Expertise in Education.* Revised and updated by Angus M. Gunn. Grand Rapids, MI: Kregel, 1998.

Knowles, Malcolm. *The Modern Practice of Adult Education: From Pedagogy to Andragogy.* Revised and updated. Chicago: Follett, 1980. (Out of print, but used copies are available at reasonable cost.)

Lingenfelter, Judith E., and Sherwood G. Lingenfelter. *Teaching Cross-Culturally: An Incarnational Model for Learning and Teaching.* Grand Rapids, MI: Baker Academic, 2003.

Palmer, Parker. *The Courage to Teach: Exploring the Inner Landscape of a Teacher's Life.* San Francisco: Jossey-Bass, 2007.

Plueddemann, James E. *Leading across Cultures: Effective Ministry and Mission in the Global Church.* Downers Grove, IL: InterVarsity Press, 2009.

Schön, Donald A. *Educating the Reflective Practitioner.* San Francisco: Jossey-Bass, 1987.

Shaw, Perry. *Transforming Theological Education: A Practical Handbook for Integrative Learning.* Carlisle: Langham Global Library, 2014.

Vella, Jane. *Learning to Listen, Learning to Teach: The Power of Dialogue in Educating Adults.* Revised ed. San Francisco: Jossey-Bass, 2002.

———. *Taking Learning to Task: Creative Strategies for Teaching Adults.* San Francisco: Jossey-Bass, 2001.

Weimer, Maryellen. *Learner-Centered Teaching: Five Key Changes to Practice.* San Francisco: Jossey-Bass, 2002.

Zuck, Roy B. *Teaching as Jesus Taught.* Eugene, OR: Wipf and Stock, 2002.

Zull, James E. *The Art of Changing the Brain: Enriching the Practice of Teaching by Exploring the Biology of Learning.* Sterling, VA: Stylus, 2002.

Appendix A

Sample Class Observation Guide and Report Form

Instructor Observed: _____

Classroom Observer: _____

Course Title: _____ Date: _____

Type of Course: ☐ General Requirement ☐ Program Requirement ☐ Elective

Number of Students: _____ Class Setting: _____ Hour: _____

This document guides one's organization of observations and expressions as documentation of evidence related to quality instruction. Evidence is what you see, hear, or experience. Please attempt to state your observations regarding activities, interactions, discourse, presentations, materials, etc., as evidence supporting the premise that good instruction is taking place in the classroom. Not all categories may be addressed during a single-session observation. If you do not see positive evidence, simply state that no evidence was observed. Please review the course syllabus BEFORE your classroom observation for additional perspective.

A. Evidence of the instructor's mastery of the subject matter

B. Evidence of the instructor's adequate preparation for and management of the classroom experience

C. Evidence that instructional objectives (i.e. learner outcomes) for this class were accomplished

D. Evidence that the instructor made the content relevant to life in the world of the students

E. Evidence that the instructor used appropriate educational methods and technologies

F. Evidence that the instructor encouraged students to actively engage in the learning process

G. Evidence that the instructor helped students develop a Christian worldview by addressing philosophical, ethical, and biblical values associated with the topic under discussion

In light of this limited observation, the observer offers the following:

<u>One</u> **Commendation** (praiseworthy statement):

<u>Two</u> **Suggestions** (practical ideas that may stimulate improvement in the teaching–learning process, or in the instructor's handling of the subject):

<u>One</u> **Opportunity** (candid feedback from one peer to another about a distraction, weakness, or shortcoming in the educational experience that the instructor should be aware of):

Appendix B

Sample Annual Performance Review Form

[Name of School] Core Values

1. How has [first core value] been modeled in the past year?

2. How has [second core value] been modeled in the past year?

[Continue this pattern for each of the school's core values.]

Position Description, Responsibilities, and Expectations

5 = Significantly exceeds expectations
4 = Exceeds expectations
3 = Meets expectations
2 = Improvement is needed
1 = Needs significant help

Using the scale above, rate the faculty member's performance   Rating

3. The teacher has a professional command of the subject matter   _____
An example of this is:

4 The teacher models integration of his/her discipline with a   _____
biblical worldview
An example of this is:

5. The teacher provides appropriate student feedback to   _____
promote learning
An example of this is:

[Continue this pattern for each item on the position description for faculty instructors.]

Previous Year's Personal and Professional Development Goals

6. Development Goal #1: [State the goal]   Achieved? Yes No
Comments:

7. Development Goal #2: [State the goal]   Achieved? Yes No
Comments:

[Continue this pattern for each goal set at the previous year's performance review.]

Next Year's Personal and Professional Development Goals

Appendix C

Sample Student Course Evaluation Form

Course Title: _____ Term: _____

This course:

	Below expectation		As expected		Exceeded expectation	
1. Taught things I can use in life and ministry						
2. Matched the description in the syllabus						
3. Used class time well						
4. Required work that was challenging but realistic						
5. Helped me develop a biblical perspective						

Comments:

The instructor:

	Below expectation		As expected		Exceeded expectation	
6. Knows the subject matter very well						
7. Was well prepared for every class						
8. Communicated effectively						
9. Responded well to students' questions						
10. Was interested in me as a person						

Comments:

11. What did you find was the most valuable part of this course?

12. What advice would you give to a student who may take this course next year?

[Many course evaluation forms are available on the Internet. This one was adapted from http://www.qvcc.commnet.edu/ce/Final%20Evaluation%20 Form-Regular%20Courses.pdf.]

5

Administrative Responsibilities of Academic Leaders in Dealing with Faculty

Les Crawford

In the past year, the theological college has had an unprecedented increase in enrollments, which meant an expansion of several programs and the need for more faculty members to teach the extra subjects. This was a great problem to have, but it also presented an urgent challenge to recruit the additional faculty. Immediate action was needed, and the academic dean[1] was responsible for it.

Over a period of several semesters the student evaluations consistently indicated dissatisfaction with a particular faculty member regarding the quality of teaching and engagement with the students. The degree of complaint could no longer be explained as out of character or one-off in nature. Something had to be done, and it fell squarely on the shoulders of the academic dean to deal with it.

Two faculty members regularly took opposing sides on items during faculty meetings, and it became obvious to all that something was wrong. Not so long

---

1. In this chapter, the term "academic dean" will be used to refer to the academic leader responsible for dealing with the faculty.

ago they were close colleagues and were often seen eating together, conversing regularly about teaching, and sharing activities outside of work. Their increasing conflict with each other was affecting the faculty, and something had to be done. The academic dean needed to address the issue.

The seminary president called the academic dean to meet him in his office on an urgent matter. Student enrollments had fallen significantly for one of the programs, which was no longer viable, and that meant major adjustments in faculty. It became abundantly clear that several long-term faculty members would lose their positions. As academic dean, she was responsible to communicate the devastating news to those affected.

These examples give some idea of the administrative responsibilities that academic leaders have in dealing with faculty. It is no easy task to source, support, and supervise faculty in the complexities of institutional operations and personal life situations. This chapter focuses on handling these responsibilities, but before venturing into that area, it is important to affirm two realities that characterize theological institutions and their faculties.

Two Fundamental Realities of Theological Institutions

First, theological institutions are first and foremost spiritual entities. Therefore, their faculties must, above all else, be spiritually alive. Competence in scholarship and teaching is essential for effectiveness in the faculty's role of developing students to their full potential for ministry, but without genuine and vital spirituality this cannot occur (John 15:5). As much as academic leaders are responsible for the practical administration of the faculty, they cannot neglect the spiritual dimension.

Indeed, the spiritual dimension provides an additional resource for success in academic administration, because it recognizes and depends on the work of the Holy Spirit in both the people and the situation. One pressing need in all administrative decisions and actions is wisdom, which is available from God (Jas 1:5–6). Another urgent need is love, which is also available from God (Rom 5:5). Wisdom and love empower the academic dean to deal with faculty in the best possible way. Academic deans must enjoy a vital and deep spirituality, which enables them to draw on God's rich provisions for their responsibilities to faculty.

The second fundamental reality is that faculty members are first and foremost fellow Christians and human beings (1 Cor 12:12–26). Therefore, they must be treated as members of the Christian community, and not as cogs in a machine or mere parts of an organization. It is easy to forget this when working with educational systems, strategic plans, budget constraints, curriculum development, and other impersonal matters that make up a large portion of academic administration. Academic deans must remember they are dealing with people, and even more than that, family members of the same Christian community.

My youngest son is a business analyst with Westpac Bank in Adelaide, Australia, and his primary task is to improve efficiency, reduce cost, and increase productivity. Most often this requires a reduction in staff, with little attention to the personal impact such actions produce. In secular business, profit is often more important than people. A Christian organization, however, cannot ignore the personal dimension of its operations, despite having to make difficult decisions regarding employees. Academic deans are faced with balancing relational responsibility with administrative efficiency; this is no easy task, but it is absolutely essential for maintaining the institution's Christian identity.

Recruiting, Retaining, and Releasing Faculty

Recruiting Faculty

With these two realities in mind, we can discuss the administrative responsibilities in dealing with faculty, starting with recruiting, retaining, and releasing faculty members. Someone correctly stated that the quality of an educational institution is grounded in the quality of its faculty, and so it is essential to employ the best possible faculty for your institution, and this is your direct responsibility.[2] As with any recruiting task, you must first create a detailed job description for the particular faculty position needing to be

---

2. Allan Tucker and Robert Bryan, *The Academic Dean: Dove, Dragon, and Diplomat*, 2nd ed. (New York: American Council on Education/Macmillan, 1991), 151.

filled.[3] Any specific essential qualifications ought to be stated in this profile, including items unique to your institution,[4] such as theological distinctions or church affiliation required of faculty.[5] This will enable you to target the right potential candidates either by headhunting or advertising the vacancy. In the case of advertising, it will screen out those who would not be suitable, saving you time and energy.

Unless headhunting, you will need to review the application, check references, and narrow down the list of applicants to serious contenders who will then be asked for an interview. It is best to conduct the interview face-to-face, but if that is not possible, a video call using Skype or another suitable service would suffice. Make sure you have prepared a list of questions specifically oriented to the vacancy, and be willing to dig deeper to expose any significant issues to ensure you select the right person. It is much easier not to employ someone than to remove that person later on.

One key consideration in this process is how well the applicant will fit with the existing faculty and institutional culture. Even someone who is well qualified for the position may not be a wise choice if you discern difficulties in these two areas. An item that needs up-front agreement is the contract of employment, including details on conditions, remuneration, sick leave, vacation and sabbatical provisions, and other standard entitlements. It is wise to have a probationary period for new faculty, so that employment can be easily terminated if difficulties arise within that period. Hopefully this will never occur, but it is a necessary contingency. These items may vary from country to country on legal or other grounds, but must be established prior to employment.

Retaining Faculty

Now that you have a new faculty member, an induction process is the next step. Orientation to the institution (its history, ethos, vision and values, strategic

3. Gary Krahenbuhl, *Building the Academic Deanship: Strategies for Success* (Westport, CT: American Council on Education/Praeger, 2004), 94.
4. Robert Ferris, "The Work of a Dean," *Evangelical Review of Theology* 32, no. 1 (2008): 66.
5. Dale Stoffer, "Faculty Leadership and Development: Lessons from the Anabaptist-Pietist Tradition," in *C(H)AOS Theory: Reflections of Chief Academic Officers in Theological Education*, ed. Kathleen Billman and Bruce Birch (Grand Rapids, MI: Eerdmans, 2011), 145–146.

plan, academic policies, and procedures), the faculty, facilities, students, and administration is essential for the faculty member's effective transition to a new position.[6] This should include a tour of the campus, a dinner with the faculty (or an alternative relaxed social setting), introduction to the students in an appropriate context, a meeting with the president/principal, and sufficient personal time with you as the primary leader of the faculty. Hopefully, these actions will quickly allow the new faculty member to function effectively in this new setting, and will counter any anxiety commonly experienced in adapting to significant new circumstances.

The old saying that "the squeaky wheel gets the oil" can soon apply to your relationship with faculty. After the initial attention given to the new faculty member, neglect can follow unless difficulties are openly published either by complaint or appeal for help. Retaining good faculty requires constant maintenance of your relationship with them and solid support for them in their responsibilities for research and writing, teaching and assessment, mentoring, and any additional assigned tasks.[7] New faculty members could be mentored by senior faculty members[8] as part of sustaining and developing them in their new environment, but this is not a substitute for your involvement. The academic dean works for the success of the faculty as a servant leader, much like the biblical metaphor of the shepherd, which requires close personal attention.

Faculty support is essential for faculty success, which enhances retention. This covers a number of areas, including adequate office space and furnishing, effective teaching space and equipment, access to resources (a good library) for research and teaching, assistance for grading if needed, provision of study leave for research, and a budget for professional development. It is important that faculty members are convinced that you want the best for them, even when limitations of finance and circumstances restrict what can be provided. Faculty understand these limitations and will readily accept them when what can be done for them is actually delivered. Even a little support can go a long way to faculty success and satisfaction.

---

6. Krahenbuhl, *Building*, 101–103.

7. Anne Yardley, "Scaffolding That Supports Faculty Leadership: The Dean's Constructive Role," in Billman and Birch, *C(H)AOS Theory*, 140.

8. David Bright and Mary Richards, *The Academic Deanship: Individual Careers and Institutional Roles* (San Francisco: Jossey-Bass, 2001), 154.

Another way to ensure success is protecting the faculty from distracting demands, such as unnecessary administration, or membership on committees unrelated to their roles.[9] The academic dean should advocate for the faculty as their representative to the institution's administrative authorities, such as the president/principal and board. This relieves the faculty of dealing with such matters directly. Another way is to guard against faculty overload, so that the demands of their combined responsibilities does not exceed the available contracted hours. A wise academic dean has a workload system that clearly outlines the hourly demand of all manner of tasks, so that the overall load can be accurately calculated.[10] This may vary from institution to institution, but an objective standard for workload counters abuse of faculty, and enables fairness across the faculty, which contributes to a healthy academic culture.

This has become a more complex task, with faculty assigned a variety of responsibilities, especially in smaller institutions. Factors to consider when evaluating workload include more than just teaching hours per week per semester. Institutions offering online delivery often add this option to an existing subject, which increases the workload on the faculty member responsible for it, even though the on-campus teaching hours are unchanged. Size of classes also affects workload in that marking students' academic work, advising students, and other administrative tasks increase or decrease proportionately to the number of students in the class. A sudden increase in enrollments may upset the balance of workload previously allocated, which will therefore need significant adjustment. Expectations for research, writing, and publishing also add to workload and should not be forgotten in the overall evaluation.

One further consideration that controls how faculty workload is viewed is a distorted view of Christian ministry. It is easy to think that extreme hard work, personal sacrifice, going beyond the call of duty, and the common saying, "I'd rather burn out than rust out" should characterize faculty to the same extent that it has been applied to church ministry, and wrongly so. This mindset can justify excessive workloads as spiritual service, without due concern for the

---

9. Ferris, "The Work of a Dean," 69.

10. One recent university example in Australia can be found here: http://www.swinburne.edu.au/corporate/hr/eb/docs/The%20proposed%20new%20Academic%20Workload_what%20it%20means%20for%20you200214.pdf.

well-being of the faculty members by the administration or even themselves. Laziness and indolence are unacceptable, but so are constant unreasonable demands for output, which carry the danger of spiritual bankruptcy.[11]

Here, the academic dean must remember that faculty members are people, not machines, and fellow Christian servants who are more than academics. They have a life outside of the institution, which may include family, recreation, church leadership, and much more. These relationships and activities are important for overall well-being and should not be undermined by excessive institutional workload. It may also be necessary to protect faculty members from creating their own overload by regular review of their actual workload, which may be more than that allocated by the institution. A healthy, balanced faculty member is a valuable asset to be preserved, rather than a resource to be consumed.

This requires the academic dean to know the faculty individually,[12] and not just as a group. Personal one-on-one engagement is an essential means of developing sufficient relationship, so that you are well informed as to what is going on in a faculty member's life.[13] Routine matters, such as academic activities, student concerns, resource needs, and so on, will probably occupy the majority of discussions, but regular engagement will provide opportunities for conversation on personal matters or concerns. In such cases, you can provide a level of support that will be much appreciated and needed, and which will enhance the faculty member's success in the institution.

Releasing Faculty

Sadly, not all faculty members will be successful, for a variety of reasons, and in such cases the academic dean will need to act, but in a genuinely Christian manner. Objective data are essential in deciding whether or not a faculty

---

11. Constant spiritual output without time for replenishing spiritual resources on account of continual overload is a recipe for spiritual bankruptcy or breakdown, from which it will be difficult to recover. The loss of a faculty member (short or long term) is a tragic outcome that transforms the benefit of past additional output into the liability of lost future output.

12. Ferris, "The Work of a Dean," 72–73.

13. Tucker and Bryan, *Academic Dean*, 156–169.

member is performing to expectations.[14] Feedback from students is one source from which patterns can be discerned. Key performance indicators, such as personal spiritual growth, grading efficiency, research and writing output, contribution to faculty meetings, mentoring effectiveness, and standard of teaching, also provide measures of success. These should be clearly established prior to employment, revised as needed during employment, and form part of annual faculty reviews to avoid unexpected or unfounded evaluations.[15]

Faculty reviews are not intended to threaten employment, but they do have an edge to them for underperforming faculty. For the most part, they serve to affirm and advise faculty, highlighting positive aspects of performance while identifying areas for improvement. Nevertheless, they also provide a basis for decisions on retaining faculty or not. If opportunities for improvement fail to achieve a satisfactory performance standard, the academic dean must release that faculty member for the overall welfare of the institution. This should be done with consideration of the impact such a loss of employment will have on the faculty member, as well as the impact on the institution if no action is taken.

Other grounds for dismissal may be more straightforward, such as serious moral failure, a change of theological position which is contrary to that of the institution, or disagreement with the institution's mission, vision, values, and philosophy. Of course, these grounds must be established without doubt and raised directly with the faculty member before any action is taken, consistent with the principles of church discipline in Matthew 18:15–20. In these cases, academic performance is not in view, and improvement is not an option. The only proper response is the loss of employment.

Regardless of the circumstances, releasing a faculty member is a delicate task and demands great wisdom, a good process, and gracious handling. It is a face-to-face experience which requires clear communication of the basis for the decision and personal readiness for the faculty member's response to the decision. Hopefully, the faculty member will respond well to the decision, but that may not be the case. Some counseling support may be necessary and

---

14. An excellent resource dealing with faculty performance is Peter Seldin and Associates, *Evaluating Faculty Performance: A Practical Guide to Assessing Teaching, Research, and Service* (San Francisco: Jossey-Bass, 2006).

15. Jeffrey Buller, *The Essential Academic Dean: A Practical Guide to College Leadership* (San Francisco: Jossey-Bass, 2007), 208–215.

should be available after the formal meeting concludes. Care should be taken to minimize the disruption caused by such a significant action. Departure from the campus, communications with faculty and students, removal of access, and other security matters must be managed well to protect both the institution, as a first priority, and also the released faculty member.

Resolving Conflict

Another delicate task for academic deans is resolving conflict among and with faculty.[16] Theological institutions are not exempt from the occurrence of conflict, even though staffed by mature, godly Christians. People are different, and such differences are potential sources of conflict. Mature Christians still battle with sin (1 John 1:8–10),[17] and sometimes that battle overflows into relationships, producing conflict. Not all conflict, however, is bad and it may provide a unique opportunity for personal growth and a stronger institutional culture. Unresolved conflict is a threat to the unity and harmony of any institution, but especially one where Christ has bound the members together into one community.

Conflict can arise from differences of perspective on curriculum structure, content, and delivery, differences in priorities regarding resource allocation, or negative responses to institutional changes in policy and/or procedure. Other origins of conflict can be more personal, such as a dispute between two faculty members over an opportunity to receive study leave for postgraduate research granted to one but not the other. It is also possible that some faculty members dislike other members on the grounds of personality, and so regularly criticize their performance. These possibilities could also include faculty conflict with the academic dean or other personnel. Such conflict can be heated or cool, but

---

16. An excellent book discussing a variety of aspects in higher education conflict is Susan A. Holton, ed., *Mending the Cracks in the Ivory Tower: Strategies for Conflict Management in Higher Education* (Bolton, MA: Anker, 1998).

17. The apostle Paul disciplined his body to maintain self-control and avoid disqualification from ministry (1 Cor 9:27), and he became increasingly aware of his sinfulness, referring to himself as "the foremost of sinners" (1 Tim 1:15 RSV) as he neared the close of his life and ministry.

no matter the type or source of the conflict, it cannot be ignored and allowed a destructive influence.[18]

Few people enjoy dealing with conflict. Most would avoid it at all costs, but the price for doing so is high. In organizations where good relationships are foundational for their successful operation – which is true of theological institutions – unresolved conflict will inflict inestimable damage. Academic deans must force themselves to act when faced with conflict, and not hope that in time it will dissipate. Such action must not be hasty or rushed, but rather be decisive and planned. This is by far the most challenging responsibility for academic deans, as indicated by McLean: "An ability to deal constructively with conflict, to resolve contentious issues, to facilitate agreement, or to recognize when issues are not resolvable are among the foremost skills required of chief academic officers."[19]

One thing to note is the possibility of irreconcilable issues which may require a parting of ways between the institution and the people involved. Sometimes leaders cannot agree and the only solution is separation, as demonstrated in the early church with the dispute between Paul and Barnabas over the inclusion of John Mark (Acts 15:36–41). In one sense, the issue is resolved, but not by bringing the two parties together. Although not the preferred outcome, God can use such circumstances to redirect people to places of more effective service. The alternative of ongoing dispute is untenable for both the institution and the people involved.

Most often, academic deans become the mediators in conflict situations, but at times they may find they are directly involved. As mediators, they enter the situation after no attempt has been made at reconciliation, or after other attempts have failed, which means the conflict is serious. Hopefully, in the case of a personal conflict, the biblical process has been applied up to this point, in that the aggrieved party has privately sought reconciliation with the offending party as a first step (Matt 18:15). Now, hopefully, the second step is

---

18. Sharon Pearson has prepared an excellent synopsis of Cynthia Berryman-Fink, "Can We Agree to Disagree? Faculty-Faculty Conflict," from Holton, *Mending the Cracks*, which includes helpful insights on strategies for conflict management, at http://ombudsfac.unm.edu/Article_Summaries/Can_We_Agree_to_Disagree.pdf; accessed 7 August 2017.

19. Jeanne McLean, *Leading from the Center: The Emerging Role of the Chief Academic Officer in Theological Schools* (Atlanta: Scholars Press, 1999), 73.

being taken: seeking the assistance of a third party with authority to arbitrate in the situation, which in this case is the academic dean (Matt 15:16); if this is not done at the initiative of those involved, the academic dean must intervene.[20]

It is critical that only the right people, those who are part of the problem or the solution, are involved in this process. Reconciliation cannot occur if key people are missing from the process. The situation increases in complexity if other people who are not part of the problem or solution are drawn into the situation. Conflicts can easily spread, so minimizing the number of people involved is essential as well as biblical (Matt 18:15–16). Maintaining privacy and confidentiality as much as possible is also required, but public issues will need a public response.

Dealing with Difficult Faculty

Even if no specific conflict is in view, a faculty member may be difficult to deal with, perhaps because of poor personal communication or other entrenched behavior that makes relationships tense or uncertain. In one sense, it is easier to address a particular known problem than to handle a generic one, because the evidence is sufficient to call on for justification of a response. This is not so for a generic problem, as the evidence is often cumulative over time and situated in personality traits. Nevertheless, action must be taken to change the situation so that it does not influence negatively the other faculty members, administrative personnel, and possibly students. Behavior that is not consistent with Christian character cannot be overlooked.

As for conflict situations, it is critical to have sufficient facts to hand to support evaluations of behavior, and it is best if the academic dean has firsthand knowledge of the concerns that make this faculty member a problem. With such data in hand, it is now necessary to meet with the faculty member to discuss the problem, but beforehand the situation should be bathed in prayer. Behavioral change is a spiritual work, only really accomplished through

---

20. Two helpful resources for handling conflict are Peacemaker Ministries, whose website has a useful summary of mediation principles and practice as well as conflict coaching and arbitration guidelines (www.peacemaker.net); and Peacewise, whose website has a similar page listing peacemaking principles that can also be downloaded as a pdf: http://peacewise.org.au/get-help-with-conflict-2/peacemaking-principles/.

the ministry of the Holy Spirit, so you need to seek his involvement before broaching the subject.

It is possible that this faculty member has a blind spot regarding the behavior that makes him or her difficult to work with, so its mention may not be understood initially. In such cases, it is best to communicate tactfully and fully, with an expectation of a positive response, especially when you have already gained the trust and respect of that person. Trust and respect provide resilience in relationships and are important prerequisites in dealing with difficult people. Both are built by investing time in and contributing beneficial input to the relationship. A further offer of help to overcome the behavior will probably be welcomed on the grounds of previous support already given. This person will have no difficulty in believing that you desire the best for him or her and that you are raising the concern primarily for his or her well-being, which fosters a positive response.

A faculty member could, however, be well aware of the behavior that causes difficulty in relationships, but has done nothing to change it. As previously, it is best to have a bank of trust and respect that you can draw on, but if not, action is still required. Raising the matter still needs a tactful approach, but you need to be ready for resistance in admitting the problem exists or in taking steps to address it. Clear and compelling evidence of the seriousness of the problem is necessary and should be fully communicated in a face-to-face meeting. In addition, possible pathways which correspond to how the faculty member responds should be clearly outlined. These will provide a way forward for a positive response, or communicate the consequences of a negative response. A non-response is unacceptable, as is acknowledgment without action. This person must realize the issue is serious and cannot be ignored.

In both cases, the interactions and outcomes must be documented. One vital part of this documentation is a written agreement of commitment to change and a contract of personal or professional development designed to accomplish that change. This will provide accountability for the faculty member, and protection for the institution if further action is deemed necessary.

Positive Relational Culture

One helpful ingredient to facilitate a successful handling of conflict and a difficult faculty member is the existence of an established positive relational culture, in which faculty members are generally supportive of each other and academic leaders are highly valued and respected. In this setting, conflict or unease are unwelcome and unacceptable intruders that stimulate and justify action to resolve them. Academic deans are most influential in creating this kind of culture and ought to make it a top priority, not only to handle conflict or deal with a difficult faculty member successfully, but also as an expression of a genuine spiritual community, which the theological institution ought to be. This kind of culture provides the best context for all faculty members to thrive and reach their individual potential.

Faculty Meetings

A primary contribution to a positive relational culture is effective communication with the faculty, and one important opportunity to achieve this is the faculty meeting. Possibly at no other time does the academic dean have a greater chance to engage all faculty members, so doing this well is a high priority. As the primary academic leader, you have responsibility to conduct this meeting[21] and ensure it delivers the outcomes expected by you and the faculty. It is not sufficient that you are satisfied with the expected outcomes; the faculty members must be also if they are to value and contribute to the meeting.

"Worthwhile" might be an understatement in describing the faculty meeting, but it is nevertheless a critical characteristic for effectiveness. All participants expect that their presence proves to be worthwhile, which means that the meeting accomplishes relevant and necessary outcomes.[22] I am sure you can recall meetings that used a large amount of time but produced very little, if any, useful outcomes. Nothing is more frustrating for talented and

---

21. One excellent resource is Patrick Lencioni, *Death by Meeting: A Leadership Fable* (San Francisco: Jossey-Bass, 2007), which gives a good analysis of meetings and how to get the most out of them.

22. Lencioni views these meetings as tactical, meaning they focus on current issues with accompanying data that can be resolved in an hour, but he advocates no advanced agenda, which I would not support.

time-pressured faculty than wasted meetings. Several components can prevent this happening at faculty meetings.

Key Components for Worthwhile Faculty Meetings

Purpose and Procedures. First, the purpose and procedures of faculty meetings must be established and communicated to all concerned. Why does the faculty meet? What governs the way the meeting is conducted? The primary purpose for meeting is to deal with academic matters directly related to the faculty, which may include curriculum content and delivery, teaching practice and resources, student progress and well-being, professional development and advancement, and future direction and planning. Faculty members must consider that their presence is essential for the items being discussed and decided on in this meeting, which is achieved by maintaining the right purpose.

Procedures clarify how the meeting will be conducted so that everyone understands what is expected of them. Commonly, this level of meeting is viewed as collaborative in nature and so requires a consultative approach, rather than a dictatorial one. As much as the academic dean must provide leadership prior to, during, and after the meeting, the style of leadership is critical for success.[23] In this setting, it is wise to take advantage of the significant range of knowledge, experience, and skills possessed by the faculty through inviting their contributions to the discussions and decisions. Such personal input reinforces the necessity of their presence, and enhances their ownership of the outcomes.

A Safe Environment. For such contributions to be heard requires a safe environment, which can be assisted by some ground rules on communication designed to control dysfunctional behaviors. Rule 1 is that all contributions are welcome and respected. Rule 2 is that each person speaks one at a time, and allows other people to finish their contributions – no interruptions. Rule 3 is that no derogatory communication is permissible. Rule 4 is to stick to the topic and focus on facts. Rule 5 is that final decisions are final and must be accepted by all. I would hope that these rules are already obeyed without spelling them out, but they cannot be presumed. It is best to ensure all attendees are committed to keeping them so that any violations can be more easily addressed.

---

23. Wilson Yates, "The Art and Politics of Deaning," *Theological Education* 34, no. 1 (1997): 91–92.

Advanced Preparation. A second component to prevent a wasted meeting is adequate advanced preparation for the meeting. Simple things such as the time and location need to be communicated well before it occurs, and reminders sent to ensure a full attendance. A proposed agenda must be prepared and distributed sufficiently in advance of the meeting to allow for any input from faculty on items already included or needing to be added. Any documents necessary for the meeting must also be prepared and distributed prior to it so that the faculty can be ready to participate, rather than spend time in the meeting to bring them up to speed. This has the advantage of placing responsibility on them, which communicates how needed they really are.

A functional agenda is essential for an effective faculty meeting.[24] It should include the agenda item, its purpose for inclusion, time allocated for the item, a starter question for discussion (if needed), the process to use in handling the agenda item, the outcome for that item, and the person responsible for it after the meeting. Table 5.1 is a suggested form that can be adapted to local settings.

Table 5.1: A Suggested Agenda Template

Agenda Item	Purpose	Time Allocation	Starter Question	Process	Outcome	Person Responsible
Introduction	Welcome participants Setting the meeting context Review the agenda	5 minutes	Are any changes needed for the agenda?	Discussion and consensus	Revised agenda	Academic dean
Item 1 Curriculum				Discussion and consensus		

---

24. Sue Brandenburg, "Conducting Effective Faculty Meetings" (EdD diss., Edgewood College, 2008), 107–108, 122.

Item 2 Teaching				Discussion and consensus		
Item 3 Students				Discussion and consensus		
Item 4 Professional Develop- ment				Discussion and consensus		
Item 5 Future Direction and Planning				Discussion and consensus		
Item 6 Other Matters				According to type of item		
Conclusion	Express appreciation	10 minutes		Brief review		
	Review decisions, tasks, deadlines, future agenda items				List of action points	Individuals allocated to the specific action points
	Schedule next meeting				Meeting date, time, and location	Academic dean and faculty

The agenda items are in suggested categories and would be more specific for any given meeting, so their purposes would also be specified. Time will be allocated according to need for any given item, as will the process used to deal with it, but most often it will involve discussion and consensus. Determining outcomes and allocating persons responsible for them are critical for the faculty meeting to make a difference in the institution as well as prove worthwhile for all participants. The faculty meeting agenda is a servant, not a master, and should be adapted according to need. It has to be flexible enough to cover all necessary faculty matters, but structured sufficiently to achieve workable outcomes in the allotted time.

For a theological institution, the elements of prayer, devotion, and theological reflection should also be incorporated into the agenda, but not at the expense of necessary faculty matters. Hopefully, faculty members will be progressing in personal prayer, daily devotion, and private theological reflection, so they will not be dependent on the faculty meeting to provide them. A vital spiritual life is expected of faculty, and this can be shared at the faculty meeting as one way of holding each other accountable for it. Another way to emphasize spiritual vitality for all is to roster the faculty members to lead the time of prayer, devotion, and theological reflection during the faculty meeting.

Keeping to Time. One more component to prevent a wasted meeting is keeping to time. This means starting on time, and finishing on time. Despite cultural differences, faculty members still expect students to arrive on time at lectures, and students expect lectures to finish on time. Academic institutions, by necessity, have a daily timetable or schedule that requires keeping to time so that significant disruption to their smooth operation is avoided. If this standard is expected for students, surely it is reasonable to apply it to faculty meetings. Waiting for late faculty members wastes the time of those already present, and going overtime abuses their schedules, which are usually pressured.

Keeping to time requires some forethought as to the composition of the agenda, so that it is not overloaded with time-consuming items. The suggested template includes six possible categories for agenda items, but it would be impossible to include all of them in any given faculty meeting. One way to make sure none are neglected is to schedule them over a semester or year, depending on how often the faculty meetings are conducted. It is better to deal with only one or a few items thoroughly and completely within the allotted time, than treat them superficially, without substantial outcomes, or extend the faculty meeting well beyond the agreed time. The faculty may agree to an extension of time for a crucial matter, but this should be done rarely, and only by consensus.

Two Other Types of Meetings

In addition to the regular faculty meetings, two other types of meeting involving the faculty are useful for effective institutional administration. The first type is a five- to ten-minute catch-up meeting at the beginning of each day to communicate one's responsibilities for the day and then commit the day to God in prayer. This meeting serves to enhance unity and provides awareness of the overall academic activities. It also provides an opportunity to inform the faculty of any specific needs for that day arising from unique challenges, special events, or other uncommon items.

The second type is a two- to three-hour monthly strategic meeting[25] which focuses on larger agenda items, primarily dealing with future planning, that the regular faculty meetings cannot address. It allows faculty to deal with such items thoroughly and completely, avoiding the frustration of either unfinished or inadequate treatment of important matters. Regular faculty meetings can identify what items need to be added to strategic meetings, allowing the more routine matters to be discussed without distraction in the faculty meeting.

Conclusion

By now, I hope you can appreciate the complexity and challenges associated with the administrative responsibilities of academic leaders in dealing with faculty, especially in a spiritual environment. Recruiting, retaining, and releasing faculty are no easy tasks. Resolving conflict and dealing with difficult faculty are also challenging demands. Leading the faculty using a variety of meetings adds yet another one, but the successful achievement of them all has great reward.

As a Christian academic dean, your ambition is to please God (2 Cor 5:9), especially in the accomplishment of his mission, which includes the mission of your institution. A successful academic dean develops a successful faculty, and a successful faculty enables the institution to accomplish its God-given mission, training students for effective service in whatever calling God has placed on their lives. No greater joy exists than seeing God's work advanced, and your efforts in these crucial responsibilities will advance God's work beyond what

---

25. See "The Monthly Strategic" in Lencioni, *Death by Meeting*, 157–163.

you can see this side of eternity. It is worth the pain and the strain (Rom 8:18; 2 Cor 4:17).

Reflection and Action Points

1. Theological institutions are spiritual entities, and faculty members are fellow Christians and human beings. As you consider these two realities, what difference do they make to how you approach your administrative responsibilities in dealing with faculty?

How does your cultural setting affect your approach, either positively or negatively?

2. *Recruiting Faculty:* What do you see as the biggest challenge in recruiting faculty for your institution in your cultural context? How can you overcome it?

3. *Retaining Faculty:* Do you have a strategy for retaining faculty? If not, what initial steps can you take to formulate one? If so, how can it be improved?

4. *Releasing Faculty:* What cultural factors, if any, would influence how you respond to underperforming faculty who are in danger of losing employment? How could you take advantage of those that are helpful, or how would you counter those that are unhelpful?

If a faculty member must be dismissed, what do you see as the biggest challenge in this process in your cultural context?

5. *Resolving Conflict:* Conflict among or with faculty is a difficult and dangerous situation to handle, but it cannot be ignored. What would you find the hardest aspect in dealing with conflict, and how would you address it in your cultural context?

6. *Dealing with Difficult Faculty:* How would you approach a difficult faculty member to address a behavioral problem that is causing a loss of respect for that person from other faculty and students?

7. *Positive Relational Culture:* Review your institution's relational culture, identify its strengths and weaknesses, and suggest ways to capitalize on its strengths as well as address its weaknesses. What steps can you take to improve the relational culture of your institution?

8. *Faculty and Other Types of Meetings:* As you reflect on the formal meetings regularly conducted with faculty, what can be done to improve their effectiveness?

Resources for Further Study

Billman, K. D., and B. C. Birch, eds. *C(H)AOS Theory: Reflections of Chief Academic Officers in Theological Education.* Grand Rapids, MI: Eerdmans, 2011.

Bright, D. F., and M. P. Richards. *The Academic Deanship: Individual Careers and Institutional Roles.* San Francisco: Jossey-Bass, 2001.

Buller, J. L. *The Essential Academic Dean: A Practical Guide to College Leadership.* San Francisco: Jossey-Bass, 2007.

Cedja, B. D., W. B. Bush Jr, and K. L. Rewey. "Profiling the Chief Academic Officers of Christian Colleges and Universities: A Comparative Study." *Christian Higher Education* 1, no. 1 (2002): 3–15.

Cooley, R. E., and D. L. Tiede. "What Is the Character of Administration and Governance in the Good Theological School?" *Theological Education* 30, no. 2 (1994): 61–69.

Douglass, J. D. "Faculty Development: A Shared Responsibility." *Theological Education* (Autumn 1991): 36–42.

Eckel, P. D., B. J. Cook, and J. E. King. *The CAO Census: A National Profile of Chief Academic Officers.* Washington DC: American Council on Education, 2009.

English, R. A. "The Deanship as a Cross-Cultural Experience." *New Directions for Higher Education* 25, no. 2 (1997): 21–29.

Fagin, C. M. "The Leadership Role of a Dean." *New Directions for Higher Education* 25, no. 2 (1997): 95–99.

Ferris, R. W. "The Work of a Dean." *Evangelical Review of Theology* 32, no. 1 (2008): 65–73.

Gillespie, K. J., ed. *A Guide to Faculty Development: Practical Advice, Examples, and Resources.* San Francisco: Jossey-Bass, 2002.

Gmelch, W. H., D. Hopkins, and S. Damico. *Seasons of a Dean's Life: Understanding the Role and Building Leadership Capacity.* Sterling, VA: Stylus, 2011.

Gmelch, W. H., and M. Wolverton. *An Investigation of Dean Leadership.* New Orleans: American Educational Research Association, 2002.

Gmelch, W. H., M. Wolverton, M. L. Wolverton, and J. C. Sarros. "The Academic Dean: An Imperiled Species Searching for Balance." *Research in Higher Education* 40, no. 6 (1999): 717–740.

Hardy, S. A. *Excellence in Theological Education: Effective Training for Church Leaders.* Green Point, South Africa: Modern Printers, 2006.

Hartley III, H. V., and E. E. Godin. *A Study of Chief Academic Officers of Independent Colleges and Universities.* Washington DC: Council of Independent Colleges, 2010.

Holton, Susan A., ed. *Mending the Cracks in the Ivory Tower: Strategies for Conflict Management in Higher Education.* Bolton, MA: Anker, 1998.

Hough, J. C. "The Dean's Responsibility for Faculty Research." *Theological Education* (Autumn 1987): 102–114.

Hudnut-Beumler, J. "A New Dean Meets a New Day in Theological Education." *Theological Education* 33 (supplement, 1996): 13–20.

Krahenbuhl, G. S. *Building the Academic Deanship: Strategies for Success.* Westport, CT: American Council on Education/Praeger, 2004.

Le Cornu, A. "The Shape of Things to Come: Theological Education in the Twenty-First Century." *British Journal of Theological Education* 14, no. 1 (2003): 13–26.

Lencioni, Patrick. *Death by Meeting: A Leadership Fable.* San Francisco: Jossey-Bass, 2007.

Lindt, G. *Managers, Movers and Missionaries: Who Leads the Graduate School?* Minneapolis: Association of Graduate Schools, 1990.

McLean, J. P. *Leading from the Center: The Emerging Role of the Chief Academic Officer in Theological Schools.* Atlanta: Scholars Press, 1999.

Moden, G. O., R. I. Miller, and A. M. Williford. *The Role, Scope, and Functions of the Chief Academic Officer.* Kansas City, MO: Association for Institutional Research, 1987.

Montez, J., and M. Wolverton. *The Challenge of the Deanship.* New Orleans: American Educational Research Association, 2000.

Nordbeck, E. C. "The Once and Future Dean: Reflections on Being a Chief Academic Officer." *Theological Education* 33 (supplement, 1996): 21–33.

Reason, R. D., and W. H. Gmelch. *The Importance of Relationships in Deans' Perceptions of Fit: A Person-Environment Examination.* Chicago: American Educational Research Association, 2003.

Seldin, P. *Evaluating Faculty Performance: A Practical Guide to Assessing Teaching, Research, and Service.* San Francisco: Jossey-Bass, 2006.

Sensing, T. R. "The Role of the Academic Dean." *Restoration Quarterly* 45, no. 1–2 (2003): 5–9.

Smith, J. I. "Academic Leadership: Roles, Issues, and Challenges." *Theological Education* 33 (supplement, 1996): 1–12.

Toulouse, M. G. "A Dozen Qualities of the Good Dean." *Theological Education* 42, no. 2 (2007): 109–126.

Townsend, B. K., and S. Bassoppo-Moyo. "The Effective Community College Academic Administrator: Necessary Competencies and Attitudes." *Community College Review* 25, no. 2 (1997): 41–57.

Tucker, A., and R. A. Bryan. *The Academic Dean: Dove, Dragon, and Diplomat.* 2nd ed. New York: American Council on Education/Macmillan, 1991.

Waits, J. L. "Developing the Community of Scholars: An Address to New Academic Deans in ATS Schools." *Theological Education* 33 (supplement, 1996): 71–76.

Wolverton, M., and W. H. Gmelch. *College Deans: Leading from Within.* Westport, CT: American Council on Education/Oryx, 2002.

Wolverton, M., W. H. Gmelch, J. Montez, and C. T. Nies. "The Changing Nature of the Academic Deanship." *ASHE-ERIC Higher Education Report* 28, no. 1 (2001): 95–108.

Yates, W. "The Art and Politics of Deaning." *Theological Education* 34, no. 1 (1997): 85–96.

6

Using Evaluation to Help Teachers Grow

Steve Hardy

Evaluation is a normal part of day-to-day life within academic training programs. A careful assessment of what applicants know, what they know how to do, and their calling, gifting, and passion helps determine whether potential students are appropriately qualified to enter our programs. An educational institution then uses evaluation to monitor the growth of students from beginning to end. For teachers to be good facilitators of learning, they need multiple ways to receive feedback in order to observe and document students' progress within the curriculum. Evaluation should allow students to demonstrate what they have mastered in order to be awarded credits and degrees. We also use program evaluation to show stakeholders, governmental ministries of education, or accrediting agencies that our academic programs are well designed and well resourced within overall administrative structures, so as to meet the standards required of all educational programs doing what we are doing at similar levels. As learning communities, educational programs ought to be really good at doing evaluation.

In this chapter, we want to ask how we can apply our skills in doing evaluation to help our faculty team do an even better job as teachers and educational facilitators. There are four broad areas that ought to matter to us.

Are Our Teachers Competent in Their Fields?

This involves two distinct areas: that teachers have competence in what they know and understand, so as to be able to teach it; and that their practical experience has given them competence in skills so as to lead the students to develop their gifts and abilities. It matters not only that the homiletics teacher knows enough about the basic practices and theory of preaching and communication to explain this well to students, but that he or she actually is an effective communicator and preacher. Biblical studies professors need to have a profound understanding of the Scriptures and biblical languages, along with ample awareness of important literature and theories about the Scriptures. But they also need good study skills in exegesis, along with a love and respect for the Word of God.

Do Our Teachers Have the Pedagogical (or Andragogical) Skills of Teaching?

Although the Bible indicates that teaching is a gift from God to the church, it is a gift that can be developed. Most teachers really do teach just as they were taught, and the sad reality is that most of us were not taught very creatively. All teachers can be taught to teach better. As teachers take on new generations of students who learn in a variety of ways and who come with vastly different experiences and backgrounds, do they have the skills to facilitate the learning of these students?

Do Our Teachers Positively Impact Students through Their Relationships with Them?

One's attitude as a teacher toward a student impacts the learning that occurs. That is true even when a teacher may not be so aware of his or her attitudes and feelings. So what *are* their feelings toward and expectations of their students? Are they good listeners, so as to understand the needs and expectations of their students? Are they supportive as students reflect on their unique backgrounds? Do they encourage students as they try out new experiences? To what extent are teachers facilitators of learning – or are they only lecturers, passing on their own knowledge and experience? Given that our students are holistic, integrating everything into their lives, to what extent do teachers build healthy relationships, so as to function as pastors, mentors, and coaches?

Are Our Teachers Responsible in Doing What They Are Supposed to Do?

This can't really be evaluated without a clear written explanation of expectations. What administrative responsibilities are required of teachers? Are teachers expected to attend retreats and be at all faculty meetings? Are teachers expected to speak in local churches or to do promotion for the school? When should grading be completed? To what extent are teachers to be advisors to their students? Does it matter if a teacher is a part of social or sports events promoted by the institution? And which of all of our rules also apply to part-time or modular teachers? Furthermore, expectations go beyond simply fulfilling requirements. Being faithful and responsible includes *how* all these things are done. Can teachers organize what needs to be learned into the time frame allotted for learning? Do they prepare adequately before coming to each class session, and can they manage their classroom time, so that what needs to be covered is covered? For that matter, do they actually show up for all of their scheduled classes? Do they come on time (or even a bit early) and stay to the very end of the scheduled class time? When they evaluate student work, is their evaluation done thoroughly and impartially? As teachers, do they dress and behave appropriately? Is the time that they spend with their students and colleagues quality time?

Evaluation will help us, and our teachers, to discern their strengths and weaknesses. All of our teachers will presumably want to be responsible, but when they (and we) consider their competence (knowledge and skills), their methodological skills, and their relationships, they may discover that they are stronger (and that they frankly like being stronger) in one of these three areas than in the other two. Intentional conversations about evaluations will then help teachers to maximize their gifts and strengths, while developing plans to grow in areas of weakness.

Some teachers absolutely love research and study. They have become content experts. They come to class with a stack of books or magazines to show students fascinating things they have discovered – whether it is a new nuance in Greek grammar, an interesting person in the history of the church, or stories of well-done cross-cultural communication. However, although they have memorized vast amounts of information, they somehow can't manage to remember the names of their students. They may not know how to put what they know into practice, or how to help students to learn what is so precious to them.

Other teachers may be brilliant practitioners, with years of solid experience as pastors, cross-cultural missionaries, peacemaking counselors in crisis situations, or urban youth workers. But if they haven't read much of anything in their fields (or anything new since their days as students), they probably know very little of theory or of what has been done by others. Neither do practitioners necessarily know how to help their students master what they themselves are good at.

There are also teachers who just love teaching. It doesn't matter to them what they teach, nor whether they actually know all that much about the subject. Their delight is in asking questions and provoking dialogue. This is a good thing, but if they are to be facilitators of learning, they would be so much more effective if they mastered some relevant content before encouraging creative interaction.

Finally, there are teachers who just love people. Both inside and outside of formal class time they interact with students, being encouragers as they carefully listen to their concerns. But while students may love such teachers, if such a teacher doesn't know enough to teach, or if he or she hasn't prepared a good syllabus with relevant assignments, there may not be much actual learning of a particular subject.

In his excellent work *The Seven Laws of the Learner*, Bruce Wilkinson states[1] that every teacher is either subject-oriented (focusing on what is taught), student-oriented (focusing on who is taught), or style-oriented (focusing on how it is taught). Wilkinson recommends that good teachers use their strengths to compensate for their weaknesses. That is good advice, but in his book he also explains how good teachers should gain some mastery in all three of these areas.

---

1. Bruce Wilkinson, *The Seven Laws of the Learner*, Textbook ed. (Sisters, OR: Multnomah, 1992), 48–54.

This is our primary purpose in developing evaluation tools. We want to help our teachers to be responsible and to gain mastery in the content and skills they teach, in the methodologies they use, and in their interpersonal skills.

Three General Comments on Evaluation

Evaluation Requires a Reference Point

We cannot do evaluation if we aren't clear on what we intend to achieve. What benchmarks or standards do we have? One does not simply shoot an arrow into the air and then declare that where the arrow landed was precisely where we meant to shoot. In the same way that an educational program has objectives and a strategic plan, our faculty team should have objectives and a plan. These should grow out of the realistic expectations that every institution has of its teachers. It is unfair to hold a teacher accountable for something that he or she was not aware of needing to do. Perhaps it feels obvious that teachers should prepare ahead of time for what is to be taught. But do they? And does our expectation include presenting a teaching plan for the term a week or so prior to when the subject matter will be taught? Does the teaching plan include a bibliography of books that the library actually has, and does it show how the various class sessions will be taught? What is the allowable time frame for grading papers and exams? How much time are teachers expected to spend with individual students during each week or semester? If teachers are to be learning new things, how much time per week or semester should they spend in reading, research, or writing? Do teachers (including part-time or modular teachers) have administrative responsibilities? If so, what exactly is expected of them? Do we have expectations about their spiritual growth, or about their involvement with community and church? All these things and many more should become part of a written job description to which teachers agree. An important part of an evaluation is determining how well a teacher has done in doing what he or she was supposed to do.

Evaluation Requires Perspective and Interpretation

It is human to assume that we are right and that what we are doing makes perfect sense. Proverbs 18:17 says, "The first to speak seems right, until someone comes forward and cross-examines." However, not only do data and observations have a context, but multiple points of view will enrich the wisdom to be gained from evaluations. Student feedback will tell us whether the students think that teachers are responsible, build healthy relationships, are competent in what they know and can do, and are methodologically creative. However, when a student is unhappy about a teacher, we may discover that the problem isn't a "bad teacher," but that there were family health issues or other serious difficulties that prevented the teacher from doing better. As teachers critically reflect on what they do, they will also provide background on why things might be as they are. We actually may discover that a student who makes particularly negative remarks about a teacher is reflecting his or her own poor performance in class. The observations of other teachers and academic leadership can provide good insights. It helps to get the perspective of time. Are these new problems, or is this an issue that has continued for years? We also need the perspective of how a particular subject fits into the overall purposes and objectives of the curriculum. A teacher may love teaching a particular course, and the students may have loved how the class was done, while in reality our regular institutional evaluations may demonstrate that this particular class contributes very little to shaping the students for life and ministry. We need perspective in order to interpret the evaluations that come to us.

Evaluation Needs to Be Done Regularly

A good evaluation is encouraging, just as negative feedback can be discouraging. But for evaluation to help our teachers teach better, we need to know whether what a teacher does is typical of that teacher. Feedback is needed from every class ever taught, and evaluation reviews need to be done at least annually with everyone. If evaluation is done only when problems arise, the wrong message is sent. Our desire is to help our teachers teach better, not just to identify problem people or to assign blame in a crisis. So is a good teacher getting better, or are some of our best teachers slowly beginning to go downhill? Has an only average teacher shown regular improvement through putting into practice the suggestions from feedback and evaluation, or do the same problems continue year after year? We can help everyone teach better if we evaluate everyone regularly.

Types of Evaluation

To help teachers teach better, we need evaluation tools to gather feedback from colleagues, administrators, and students, as well as from teachers themselves. The tools to be used will be different for different groups of people.

Teachers need to be critically reflective, evaluating themselves on how they have done what they have done (or not done) as facilitators of learning. As they increasingly become masters of what they know and know how to do, we want them to see how they are impacting their students as they pass on knowledge, skills, and character. Teachers need broad, open-ended questions to allow them to explain why things are as they are, and to make their own suggestions as to how they might do better in what they are doing.

Students are in the best position to note what teachers actually do. We need data from them that will allow us to assess how teachers have (or have not) been responsible, competent, methodologically creative, and relational. It is helpful to document how teachers are perceived in the different classes that they teach, and to note how they have changed from year to year. It is also useful to compare teachers with other teachers. Open-ended questions make the collection of data much more complicated. Rather, it is more helpful to have a single-paged tool with phrases or tick-boxes for students to indicate what has or has not been true.

General feedback from colleagues or administrators can be very helpful, although the reality is that most have minimal opportunities to see their colleagues actually teaching. However, as they observe interaction, or sense positive or negative impact by attitudes and behaviors, valuable insights will be gained. These evaluation tools will necessarily be uncomplicated.

The conclusions reached through systematic institutional assessments probably won't provide much direct feedback concerning the performance of individual teachers. The tools for this kind of evaluation are best found in the guidelines for institutional accreditation. Nevertheless, as we see later in this chapter, as the impact or success of an institution is documented, there are implications that can help teachers teach better within the purposes of their institution.

In the remaining pages of this chapter, we want to look specifically at how each of these evaluation tools can be developed and used to help our teachers teach better. What is important to affirm is that the academic dean, or the "Coordinator of Academic Affairs" (or whatever title your institution gives to this person), should be the primary collector and interpreter of these evaluations. The academic dean knows what is expected of teachers as he or she is the one responsible for developing job descriptions for them, as well as the one who reviews teaching plans and monitors teaching during an academic term. As a pastor and coach to the faculty team, the academic dean is in the best position to listen to the critical reflections and plans of teachers. It is the dean, and not individual teachers, who should administrate and collect surveys done with students in their classes at the end of each term. The comments made by colleagues to the academic dean should not become part of a public forum. They provide information for the dean to digest. What can be shared should be done confidentially with the teacher concerned. For all these reasons, the academic dean is in the best position to evaluate the evaluations, and to intelligently discuss with teachers how their teaching could be even better.

Self-Evaluation

A self-evaluation survey gives a teacher the opportunity to reflect on himself or herself. How "responsible" do our teachers feel? What explanation do they offer for things that they did and didn't do? How do they assess themselves in their competence, methodological skills, and relationships?

Reflective evaluation allows teachers to place their performance in the context of their own complicated lives. For example, a teacher may know that he or she has not done particularly well in always coming to class on time, in being prepared for each class session, or in the timeliness of grading and returning student work. Self-evaluation allows teachers to indicate what factors they feel have contributed to this. People are holistic, which means that everything ultimately has an effect on almost everything else. Furthermore, students often learn more from the life of the teacher than from anything done or said in a class. So, in assessing how a teacher has done, it is indeed important to be aware of spiritual, physical, and emotional health, and to know about conflicts, family and financial problems, health concerns, or doubts.

A self-reflection tool may include a handful of broad questions like the following:

- How do my subjects relate to the rest of the curriculum?

- What more do I need to know in order to teach my classes more effectively?
- How can I become more creative in my teaching methodologies?
- How are my relationships with colleagues, students, and the administration?
- What would strengthen the teaching team that I am a part of?[2]

Alternatively, a self-evaluation tool might look something like that in figure 6.1. Note that the questions are open-ended. By requiring that responses be written separately, there is no limit on what can be said. This is an evaluation that needs to be discussed, perhaps with family and colleagues as it is being prepared, but ultimately with the academic dean. And what is written should remain confidential.

Critical self-reflection also asks a teacher to suggest how he or she may improve or grow, and to indicate ways that the institution might help in these areas. Open-ended questions show the extent to which a person is aware of his or her job description and to hearing ways in which the job description could be changed for the better. Our teachers will become better teachers as we listen to them and discuss with them their ideas and plans as to how they could become better teachers.

---

2. Steven A. Hardy, *Excellence in Theological Education: Effective Training for Church Leaders* (Peradeniya, Sri Lanka/Edenvale, South Africa: The Publishing Unit, Lanka Bible College and Seminary; distributed by SIM, 2007), 304.

Figure 6.1: A Self-Evaluation Tool

Self-Evaluation Form (Confidential)

Please reflect carefully on the following questions and respond on a separate piece of paper. Indicate your name and the date on which the evaluation was done. Return this in a sealed envelope to the academic dean's office no later than ___/___/_____. Thanks.

1. Personal Concerns

- Please comment on issues such as family, health, finances, or interpersonal relationships that caused you concern in the past year, or that affected your ministry or your relationships.
- What might make things better for you in this coming year?

2. Spiritual Growth

- During the past year, in what ways have you grown spiritually? Comment on things like your personal devotional time, mentoring relationships, ministry, worship in your local church, etc.
- What are your plans for spiritual growth in the coming year?

3. Personal and Professional Growth

- In what ways have you grown and learned in the last year? Include significant books that you have read, any courses or training that you have taken, etc.
- What are your plans for personal and professional growth in the coming year?

4. Professional Competence

- How do you assess your competence as a teacher? Do you feel that you know enough to teach this subject well, and that you have enough practical experience to serve as a model to your students in areas in which you have been asked to teach?
- What are your plans for growing in competence, and how can this institution help you in this?

5. Methodological Competence

- How do you assess your effectiveness in creatively facilitating learning for your students?
- In what ways would you like to teach differently?
- How can you help yourself, and how can this institution help you to be a better teacher?

6. Relationships

- How do you assess your relationships with your students?
- How are your relationships with colleagues and those in administrative roles?
- How could you help yourself to strengthen your relationships with others, and how can this institution help you with this?

7. Specific Responsibilities

- How much of your time is given to your ministry of teaching here, and to what extent has balancing your time been a problem for you?
- Do you feel clear in your understanding of what you are supposed to be doing? Are there things that you have been asked to do that don't feel appropriate for you?
- Are there things you feel you ought to be doing, but which haven't been asked of you in your written job description?

Evaluation from Students

Students are in the best position to make observations about what teachers do and do not do, and to share their sense of whether or not these teachers are competent to have the responsibilities that they have. But as we noted earlier, what we most need from students is data, not their conclusions. Students are not aware of background issues. Furthermore, it will be a few more years before they will be in a position to evaluate the impact that a teacher or the class has had on them.

We do want to gather data from students at the end of each term for every subject that is taught in the curriculum. Class evaluations should be brief (one page is ideal) and as objective as possible, so that the results can be compiled and compared.

There are lots of ways in which we will fail to get helpful input from students. Read through the brief evaluation in figure 6.2 and note some of what should *not* be done.

It is good to keep evaluation forms brief; but the example shown in figure 6.2 given to students presents at least eight problems.

1.   Student evaluations should never ask for names. Students may imagine (and often with good reason) that there will be negative consequences for

Figure 6.2: Sample Student Evaluation Form

Teacher: _____ Your name: _____

Note: When you have finished this evaluation, please drop it off at the school office.

1. On a scale of 1 to 10, rate the teacher and the class that you just finished.
   1   2   3   4   5   6   7   8   9   10

2. Why did you find this class useful?

3. What was it about the teacher that you liked most?

4. On a scale of 1 to 10, evaluate the methodology used in teaching this course.
   1   2   3   4   5   6   7   8   9   10

5. What recommendations would you make to other students who might consider taking this course in the future?

---

negative comments. Even without their name being given, most teachers recognize handwriting. So, besides not asking for a name, someone other than the teacher should compile these responses. If students think that someone will know who they are, they are unlikely to be honest.

2.   If our intent is to evaluate specific classes that were offered, we need to know which subject this evaluation is for, and when the subject was taught or evaluated. On this form there is no date, nor do we know which class was taught by the teacher.

3.   If we want good feedback from all of our students, we should not leave it to them to do the evaluation whenever they get around to it, and to return it somewhere else. Evaluations should be given out in class and then collected by someone other than the teacher before the students are allowed to leave the room. This may be a problem for online courses or evaluations done through the Internet. One needs to find ways to include course evaluations in the course itself.

4.   The first question is both too vague and too broad. But even if our desire is to get an overall sense of how the students felt about the educational package that includes both class and teacher, in what sense is the teacher and/ or the class to be "rated"? And, is a "1" a positive response and a "10" a negative response, or is it the other way around? In any case, a scale of 1 to 10 is too wide. Maybe 1 to 5, or even 1 to 3, would be better, making it clear what a "2" or "3" is supposed to indicate.

5.   Question #2 actually isn't a bad question, but the reality is that most students will not know how "useful" the class really was until sometime in their future. But in any case, an open-ended question like this doesn't give us data that helps a teacher teach better, since we learn little that demonstrates what the instructor did or did not do.

6.   For the third question, although it might be useful to find out what students did *not* like about a teacher, we honestly don't need feedback as to what they "liked" since this is more related to personality quirks than to qualities that should be present in a good teacher.

7.   For the fourth question, besides the problem with an undefined list from 1 to 10, we don't learn anything specific from it. Even if a teacher is given a top score, we won't have a clue as to what was done that we can affirm, so that it will be done again.

8. For the last question, we don't care whether or not students have advice to give to future students. What might be interesting is advice that might help the teacher do a better job of teaching this class in the future. Rephrasing this could be the one open-ended question that you include.

What might a better evaluation tool look like to gather the information that you want from your students? Figure 6.3 is an adaptation of an evaluation form developed by ISTEL, a very good theological education program in Lubango, Angola. Note that most of the questions offer possible answers that students might have in response to specific questions that the institution would like to learn about. While students might respond with different words, the academic dean's educational experience helps in suggesting responses with tick-boxes that allow the compilation of a more objective assessment.

Figure 6.3: Student Evaluation Form, Adapted from Evaluation Form Developed by ISTEL

Advanced Institute of Theological Studies

Subject taught:_____ **Name of the instructor:**_____
Today's date: ____/____/_____

1. How qualified was the teacher to teach this course?
( ) Excellent experience, but didn't seem to know much of what has been written in the area
( ) Had lots of knowledge, but didn't seem to have much practical experience
( ) Good, both in experience and in knowledge
( ) There were days when I felt that the students knew more than the teacher did

2. How would you describe the style of teaching used? Indicate all of the responses that apply:
( ) Lectured   ( ) Organized class debates over issues
( ) Work in small groups   ( ) Provoked discussion and encouraged questions
( ) Used PowerPoint   ( ) Used the white (or black) board
( ) There was little reflection required; we mostly memorized facts and details

---

3. How well was the class time managed and structured?
( ) Used time well; we covered all of the material in the syllabus
( ) The course was well structured, but the teacher was easily distracted, and disorganized
( ) There did not seem to be a clear and coherent plan for teaching this subject

4. Was the amount of work required of students appropriate for this class?
( ) No, there was far too much work for the credits that were offered
( ) Perhaps, but it would have been better had we understood the expectations at the beginning
( ) Yes, I enjoyed the assignments, and felt that I learned from doing them

5. How was evaluation done for this class? Indicate all the responses that apply:
( ) We knew ahead of time the criteria for the assignments
( ) Our work seemed to be graded objectively
( ) The evaluations/grading was done in a timely way

6. Describe the relationship between the teacher and the students. Indicate all the responses that apply:
( ) Affirmed our ideas, and expressed appreciation for our contributions
( ) Our questions seemed to bother him/her as he/she had strong opinions of his/her own
( ) Seemed as if some students were liked more than others
( ) At times became nervous or irritated over things that didn't really matter very much
( ) Was interested in us and took time to be with us outside of class
( ) Could be trusted. I shared some of my personal issues with the teacher

7. In general, how would you rate this teacher?
( ) One of the best that I have had
( ) About the same as other teachers at this institution
( ) OK, but not as good as most of the other teachers at this institution
( ) Not a good teacher. It would be better for the school to find someone else for this class

8. What suggestions would you make to help this teacher teach better?

In the first question, we want to hear how students perceive the competence of their teacher. There isn't space for answers other than "yes" or "no," as we want them to indicate one of these four responses. Exactly how these get worded is up to you.

The second question concerns teaching methodology, so a variety of ways in which teachers teach are suggested. Students will hopefully tick more than one box to show what was actually done (or regularly done) as the class was taught. These responses provide objective data from which we can help teachers to be more creative. You may have other areas that you want to ask.

The third question asks two things: whether there was a teaching plan for the course, and how well time was managed in order to follow that plan. There are more options for responses than the three listed here, but what is here should provide valuable feedback.

The fourth and fifth questions go together to ask for feedback on class assignments and homework. Was this perceived as too much (or too little)? Were assignments clearly explained, along with expectations as to what was required in the work to be done? And were these homework assignments evaluated fairly, and in a timely fashion? This feedback will help us help our teachers to carefully think through how they can craft and evaluate good learning exercises, as well as prepare their students to learn more from those assignments.

The sixth question asks about perceptions concerning relationships. This question could easily become two separate questions, since there are many possible answers that could be given by students. What you ask depends on what you want to learn, bearing in mind that it is good to limit an evaluation form to a single page. Most of the possible responses should reflect issues from your past. However, be careful that you focus on affirming good relationships, and not simply on identifying things that didn't go so well.

In the seventh question students are being asked to "rate" the teacher, with the standard being other teachers at "this institution." Maybe we don't need data to compile a ranking of our faculty, but we do need to give our students an opportunity to state whether they think that our teachers should be honored, helped along, or sent packing.

And the final question allows students an open-ended opportunity to make suggestions as to how a teacher can teach better. My experience is that even with verbal encouragement to make such suggestions, only about half of our students will ever write anything in this space.

It shouldn't take more than fifteen minutes for all the students to fill in a one-page evaluation form like this. When they are finished, someone from the dean's office should collect the forms and then collate the information. That includes listing the comments from the last question, although sometimes I will shorten them or indicate that several people made the same suggestion. This collated evaluation form should be studied by the academic dean, with a copy shared with the teacher as part of the annual (or semi-annual) review process. A copy should be filed in the teacher's confidential file.

Evaluation from Colleagues

Mutual feedback and encouragement from colleagues is perhaps the most powerful tool to shape what teachers do, both in affirming their good habits and in pushing them to change. We should work toward being learning communities where people will interact informally over what they have learned, and where we sit together in seminars or workshops to learn how to be more effective teachers. It would be excellent for teachers to routinely visit one another's classes, to learn from what colleagues do and to offer encouragement and counsel to one another in response to what they have seen.

Working together is what makes a curriculum work well. What I teach builds on things that others have taught, while at the same time preparing the way for courses yet to come. What I teach is carefully designed in a curriculum to fit together with other subjects, so that in the end our students are well equipped in accordance with the purposes and objectives of the institution. For me to teach well, I need to know what and how others are teaching.

Furthermore, the sobering reality is that a good share of what students learn doesn't come from the things done within a formal curriculum, but from what they absorb from the community in which they study. Attitudes and informal relationships will be modeled. It is who we are as individuals and as a community that impacts who our students will be.

Essentially, there are four important things that should be learned about teaching better from the feedback/evaluation that comes from colleagues.

Confidence in the Teaching Team

Learning from (and about) colleagues gives us confidence in the quality of the teaching team. As we get to know the personal stories and passions of those who teach with us, it should increase the respect we have for others, as it increases the trust we have in what they are doing as teachers. Sensing that we are part of a good teaching team helps all of us to teach better.

Understanding How Things Fit Together

Most people are just too busy to note how others are doing. In much of the Majority World teachers tend to have two or three different "full-time jobs." So, when it comes to teaching, they rush into their class at the last minute, and then rush back to their busy lives as soon as class is over. If they haven't taken the time to study the course catalogue, or if they weren't part of the curriculum-development work group, they probably don't know how their class fits in. They would be better teachers if they did. We don't need to re-teach what our students have already learned, but we may lose them altogether if we assume that they have learned something important that in fact they don't know anything about. And we ourselves have important things to teach so that our students will be properly prepared for what is yet to come.

Awareness of the Community

Our students are aware of the relationships that exist between teachers as well as between faculty and staff. How we relate to one another is likely to be the way that they will relate to others as they move into life and ministry. The way that we interact with our families as we do ministry will affect the way they will interact with their families as they enter ministry. We need feedback to be aware of our role in shaping a healthy learning community.

Learning from Others as They Teach

As mentioned above, it would be good if teachers could periodically visit one another as they teach. Our confidence in one another's competence should give us courage to want to learn from what others are doing. But the reality is that most of our colleagues know little of what actually goes on in our classes. It isn't realistic to think that teaching colleagues will be able to give much input to this part of the evaluation process. It may be helpful to designate an especially good "senior" faculty member to serve as "master teacher" to coach and evaluate other teachers. This may make it easier for some teachers to receive suggestions. In any case, it should be helpful to hear the input of any of one's colleagues. In a smaller institution, one can ask every teacher to comment on everyone else. In larger institutions, one needs to be selective in who is asked for input. This kind of feedback needs an evaluation form, but one that contains only a handful of questions. These are confidential observations to be given to the academic dean, and since there may be need for clarifications or further information, in this case it is helpful to ask for the name of the person doing the evaluation, as well as to note the name of the one being evaluated and the date of the evaluation. The form might look something like figure 6.4.

Figure 6.4: Peer Teaching Evaluation

Evaluation comments on: _____
Your name: _____
Today's date: ___/___/_____

What is your relationship with the person you are evaluating?
( ) A colleague and friend that I have known for years
( ) Someone I work with, but not someone that I know well personally
( ) Someone I hardly know at all

1. In your opinion, in what way does this person fit well, or not, into our academic community?

2. In what ways are you aware that he or she may, or may not, be an outstanding teacher?

3. Have you noticed anything that would indicate that the person is, or is not, contributing to the academic community beyond what he or she does in the classroom?

4. In what ways does this person seem to be wise and caring in his or her relationships with students, colleagues, and the administrative staff team?

5. Do you have any suggestions that might help this person to have greater impact as a teacher?

Note that these are broad general questions that draw on the personal perceptions of the evaluator to comment, positively or negatively, on the teacher's competence, non-teaching roles, and relationships in the context of the institution. There also should be an opportunity to offer suggestions. Not all of this information will necessarily be passed on to the one being evaluated, especially if it contains accusations that are shown to be untrue or unhelpful. This is an evaluation form to help the academic dean in his or her conversation with the person involved at the time of the annual review.

Evaluation from Institutional Assessments

Every educational institution should periodically do a systematic review of everything. These reviews are usually motivated by a need to show one's constituency that the institution is doing a good job, as well as to establish that it is a credible institution for the accreditation or licensing bodies. A good example of the kinds of questions that you may want to ask yourself in order to do a thorough and systematic institutional evaluation is found in the "ACTEA Standards and Guide to Self Evaluation," a document developed by the Association for Christian Theological Education in Africa.[3]

An additional and very important value of a broad institutional self-study is the impact that it will have on internal quality. "An excellent leadership training institution takes the time to develop and routinely review a strategic plan that includes discovering its values, defining its mission in the light of needs, assessing its own strengths and weaknesses and then prayerfully dreaming in order to develop a doable plan that takes it to where it ought to go."[4]

What is learned from an institutional assessment has implications for the teaching team. You may already know from self-evaluations and evaluations from students and colleagues that you have teachers that could be even better. But from an institutional perspective, we may now learn how well our faculty functions as a team. Feedback from graduates and the community will help us to understand the extent to which teachers have modeled respect for others or have taught the skills of conflict resolution. Through this broad evaluation we

---

3. The Accrediting Council for Theological Education in Africa, "ACTEA Standards and Guide to Self Evaluation," 2011, http://www.acteaweb.org/downloads/ACTEAStandards GuideToSelfevaluation.pdf.
4. Hardy, *Excellence in Theological Education*, 64.

can develop plans to help shape our faculty community to be more effective in the impact that they have.

Institutional assessments also let us see whether we have the right teachers for the programs that we are offering. For example, if seven of our eight faculty members have their training in cross-cultural studies, we might have a fabulous missions program. However, we do not have the staff to justify offering specialized studies in church history, or biblical studies. These are conclusions that will not affect existing teachers, but they certainly should affect your priorities as you look for new teachers in order to have a better teaching team.

A clearer understanding of our students, mission, and context will require us to rethink what is offered in our curriculum and reshape the way that our current teachers teach. For example, if part of our focus is to equip men and women to be mature in Christ, how can every class session encourage character formation? If feedback suggests that others see us as an institution whose students lack passion and a love for God, how can every teacher make worship and a love for God a part of every class that is taught? If ethnic tensions are a significant issue in the world of our institution, how can every class help our students to deal with this? If our expectation is that every student will become a teacher and mentor, learning to teach can be part of what is structured into all the things that are taught. These aren't necessarily subjects to be added to a curriculum, and they will not necessarily change the content in any given class session, but they should inform the attitudes and shape the methodologies that teachers use.

Interpreting Evaluation

In a learning community, evaluation will happen in multiple ways all the time. Both students and teachers should be learning from what they see and hear. We don't just acquire knowledge and information, we want to see how we can put what we have learned into practice. This is a good thing, and so we should ensure that there is a specific time each year to focus on helping our teachers to teach better.

Every teacher should have the "right" to thirty minutes each year with the academic dean. Finding time for a focused conversation with teachers is one of the most important responsibilities of an academic dean. This may be a formal "annual review," although as a tool to help teachers teach better, it may be even better if it can be a conversation that occurs at the end of a term or module.

Both the academic dean and the teacher need to prepare for this thirty-minute conversation. If the teacher submitted a teaching plan or syllabus, the academic dean will hopefully have been following what is happening in class. Perhaps the dean can visit or listen in on one of the class sessions during the term. As a way to make sure that students are receiving fairly what they are supposed to be receiving, the academic dean should periodically verify that the class is on track, and that assignments have been graded and returned within the appropriate time frame. The academic dean will also give the self-evaluation review to the teacher, an evaluation form to a handful of the teacher's colleagues, and administer the evaluation form to the students on the last day of class. He or she will then collect and collate these evaluations. Admittedly, this is a lot of work, but if we want quality in our educational program, this is perhaps the most important part of what an academic dean should be doing.

The teacher also should prepare by carefully working through the self-evaluation review. The academic dean should have this prior to their conversation, so that it can be read through carefully. The dean will also want to review the teacher's job description.

However, the thirty-minute conversation itself is not a time for a summary of what everyone has said. If this is to be an opportunity for the growth of teachers (as opposed to a time to raise or lower their salaries – or to fire them), then the thirty minutes should become a time to listen as a teacher responds to such not-so-complicated questions as, "How did it go?," or "How are you doing?"

The teacher may say, "I love teaching! And this last year has been a very satisfying time with these students." That's good – assuming that the students also affirm that it was a satisfying time of learning. But if the students (and colleagues) suggest that this isn't reality, there is a need for some serious conversation.

On the other hand, if the teacher says, "I really struggled this term. I'm not sure what happened, but things were really hard," and if the students agree that it was a difficult term, the discussion can focus on what could be done differently. Alternatively, if the students actually liked the class, there will be a need for encouragement. Everyone goes through times of discouragement. Academic deans should listen for signs of stress or burnout. Or perhaps the teacher has developed theological doubts, or has serious concerns about practices and people at our institution. Although these are hard issues to deal with, by scheduling this thirty-minute conversation at least once a year your problems will at least not continue to grow invisibly. This is where administrative roles include pastoral counseling and professional development.

A brief confidential report should be written up after this thirty-minute conversation. It will be archived in the teacher's file, along with copies of whatever evaluations were done. Although this could become the basis for letting a teacher go, its primary purpose is to help teachers to teach better. It thus can be very helpful to review the file before the next thirty-minute conversation next term.

It is likely that common themes will arise from individual conversations with all of the teaching team. The academic dean will want to help each teacher develop plans to improve his or her teaching. The dean will also want to develop institutional plans, such as training workshops, designed to strengthen the curriculum and the teaching team.

Conclusion

As we have noted, learning institutions do evaluation in multiple ways all the time. It is our opportunity to help our teachers to teach better. Self-evaluations allow for teachers to reflect on their own practice in order to come to a better understanding of the impact that they have as teachers, and to develop their own plans for continued growth in the ministry that God has given them.

In order to give good advice to our teachers, we need information. Much of this should be regularly gained from students to see the extent to which our teachers are perceived as being credible and competent in their knowledge, skills, and experience. We want to know whether our faculty are methodologically creative, and how their relationships impact the learning of students. We'd like to know from students and colleagues whether our teachers are being responsible in doing what their job descriptions require of them. And we'd like to understand how their contributions fit into all that is being done by our educational institution.

However, evaluation needs to be interpreted. This is fundamentally the responsibility of the academic dean, who coordinates whatever surveys are done. Each teacher should have a confidential conversation with the academic dean, at least annually. In this conversation, the academic dean should listen carefully to each teacher in the light of the input gained from the multiple evaluations. What the academic dean says as pastor and mentor will have a powerful impact on the quality of teaching in the institution.

Reflection and Action Points

1. To what extent does your institution have evaluation tools for helping your faculty team to teach better?

Self-evaluation for teachers
( ) Yes, we have this
( ) Yes, we have this, but it could be a lot better
( ) No, we don't have this evaluation tool

Evaluation of teachers by students
( ) Yes, we have this
( ) Yes, we have this, but it could be a lot better
( ) No, we don't have this evaluation tool

Evaluation from colleagues
( ) Yes, we have this
( ) Yes, we have this, but it could be a lot better
( ) No, we don't have this evaluation tool

Institutional evaluation
( ) Yes, we have this
( ) Yes, we have this, but it could be a lot better
( ) No, we don't have this evaluation tool

If you are not satisfied with the evaluation tools that you have, or if you don't have these tools at all, take the time to revise or write them. Then schedule an unhurried time when you can review with your faculty team all the evaluation tools that you have.

2. What are some of the specific areas that you have discovered in which your teachers are already pretty good?

3. What are some of the specific areas that you have discovered where your teachers could improve?

4. What specific plans or programs could you develop to both share the strengths that exist and help others to improve?

5. As you listen to feedback, what makes mentoring a difficult task? How could those who know how to teach well within your institution help those who need to learn these skills?

Resources for Further Study

Blumberg, Phyllis. *Developing Learner-Centered Teaching: A Practical Guide for Faculty*. San Francisco: Jossey-Bass, 2009.

Gillespie, Kay J., Douglas L. Robertson, and Associates, eds. *A Guide to Faculty Development*. 2nd ed. San Francisco: Jossey-Bass, 2010.

Hardy, Steven A. *Excellence in Theological Education: Effective Training for Church Leaders*. Peradeniya, Sri Lanka/Edenvale, South Africa: The Publishing Unit, Lanka Bible College and Seminary; Distributed by SIM, 2007.

Kane, Thomas, Kerri Kerr, and Robert Pianta. *Designing Teacher Evaluation Systems*. San Francisco: Jossey-Bass, 2014.

Marshall, Kim. *Rethinking Teacher Supervision and Evaluation*. 2nd ed. San Francisco: Jossey-Bass, 2013.

Nolan, James. *Teacher Supervision and Evaluation*. 3rd ed. San Francisco: Jossey-Bass, 2011.

Posner, George J., and Alan H. Rudnitsky. *Course Design: A Guide to Curriculum Development for Teachers*. 6th ed. New York: Addison Wesley Longman, 2001.

Shaw, Perry. *Transforming Theological Education: A Practical Handbook for Integrative Learning*. Carlisle: Langham Global Library, 2014.

Vella, Jane. *How Do They Know They Know: Evaluating Adult Learning*. San Francisco: Jossey-Bass, 1998.

———. *On Teaching and Learning: Putting the Principles and Practices of Dialogue Education into Action*. San Francisco: Jossey-Bass, 2008.

Wilkinson, Bruce. *The Seven Laws of the Learner*. Textbook edition. Sisters, OR: Multnomah, 1992.

Part III

Strategic Processes in Faculty Development

7

Building a Faculty Team

Pieter Theron

L et's imagine two scenarios:[1]

- *School #1:* This school has faculty members who are excellent scholars in their respective disciplines, and generally good teachers. They have good intentions, and care about students' learning in their subjects. But they don't spend much time talking and thinking together about the mission, vision, values, goals, and educational philosophy of the school's theological education program. Every faculty member is busy with his or her own research and teaching. There is not much coordination between the different subject areas. There is very little interaction between faculty regarding the learning of students and teaching methods. Faculty usually meet only for official school events and faculty business meetings. Most faculty have limited knowledge about the interests and responsibilities of their peers.
- *School #2:* The faculty share a common vision and passion for what they are doing. They are committed to the same set of values and educational philosophy, which were developed through purposeful and creative conversations. They have clear goals for theological education, and a strategy for developing the program. They know

---

1. These scenarios are an adaptation and paraphrase of Patrick Lencioni, *The Advantage: Why Organizational Health Trumps Everything Else in Business*, Kindle ed. (San Francisco: Jossey-Bass, 2012), 72, to apply them to faculty teams.

the strengths of each member, trust each other, and understand how each member contributes to achieving the goals. During regular meetings and conversations faculty think, learn, and create together, as well as coordinate and facilitate interaction between the different subject areas. Faculty serve as peer mentors to help one another grow professionally and spiritually.

Sadly, many faculties of theological schools function like that in school #1. I believe that the faculty of a theological school should function as a team like the faculty team in scenario #2. Why?

Most of the church's ministry and missions involves teams and team work. The faculty are developing Christlike leaders who are going to engage in, lead, and build teams. They should not only prepare their students for team work, but also model it. The faculty should function as a learning community. "Learning community" here refers to a community, a team, that continuously learns to improve and enhance its members' capacities to achieve their shared vision. It is a learning community that continuously grows together in Christlikeness. Thus, the academic leader, whether provost, dean, or head of department, has the special calling to build a faculty team.

There are many resources on teams and team building, with various approaches to team building, and a vast array of team building methods and activities. Despite so many studies on teams, so many resources available, and so many team building activities being done, nothing seems to change. Organizations spend time and money on team building activities. Everyone enjoys it and has a good time together, but when they are back in the office or work situation, it is back to the status quo in dealing with each other and working together. True synergy is not achieved – or when it is achieved, it is only for short periods of time and is not maintained. What is the problem?

Trust is foundational to team building. Without trust, there is no team. Thus, trust building is essential, and should receive priority. However, to build trust, the art of conversation, of dialogue, needs to be recovered.

This chapter does not present a method or process for team building. There are many excellent resources available for this, and any attempt on my part will not do justice to the complexity and importance of the process, nor to these available resources. I focus only on some foundational disciplines and skills that are required for any team building process, no matter which methods or tools are used. Without these in place to guide and support the process, team building will not work. As I discuss these disciplines, I refer to resources that would help teams with tools and processes to acquire and in using these disciplines and skills. At the end of the chapter, in the section "Resources for Further Study," I give a survey of some additional team building resources.

The Foundational Team Disciplines

The Lost Art of Conversation

Isaacs begins the first chapter of his book *Dialogue and the Art of Thinking Together* by asking the reader the following:

> When was the last time you were really listened to? If you are like most people, you will probably find it hard to recall. Think about a time when you saw others try to talk together about a tough issue. How did it go? Did they penetrate to the heart of the matter? Did they find a common understanding that they were able to sustain? Or were they wooden and mechanical, each one reacting, focusing only on their own fears and feelings, hearing only what fit their preconceptions?[2]

He goes on to say that most of us "tend to spend our conversational time waiting for the first opportunity to offer our comments or opinions."[3] Our conversations many times look like a gun fight in the main street of a town in a Western movie. "The points go to the one who can draw the fastest or who can hold his ground the longest. . . . People do not listen, they reload."[4] They take position, and listen to defend or attack. "Instead of creating something new, we polarize and fight . . . we tend to harden into positions that we defend by advocacy. To advocate is to speak your point of view. Usually we do this

---

2. William Isaacs, *Dialogue and the Art of Thinking Together: A Pioneering Approach to Communicating in Business and in Life* (New York: Currency, 1999), 17.

3. Isaacs, *Dialogue*, 17.

4. Isaacs, 18.

unilaterally, without making room for others."[5] Thus, instead of dialogue, our teams are actually involved in a series of monologues. Teams "have not learned to think together."[6] It seems we have lost the art of conversation.

What we need is to learn to "kindle and sustain a new conversational spirit that has the power to penetrate and dissolve some of our most intractable and difficult problems."[7] We need "a powerful set of practical tools and practices" – disciplines – that can help us to recover the art of talking and thinking together that would enable us to act together in more effective and creative ways.

I would like to share with you such a set of disciplines. There are four disciplines that are foundational to team work. They are foundational because all other team building activities and team work are based upon, and flow out of, these activities. Team building activities will not work or achieve their full potential if these foundational principles and disciplines are not part of a team's culture and environment. They are also integral and are integrated with one another. They are integral to the process of team building. They are integrated because they work together, affect, and need one another.

They are disciplines because you must work intentionally at establishing them and maintaining them as habits. In other words, they will not happen by themselves. They are also called disciplines because you must develop and practice them on an ongoing basis if you want to be effective in them.

These foundational disciplines are shared vision, trust, mental models, and dialogue. Of these three, trust is the underlying one. And all of them are bound together in love (Col 3:14).

In this chapter I focus on the discipline of dialogue with brief discussions of trust and mental models. The discipline of mental models goes hand in hand with, and is essential for, the practice and discipline of dialogue. And both of these are founded on trust. These disciplines will help us to become aware of and think about how we are thinking and talking. I do not discuss shared vision because there are many excellent resources on building a shared vision. Suffice it to say that a team without a shared vision is not a team. I focus on dialogue because it is essential for building trust and a shared vision. Mental

---

5. Isaacs, 18.

6. Isaacs, 2.

7. Isaacs, 6.

models facilitate dialogue and building trust. And trust is the foundation of a high-performance, creative team that is also a true learning community.

Trust

Of the foundational disciplines, trust is the underlying one. We could say it is the root discipline. Without establishing and building trust continuously, the other disciplines will not be effective and team building may not happen.

The importance and essential role of trust is confirmed and emphasized by the following sources. These are excellent resources for building trust. The theory and principles underlying this process are discussed in these sources. Therefore, I do not discuss building trust in this chapter; I would just be repeating what is already stated elsewhere. I focus on dialogue as one of the foundational and essential disciplines for team building. Dialogue is required for building trust. Dialogue is also enabled by trust. It is interesting that all these sources discuss the importance of open discussions, constructive communication, conversation, or dialogue as a key practice in developing trust and building teams.

I believe that Patrick Lencioni's books are one of the best places to start the team building process and to understand trust. They offer not only the theory, but also the tools and processes for developing trust and building the team.[8]

Another set of resources that emphasize the importance of developing relationships of trust and environments of grace, which are essential for team building and helping team members grow spiritually and in character, are those of Bill Thrall and associates.[9]

---

8. P. Lencioni, *The Five Dysfunctions of a Team: A Leadership Fable* (San Francisco: Jossey-Bass, 2002); P. Lencioni, *Overcoming the Five Dysfunctions of a Team: A Field Guide for Leaders, Managers, and Facilitators* (San Francisco: Jossey-Bass, 2005); P. Lencioni, *The Five Dysfunctions of a Team: Facilitator's Guide: The Official Guide to Conducting the Five Dysfunctions Workshop* (San Francisco: Pfeiffer, 2007); Lencioni, *The Advantage*.

9. Bill Thrall, Bruce McNicol, and Ken McElrath, *The Ascent of a Leader: How Ordinary Relationships Develop Extraordinary Character and Influence* (San Francisco: Jossey-Bass, 1999); Bill Thrall, Bruce McNicol, and Ken McElrath, *Beyond Your Best: Develop Your Relationships, Fulfill Your Destiny* (San Francisco, CA: Jossey-Bass, 2003); Bill Thrall, Bruce McNicol, and John Lynch, *Truefaced: Trust God and Others with Who You Really Are*, rev. ed. (Colorado Springs, CO: NavPress, 2004).

Two more good resources on trust are Covey and Merrill, *The Speed of Trust*, and Ryan and Oestreich, *Driving Fear Out of the Workplace*.[10]

Mental Models

An excellent story by David Hutchens, *Shadows of the Neanderthal: Illuminating the Beliefs That Limit Our Organizations*,[11] illustrates well what mental models are and how they function. In addition to the story his book contains an explanation of mental models, guidelines, and discussion questions for using mental models as a discipline for team building.

"Mental models are the deeply held beliefs, images, and assumptions we hold about ourselves, our world, and our organizations, and how we fit in them."[12] The Greek philosopher Plato, in his Parable of the Cave in *The Republic*, stated, "We are all misguided cave dwellers, operating under incomplete or distorted perceptions of reality . . . and violently resistant to having those perceptions challenged."[13]

Mental models are the assumptions we have about the world, people, and reality, and they influence how we act and react, behave, and interpret and view reality, people, and experiences. They are usually tacit, existing below the level of awareness, and therefore remain unexamined and unchanged.[14] The discipline of mental models refers to the actions of reflecting upon, continually clarifying, and improving our internal pictures of the world, and seeing how they shape our actions and decisions.[15] This discipline aims to bring our

---

10. Stephen M. R. Covey and Rebecca R. Merrill, *The Speed of Trust: The One Thing That Changes Everything* (New York: Free Press, 2006); Kathleen Ryan and Daniel K. Oestreich, *Driving Fear Out of the Workplace: Creating the High-Trust, High-Performance Organization*, The Jossey-Bass Business & Management Series, 2nd ed. (San Francisco: Jossey-Bass, 1998).

11. D. Hutchens, *Shadows of the Neanderthal: Illuminating the Beliefs That Limit Our Organizations* (Waltham, MA: Pegasus Communications, 1999).

12. Hutchens, *Shadows*, 61.

13. Quoted by Hutchens, 62.

14. Peter M. Senge, *The Fifth Discipline: The Art and Practice of the Learning Organization* (New York: Doubleday/Currency, 1990), 176. Peter M. Senge, *The Fifth Discipline Fieldbook: Strategies and Tools for Building a Learning Organization* (New York: Doubleday/Currency, 1994), 236.

15. Senge, *Fifth Discipline Fieldbook*, 6.

"mental models to the surface, to explore and talk about them with minimal defensiveness."[16]

Mental models limit our organizations, teams, and ourselves every day. Many good ideas never get off the ground because they don't match the prevailing assumptions and beliefs.[17] This sometimes leads to polarization and highly politicized conflicts. When you look into the heart of such conflicts you will often find different sets of assumptions at work, and labeling begins, which sets into action a reflexive cycle in which groups actually become the labels they have been given. "Mental models are built over time, incrementally, as we observe data and draw conclusions every day. By understanding how this happens, we can begin to achieve some mastery over this hidden process."[18]

"The Ladder of Inference" is a helpful tool for understanding how our mental models are formed and function. The ladder is a tool of Action Science, developed by theorists Chris Argyris and Donald Schön. It traces the mental processes (or leaps of inference or abstraction) that lead us to form and maintain mental models.[19]

Many times the process of racing up the ladder occurs within our subconscious thoughts, and almost instantaneously, within seconds. "We make these leaps of inference instantly and silently . . . even multiple times in the course of one simple interaction. Over time, these leaps, combined with the action in the Reflexive Loop" – our beliefs affecting what data we select next time – form and shape our mental models.[20]

Using Mental Models

Why have I provided this overview of mental models? The discipline of mental models is integrated with and facilitates the discipline of team dialogue. Without this discipline and using tools like the Ladder of Inference, dialogue would be very difficult. The following skills are required to use the Ladder of Inference effectively. We will see that similar skills are required for effective dialogue.

---

16. Senge, 236.

17. Hutchens, *Shadows*, 62.

18. Hutchens, 72.

19. Hutchens, 72. See also the writings of Peter Senge that explain the "Ladder of Inference" with good examples.

20. Hutchens, 73–74.

- *Reflection:* Becoming more aware of our own thinking and reasoning. We need to slow down our thinking processes to become more aware of how we form our mental models.
- *Inquiry:* Inquiring into others' thinking and reasoning
- *Advocacy:* Making our thinking and reasoning visible to others.[21]

The last two skills involve holding conversations in which we openly share views and develop knowledge about each other's assumptions. This is the art of conversation, or dialogue.

Because of our mental models we are trapped in what Argyris calls "defensive routines" that insulate our mental models from examination, and we consequently develop "skilled incompetence."[22] We are afraid to expose our thinking and reasoning to others, fearing that they may discover flaws in our reasoning, or use it as counter arguments. We need to break out of these defensive routines and open up ourselves and our mental models for examination by ourselves and others.

This knowledge about mental models is not enough. "Insight alone does not produce change."[23] We need to practice what we have learned. The following questions and steps can help team members to practice the discipline of mental models, use the Ladder of Inference, and therefore have real dialogue. These will help us "to limit the likelihood that our mental models will constrain our ability to take effective action." They will help us "by illuminating their presence, and by taking deliberate steps to challenge our thinking against the Ladder of Inference."[24]

The following questions can help you to stop a conversation, and to identify your and your teammate's movement up the ladder:

- What is the observable data behind that statement?
- Does everyone agree on what the data is?
- Can you run me through your reasoning?
- How did we get from the data to these abstract assumptions?

---

21. Senge, *Fifth Discipline Fieldbook*, 245.
22. Senge, *The Fifth Discipline*, 182.
23. Hutchens, *Shadows*, 74.
24. Hutchens, 74.

- When you said "[your inference]," did you mean "[my interpretation of it]"?[25]

Use the following guidelines to practice the discipline of mental models in your dialogue and team building.[26]

- Notice that your conclusion may be based on your inferences, and that they may not be self-evident facts.
- Assume that your reasoning process could have gaps or errors that you do not see.
- Use examples to illustrate the data you selected that led to your conclusions.
- Paraphrase (out loud) the meanings you hear in what others say, so that you can check if you are understanding them correctly.
- Explain the steps in your thinking that take you from the data you select and the meanings you paraphrase to the conclusions you reach.
- Ask others if they have other ways of interpreting the data, or if they see gaps in your thinking.
- Assume that others may reach different conclusions because they have their own Ladder of Inference with a logic that makes sense to them.
- Ask others to illustrate the data they select and the meanings they paraphrase.
- Ask others to explain the steps in their thinking.

How can we apply this in our team building?

- Explain to the faculty team the disciplines of mental models and the Ladder of Inference, and their impact on team learning and dialogue.
- The team must commit to these disciplines.
- Then they must practice them during their meetings or interactions.
- The team could develop ground rules for their interactions, meetings, and work based on the above questions and steps.

---

25. Senge, *Fifth Discipline Fieldbook*, 245.

26. These guidelines were taken from Hutchens, *Shadows*, 74–77. They were "developed by the partners of Action Design (Diana Smith, Bob Putnam, and Phil McArthur)."

Dialogue or the Art of Conversation

Senge calls this the most challenging discipline – intellectually, emotionally, socially, and spiritually[27] – and we will see why as we discuss it. What is dialogue?

- David Bohm and L. Nichol, in their book *On Dialogue*, say, "Dialogue is a set of practices based on the idea of people coming together to create collective understanding. In its simplest sense, it is a form of conversation whose purpose is to promote understanding and learning."[28] Its primary intention is learning, and it is most interested in understanding others' perspectives and in clarifying together what we are trying to accomplish.[29]

- According to William Isaacs, as cited by Peter Senge and associates, dialogue is "a sustained collective inquiry into everyday experience and into what we take for granted."[30]

- Peter Senge states that dialogue is the "deep listening to one another and suspending of one's own views." It is a "free and creative exploration of complex and subtle issues."[31]

Perhaps we will understand dialogue better if we compare it with discussion or debate, which usually characterizes our team meetings. This comparison is done through what Ellinor and Gerard call the "Conversation Continuum:"[32]

Dialogue is	Discussion or Debate is
Seeing the *whole* among parts	Breaking issues/problems into *parts*
Seeing the *connections* between parts	Seeing *distinctions* between parts
Inquiring into assumptions	*Justifying/defending* assumptions
Learning through inquiry & disclosure	*Persuading, selling, telling*
Creating *shared* meaning	Gaining agreement on *one* meaning

---

27. Senge, *Fifth Discipline Fieldbook*, 355.

28. David Bohm and L. Nichol, *On Dialogue* (London/New York: Routledge, 1990), 1.

29. L. Ellinor and G. Gerard, *Dialogue: Rediscover the Transforming Power of Conversation*, Kindle ed. (Hertford, NC: Crossroad Press, 2014).

30. Peter M. Senge, Nelda Cambron-McCabe, Timothy Lucas, Bryan Smith, and Janis Dutton, *Schools That Learn: A Fifth Discipline Fieldbook for Educators, Parents, and Everyone Who Cares about Education*, 1st ed. (New York: Doubleday, 2000), 75.

31. Senge, *The Fifth Discipline*, 237.

32. Ellinor and Gerard, Kindle loc. 1126–1127 (author's emphasis).

Why Dialogue?

As a leader, dialogue "can help you to uncover the undiscussed thinking of the people in your organization. . . . The problems we face today are too complex to be managed by one person. We require more than one brain to solve them. Dialogue seeks to harness the 'collective intelligence' . . . of the people around you; together we are more aware and smarter than we are on our own."[33]

In our rapidly changing world, organizations and schools have to continuously reinvent themselves to remain relevant and effective. To achieve this, "this capacity for collective improvisation and creativity [dialogue] is essential."[34] In order to achieve this as a leadership method, dialogue is an approach that "you must develop within yourself, and model . . . to others, before you seek to apply it to the teams you lead or the problems you face."[35]

In addition, dialogue can help us deal with the intercultural relationships and cross-cultural problems many of our schools have. "Dialogue can enable people to bring out these differences and begin to make sense of them, fostering communication and understanding among people."[36]

Skills for Dialogue[37]

To practice dialogue, Isaacs identifies four skills that we need to develop:

- Listening
- Respecting
- Suspending
- Voicing

Listening

The skill of listening is to listen without resistance or imposition. This begins with recognizing how I am listening now. I need to listen to myself and my

---

33. Isaacs, *Dialogue*, 11.

34. Isaacs, 11.

35. Isaacs, 11.

36. Isaacs, 11.

37. The following four sections are adapted and summarized from Isaacs's chapters on these skills: chapters 4–7, pp. 83–184.

own reactions. I should ask myself: What do I feel here? How does this feel?[38] I should take notice of what I am thinking while listening.

Second, listening requires sticking to the facts. We should listen with a great deal more humility. This means we need to come down to earth, overcome the overinflated views or senses of ourselves, and realize that we don't know everything. Many times what we know are our own conclusions based on selected data from our specific experiences. We continuously jump to conclusions, so we need to climb back down the ladder of our inferences, and go back to the data of our experiences. Isaacs also recommends the Ladder of Inference as a powerful tool for helping with the skill of listening.[39]

Often, we are also listening from disturbance. For example, someone says something that I don't like, and I am triggered by what he or she says. This happens because we are listening from our emotional memory rather than from the present moment.[40] One way to deal with this is to "follow the disturbance" – that is, to learn to listen for the sources of the difficulty. "Instead of looking for evidence that confirms your point of view, you can look for what disconfirms it, what challenges it."[41] Listening then becomes reflective. "We begin to see how others are experiencing the world."[42]

To listen without resistance is actually listening while noticing the resistance. The challenge here is to "become conscious of the ways in which we project our opinions about others onto them, how we color or distort what is said without realizing it."[43]

Standing still is another skill for listening. Isaacs calls this "perhaps the simplest and most potent practice," but not the easiest, "for listening is simply to be still."[44] It is to quiet the inner chatter of our minds, so that we can listen from the silence within ourselves. "Listening from silence means listening for and receiving the meanings that well up from deep within us."[45]

---

38. Isaacs, 92.
39. Isaacs, 93–98.
40. Isaacs, 98–101.
41. Isaacs, 99.
42. Isaacs, 100.
43. Isaacs, 101.
44. Isaacs, 101.
45. Isaacs, 101–102.

Asking ourselves the following core questions can help us learn and practice listening:

- What am I feeling in my body?
- How does this feel?
- How is this affecting people?
- What are the different voices trying to convey?
- What voices are marginalized here?
- What happens when controversial things are raised?
- Am I acting consistently with what I profess?
- In what ways am I behaving?
- In what ways am I doing to others the very things I claim they should not do?[46]

Respecting

Respecting as a behavior in dialogue involves developing and having the awareness of the integrity of another's position, and the impossibility of fully understanding it. Respecting is "to be able to see a person as a whole being."[47]

"The act of respect invites us to see others as legitimate."[48] "Respect also means honoring people's boundaries to the point of protecting them. If you respect someone you do not intrude. At the same time, if you respect someone, you do not withhold yourself or distance yourself from them."[49] Leaving someone alone is not respecting that person, but is distancing yourself from something you don't want to deal with. "When we respect someone, we accept that they have things to teach us. . . . Treating the people around us with extraordinary respect means seeing them for the potential that they carry within them . . . to treat the person next to you as a teacher. What is it they have to teach you that you do not now know?"[50]

Respecting in dialogue requires that we listen to the whole flow of a conversation, and do not select only pieces of it, aspects that matter to us or

---

46. Isaacs, 101–102.
47. Isaacs, 110.
48. Isaacs, 111.
49. Isaacs, 114
50. Isaacs, 114–117.

perhaps that irritate us. "This requires that we step back from the details, soften our focus, and hear what is going on in the overall space of the conversation."[51] According to Isaacs,

> Respect also implies taking seriously the fact that there is an underlying coherence in our world, and that we fit into this scene. We are participants, not just observers of what is happening. Accepting this means taking responsibility for ourselves. In this state, it is no longer possible simply to blame others for what happens. Our fingerprints are all over our world. The adage coined by Walt Kelly in a Pogo cartoon applies here: "We have met the enemy and it is us."[52]

He summarizes and defines respect in the following way: "Respect is . . . looking for what is highest and best in a person and treating them as a mystery that you can never fully comprehend. They are a part of the whole, and, in a very particular sense, a part of us."[53]

This is made even more profound when we add to this the awareness that the other person is, as am I, created in the image of God. We are both part of God's creation, and God is somehow represented in the other person. And if the other person is also a believer, then Christ is also in him or her as he is in me. Even more, the other person is also loved by God. And I am expected to love him or her as I love myself.

If we can become more aware of these facts, and intentionally maintain this awareness in our conversations, it will enable real dialogue. The following core questions can help us to learn and practice respect:

- How does what I am seeing and hearing here fit in some larger whole?
- What is happening right now?
- What is at risk in this situation?
- What is the dominant preoccupation?
- Can the conversation be drawn wider to include those who might be impacted?[54]

---

51. Isaacs, 120.
52. Isaacs, 124.
53. Isaacs, 117.
54. Isaacs, 117.

Suspending

When we listen to someone speak we usually begin to form an opinion. We can do one of two things: "First we can choose to defend our view and resist theirs. We can try to get the other person to understand and accept the 'right' way to see things (ours!). We can look for evidence to support our view that they are mistaken, and discount evidence that may point to flaws in our own logic."[55] When we make our stands, we remain frozen, unable to move, and we end up in advocacy and debate. Debate very rarely changes things or resolves problems. Instead, we get bogged down more and more.

Alternatively, "we can learn to *suspend our opinion* and the certainty that lies behind it. Suspension means that we neither suppress what we think nor advocate it with unilateral conviction. Rather, we display our thinking in a way that lets us and others see and understand it."[56]

This is perhaps the key skill for dialogue. It is to refrain from imposing our views on others, and to avoid suppressing, or holding back, what we think. "To suspend is to change direction, to stop, step back, see things with new eyes"; suspension is "the art of loosening our grip and gaining perspective."[57] Suspension involves the act of looking at our thoughts. Suspending involves the following activities:

- First, *surfacing assumptions*: "one must be aware of your assumptions before you can raise and suspend them."[58]
- Second, *display of assumptions*: this involves "unfolding your assumptions so that you and others can see them." It is "to hang them in front, out there," so that you and others can reflect on them.[59]
- Third, *inquiry*: "to suspend with the intention of inviting others to see new dimensions in what you are thinking and saying." This means "exploring your assumptions from new angles: bringing them forward, making them explicit, giving them considerable weight, and trying to understand where they came from."[60]

---

55. Isaacs, 134.
56. Isaacs, 134–135 (emphasis by author).
57. Isaacs, 135, 141.
58. Senge, *Fifth Discipline Fieldbook*, 378.
59. Senge, 378.
60. Senge, 378.

This is a very difficult practice because our assumptions are tied closely to our deepest beliefs and values. Therefore, an important value must guide this process. That is "to honor the passion of everyone underlying their viewpoints."[61] Suspension does not mean giving up our views, but to place, hang out, our assumptions "in the midst of the room, available for everyone to question and explore." It is asking this core question of my teammates and of each other: "Can you help me see something else about my deepest beliefs that I'm not now seeing?"[62]

Asking ourselves the following core questions can help us learn the skill of suspending:

- What are my "noble certainties"?
- What makes me so darned sure that I am right?
- What leads me to view things as I do?
- What is the question beneath the question?
- What themes, patterns, links, do I perceive underneath what is being said?
- In what alternative ways can I perceive or frame these things?[63]

Voicing

This is a very challenging aspect of dialogue. "Speaking your voice has to do with revealing what is true for you regardless of other influences that might be brought to bear . . . Finding your voice in dialogue means learning to ask a simple question: What needs to be expressed now?"[64] Voicing involves "taking seriously the possibility that what you think might be in fact valid for others."[65] Others can learn from me as I can learn from them. Thus, voicing is "listening for and speaking my authentic voice."[66]

In a team setting it also involves asking: "What is it that people together are endeavoring to say here? What is it that they want to say all together?"[67] This

---

61. Senge, 378–379.
62. Senge, 378–379.
63. Isaacs, *Dialogue*, 155.
64. Isaacs, 159.
65. Isaacs, 162.
66. Isaacs, 168.
67. Isaacs, 172.

does not mean that they all agree. "It is a matter of listening for an emerging story or voice that seems to capture more than what any one person is able to articulate, and saying that. The voice of a group of people is a function of the emerging story among them."[68]

Asking ourselves the following core questions can help us to practice voicing:[69]

- What needs to be expressed here? By you? By others? By the whole?
- What is animating this conversation, relationship, system?
- What is trying to emerge? What is it?

Jump into the Void

Among several voicing practices described by Isaacs, I find this one, "Jump into the Void,"[70] a very interesting and helpful practice for dialogue.

Voicing does not mean that we must always be prepared before we speak, or know what we are going to say. Sometimes voicing requires what Isaacs calls "a leap into the void." It is to discover in dialogue that in speaking I can create. It is a "willingness to speak in the circle without knowing what you will say."[71] Thoughts and ideas unfold and emerge as we talk. Voicing is "to step into the improvisational spirit of the conversation. . . . To speak spontaneously and improvisationally requires a willingness not to know what one is going to say before one says it."[72]

This can be a powerful experience for a team when this happens, and when they realize that they have collectively created new ideas.

Applying Dialogue as a Team Building Discipline

Perhaps you are overwhelmed by the discussion so far. It may seem somewhat abstract and theoretical. How can we use or apply this? I shared the above

---

68. Isaacs, 172.
69. Isaacs, 172.
70. Isaacs, 170–171.
71. Isaacs, 164, 165.
72. Isaacs, 170.

principles because they are very important for the academic leader to understand the theory underlying the disciplines for team building.

The good news is that there are some great resources, tools, and processes that enable the leader and the team to apply dialogue as a team building discipline.

One of these is the book by Muehlhoff, *I Beg to Differ: Navigating Difficult Conversations with Truth and Love*.[73] He applies the principles of dialogue, trust, mental models, and love in practical and easy-to-use steps. Any team that uses this approach as a foundation for its conversations will experience the powerful outcomes of dialogue.

In Section One, "Understanding Communication" (chs. 1–4), Muehlhoff discusses principles similar to those above. He provides the underlying communication theory for his steps for conducting a conversation. In Section Two, "Organizing a Conversation" (chs. 5–9), he identifies the following four steps or questions for conducting a conversation. He discusses also the rule of reciprocation (ch. 8), and proposes that this rule enables these steps to work.

- Question 1: What does this person believe?
- Question 2: Why does this person hold this belief?
- Question 3: Where do we agree?
- Question 4: Based on all I have learned, how should I proceed?[74]

Space does not allow us to discuss these in detail. Muehlhoff explains each of these steps with practical guidelines to using them, with a summary of the steps that could be used as a short-cut by faculty teams. Section Three, "Putting It into Practice" (chs. 10–12), provides case studies to illustrate how these methods work in practice.

Another powerful process for applying dialogue is described in Baldwin and Linnea, *The Circle Way: A Leader in Every Chair*.[75] They explain the structure and process for circle conversation. The circle-based model is an effective process for building sustainable teams. Circle practice also underlies

73. Tim Muehlhoff, *I Beg to Differ: Navigating Difficult Conversations with Truth and Love*, Kindle ed. (Downers Grove, IL: IVP Books, 2014).

74. Muehlhoff, *I Beg to Differ*, 85–159.

75. C. Baldwin and A. Linnea, *The Circle Way: A Leader in Every Chair* (San Francisco: Berrett-Koehler, 2010).

other group processes like "World Café,"[76] "Open Space Technology,"[77] and "Art of Hosting."[78] Still another helpful resource for facilitating conversation is *The Art of Focused Conversation* by Stanfield.[79] After discussing the guidelines for, structure of, and leading of a focused conversation, it presents a hundred tools for various types of conversations.

Once a faculty team decide to pursue serious team building and to practice the discipline of dialogue or conversation, I recommend that they choose from these tools to help them learn and apply dialogue.

Dialogue: A Fantasy or Possibility?

You may say, "This all sounds well and good, but to think that this can work is to live in a fantasy world. This is not possible." So I will first discuss some of the problems associated with implementing and practicing dialogue. These problems also illustrate the reasons why many are skeptical about it, and why dialogue often fails. Then I will affirm that this is indeed possible.

The inability to think together has become such a part of our daily interaction that people are actually skeptical about whether true dialogue can happen. Some feel it is counterproductive, that it brings us too closely to one another's thoughts, and "to do so is to risk losing our objectivity, our distance, our cherished beliefs."[80] Others feel that the practices and processes involved in dialogue and the other team building disciplines, like trust, are too "fussy," too soft. They want to get down to business, to deal with the hard, concrete things and issues. Or the effort involved and required by these practices is seen as a waste of time. For these and other reasons (like lack of trust) people avoid real dialogue, and because of this we may fall into one of two extremes.

---

76. J. Brown and D. Isaacs, *The World Café: Shaping Our Futures through Conversations That Matter* (San Francisco: Berrett-Koehler, 2005).

77. H. Owen, *Open Space Technology: A User's Guide* (San Francisco: Berrett-Koehler, 2008).

78. See Art of Hosting, http://www.artofhosting.org, for an explanation of this group process for conversation.

79. R. B. Stanfield, ed., *The Art of Focused Conversation: 100 Ways to Access Group Wisdom in the Workplace* (Gabriola Island, BC: New Society, 2000).

80. Isaacs, *Dialogue*, 5.

On the one hand, our quest for harmony may result in a false harmony in which people may sacrifice their individuality. Many good ideas and thoughts are never shared, and are therefore lost. On the other hand, we may end up in an "argument" mode, in "polarized argumentative stagnation." In both cases people stop thinking.[81]

"Dialogue presents a paradox. It is both something we already know how to do and something about which there is much to learn."[82] This has caused many to view dialogue not as something mysterious and complex, and therefore they romanticize and oversimplify the practice. This results in breakdowns and fragmentation of communication. Some believe true dialogue is not possible; it is a fantasy. Perhaps they feel that way because of a romanticized image of the simplicity of dialogue, on the one hand, or because of defensiveness about their own positions, on the other.[83]

People try to minimize the complexity of dialogue by reducing it to a few simple techniques, but doing so fragments conversations in new ways. "What is needed instead is a way of evoking what people already know about dialogue, while recognizing the ways we systematically undermine ourselves or fail to live up to the potential of our conversations."[84]

Dialogue Is a Leadership Issue

As leaders we must train and require our teams "to confront their assumptions, concerns, fears, animosities, and dreams," and in the process embrace "the possibility of coming to a much more powerful, jointly committed course of action."[85] Dialogue, and for that matter trust and team building, will not happen by itself; it is a discipline we must intentionally learn and practice on a daily basis. As leaders we should model it to our teams, train them in this discipline, and require them to practice it.

Dialogue has worked and brought about transformational change in all walks of life; the resources mentioned in this chapter attest to that fact with

---

81. Isaacs, 5.
82. Isaacs, 24.
83. Isaacs, 24, 25.
84. Isaacs, 25.
85. Isaacs, 5.

numerous case studies and examples. I could have listed many more resources, and many websites of communities of learning where dialogue is practiced. The resources listed in this chapter open the door to many more resources, tools, processes, and case studies of effective dialogue in successful teams. So dialogue is possible. Therefore, trust is possible, and so real teams are possible. When dialogue is happening, "people begin to realize that they are speaking to the common pool of meaning being created by all the people together and not to each other as individuals. They are seeking to gather a new quality of meaning and understanding together. In a dialogue, people are not just interacting, but creating together."[86]

But the question is, are we as leaders willing to help our teams to work more effectively together through this powerful discipline? Dialogue, building trust, building teams: this is a leadership issue.

I conclude by quoting Peter Senge in his foreword to Isaacs' book *Dialogue*:

[Goethe, the German poet] once called conversation the "most sublime of experiences." I have come to conclude that there is a deep hunger in the modern world for meaning and the core practices whereby human beings make meaning together. We may not go back to living in tribes. But we have an insatiable desire to live lives of dignity and meaning, and when we discover ways to do this, there is a quiet sigh of relief. We have found our way. Now we must move along it.[87]

Dialogue based upon trust and Christian love is such a way. "Come now, let us reason together . . ." (Isa 1:18 RSV).

Reflection and Action Points

1. Lencioni's team building roadmap[88] presents well-laid-out action steps for team building. But before a team embarks on this or any other process, it must first reflect on, discuss, and answer with honesty the following questions:

---

86. Isaacs, 174.
87. Isaacs, xx.
88. Lencioni, *Overcoming the Five Dysfunctions of a Team*, 9.

- Are we really a team?
- If not, do we want to become a real team?
- Are we ready for heavy lifting? Team building is hard work, and will require humility, vulnerability, submission, and honesty from all team members.

I would add a question for the academic leader: Are you ready to provide the leadership required for team building? Team building is a leadership matter, and requires hard work and sacrifice from the leader.

2. Once the team agrees and commits to do the hard work to build a team, the team should choose the process it would like to follow. The sources listed in the chapter present several such processes. I highly recommend Lencioni's process,[89] but there are others that may fit the faculty culture and situation better.

3. From the beginning, and simultaneously with the process decided upon in action point 2, the team should begin to learn the disciplines of mental models and dialogue. I recommend Muehlhoff's approach,[90] and the use of the Ladder of Inference. Using circle-based processes with Muehlhoff's questions throughout the team building process will be highly effective. A team can select from the resources mentioned. *The Circle Way*[91] is highly recommended.

4. Also, simultaneously with the above two steps, but especially for ongoing team building after the process in action point 2 is completed, the team should use various team building activities to continue practicing the disciplines and team building. There are many resources available for this, both in literature and on the Internet. However, these should be selected carefully and purposefully, not just for the sake of doing a team activity. They should also be relevant and appropriate to the faculty team's needs, situation, and culture. Many of the resources mentioned have such tools. Two additional resources are:

- E. Biech, ed. *The Pfeiffer Book of Successful Team-Building Tools: Best of the Annuals*. San Francisco: Jossey-Bass/Pfeiffer, 2001.

---

89. Lencioni.
90. Muehlhoff, *I Beg to Differ*.
91. Baldwin and Linnea, *The Circle Way*.

- L. B. Sweeney and D. Meadows. *The Systems Thinking Playbook: Exercises to Stretch and Build Learning and Systems Thinking Capabilities.* White River Junction, VT: Chelsea Green, 1995.

5. I end by reminding the leader and team that team building does not stop when any of these processes, activities, or workshops are complete. Team building must be maintained through the continuous practice of the team building disciplines discussed in this chapter. Without these the team will weaken, and will eventually stop being a real team.

Resources for Further Study

The following is a survey of additional literature and tools.

General Team Building

Dolny, Helena, ed. *Team Coaching: Artists at Work.* Johannesburg: Penguin, 2009.
    This book presents an overview, a "repertoire," of team-building tools. This would be a good place to start for a team or team leader to explore various tools for team building. However, this book alone is not sufficient to use as a specific tool; it gives only an overview of the tool. You will need to go to the original sources for learning about and how to use a specific tool. It also discusses the use of personality types in team building, which can be very effective if used correctly and with wisdom. We should be aware that there are some dangers related to the use of personality types. One is that we could label and stereotype team members, or team members could use their personality types as an excuse or defense mechanism, making them less open to change and unwilling to deal with the flaws of their personality types. *Team Coaching* discusses two tools related to personality types: the Myers-Briggs Type Indicator (MBTI) and the Enneagram. The MBTI is a well-known tool that can be used effectively in team building. There are many resources that could guide a team in using this tool. An Internet search and the counseling faculty members can help identifying these.

Aspell, Patrick J., and Dee Dee Aspell. *The Enneagram Personality Portraits: Enhancing Team Performance – Trainer's Guide.* San Francisco: Pfeiffer, 1997.
Riso, Don Richard, and Russ Hudson. *The Wisdom of the Enneagram: The Complete Guide to Psychological and Spiritual Growth for the Nine Personality Types.* New York: Bantam, 1999.

Rohr, Richard, Andreas Ebert, and Peter Heinegg. *The Enneagram: A Christian Perspective*. New York: Crossroad, 2001.
A lesser-known – but in my view a much better – tool is the Enneagram. The difference is that the Enneagram aims to be a tool for personal, psychological, and spiritual growth, and does not just place you in a box. These resources explain and provide guidelines in the use of the Enneagram. However, some training in its use is recommended.

Jones, Laurie Beth. *The Four Elements of Success: A Simple Personality Profile That Will Transform Your Team*. Nashville, TN: Nelson Business, 2005.
This resource is a fun but very helpful personality type tool for team building. It includes a twenty-eight-day tool for team development.

Rath, Tom. *StrengthsFinder 2.0*. New York: Gallup, 2014.
An effective team knows and understands each other's strengths. *StrengthsFinder 2.0* is a great tool to help with this is. For more information see their website, http://strengths.gallup.com/default.aspx.

Hibbert, E., and R. Hibbert. *Leading Multicultural Teams*. Pasadena, CA: William Carey Library, 2014.

Takagi Silzer, S. *Biblical Multicultural Teams: Applying Biblical Truth to Cultural Differences*. Pasadena, CA: William Carey International University Press, 2011.
Many teams are multicultural teams. This complicates team building. These are two resources to help in this regard.

Conflict Management

Sande, Ken. *The Peacemaker: A Biblical Guide to Resolving Personal Conflict*. Grand Rapids, MI: Baker, 2004.
Conflict is unavoidable, even with the best of teams. How will the leader and the team deal with the conflict – manage and resolve it creatively and biblically? Sande's approach and theology should be part of every faculty team's culture. It will be very helpful if the academic leader and some other team members undergo the peacemaking training for conflict mediation.

Runde, Craig E., and Tim A. Flanagan. *Building Conflict Competent Teams*. Center for Creative Leadership. San Francisco/Greensboro, NC: Jossey-Bass, 2008.

8

Coaching Faculty Members in Their Career Development

Ralph Enlow

I f you are reading this book in chapter order, you will already have received a great deal of helpful instruction concerning the *what*, *why*, and *how* of faculty development. This chapter is predicated upon and flows from the preceding ones. Although I will attempt to limit the scope of this chapter to its title and editorial intent, you may discover that I also will review and reiterate certain previously discussed faculty development principles since they bear so indispensably upon the subject of this chapter.

What precisely, then, is the subject of this chapter, "Coaching Faculty in Their Career Development"? In order to address accurately and thoroughly what this chapter title implies, we must explore two essential subjects: (1) coaching; and (2) career development. What do we mean by *coaching*? And what do we mean by *career development*?

Coaching

Coaching vs. Training

It is easy to make the mistake of equating coaching with training. After all, it would appear the objective of each is the same – improvement and advancement. But, notwithstanding ambiguity and inconsistency of usage relative to the terms coaching, training, and mentoring, there exist, in fact, crucial differences between coaching and training that are likely to have an immense impact upon what kind of faculty development actually emerges from these similar but ultimately divergent activities. The two concepts differ in terms of both ends and means.

The Ends of Coaching

Training has as its primary object meeting the needs and advancing the purposes of the *institution*. Whether the objective involves acquisition of or growth in certain skills and scholarly competencies, or even the reputational enhancement that accompanies faculty members' records of advanced postgraduate studies or scholarly publications and presentations, the *training* mindset has the institution in view. Coaching, on the other hand, has as its primary object the needs of the individual.[1] The training question is, what can my/our investment allow this faculty member to *contribute* to the goals, priorities, and reputation of this institution? The question for the coach is, by contrast, what can my investment allow this colleague to *become*?

I hope you readily recognize these are not mutually exclusive questions. In fact, I would venture that when you set out to foster faculty members' development through coaching, you get most of the benefits of training into the bargain. Conversely, when you limit your vision and purpose to institution-focused training, you may diminish both the appeal and the effectiveness of your faculty development efforts. That said, the choice to adopt a coaching over a training mode must be genuine. You cannot disguise institution-serving motives. After all, faculty members are schooled to be skeptical, and they can readily detect a disingenuous enterprise.

Career development must never be isolated from, or subordinated to, personal development. Put another way, faithful coaching will never permit disconnect of faculty members' personal development from their career development and guild advancement. The faculty, after all, *are* ultimately your

---

1. Michael K. Simpson, *Unlocking Potential: 7 Coaching Skills That Transform Individuals, Teams, and Organizations* (Grand Haven, MI: Grand Harbor Press, 2014), 3.

institution's "curriculum." As the speaker in my friend and colleague Robert Ferris's brief faculty meeting vignette puts it:

> The real curriculum is this faculty. It is the way we handle God's Word. It is the way we relate to God. It is the way we relate to one another. It is the way we relate to our students. It is the way we relate to Christ's church. It is the way we relate to this lost world. That is the real curriculum of this seminary. This list of courses which we have adopted only is a vehicle through which we will communicate ourselves to our students. If we have acted wisely, these courses will facilitate rather than inhibit that process. In the end we must not forget, however, that the faculty is the curriculum.[2]

Ferris goes on to posit corollaries to this truth. Among them is this: "Faculty development is the shortest route to curricular improvement."[3] Simply put, if you wish to improve your institution's curriculum, invest yourself in the improvement of its faculty. Such improvement, however, must be first and foremost personal rather than professional. One's professional advancement must never be allowed to supplant personal growth, and one's career accomplishments must never be permitted to excuse personal flaws. Failure to observe and foster these priorities sends a clear and contradictory message both to students and to faculty members as to what you really believe constitutes faculty merit.

The Means of Coaching

Inquiry

Coaching differs from training not only in terms of its orientation to the individual over that to the institution, but also in terms of the primary *mode* in which it is conducted. We train by *instructing*, but we coach by *inquiring*.[4] Coaching is more about asking questions than giving answers. We pursue

---

2. Robert W. Ferris, "The Faculty Is the Curriculum: A Vignette" (Unpublished manuscript, n.d.).

3. Ferris, "The Faculty Is the Curriculum."

4. Perry Zeus and Suzanne Skiffington, *The Complete Guide to Coaching at Work* (Roseville, Australia: McGraw Hill-Australia, 2001).

coaching not by poking and prodding, dictating and directing, but by suggesting and supporting, resourcing and reflecting. Coaching takes the form of conversation rather than command. Probing questions can allow fruitful reflection upon and clarification of obstacles, fears, questions, and aspirations. Skillfully framed questions are more likely to produce self-motivation and follow-through than directives, no matter how meritorious or specific.

Assessment

For this reason, coaching should flow from the practice of assessment. Threatened by what they fear may be unqualified or unfair scrutiny, faculty members frequently seek to avoid assessment and to discredit, or dismiss, its findings. While there are undoubtedly inappropriate reasons for faculty members to resist assessment, it is also possible that some resistance is justified. Too often, faculty evaluation consists exclusively of *instructional* evaluation, limited in many cases to evaluation by students. You should make it clear that instructional effectiveness is only one of several dimensions of faculty excellence.[5] And you should explicitly include faculty members' growth in scholarly competence and professional contributions as one such dimension. In my own experience, I have insisted on comprehensive faculty evaluation that includes the following six dimensions:[6]

- Modeling Christlike living, and service
- Excellence in instruction
- Effective academic and career advising
- Fostering formative student relationships
- Professional development and scholarly contributions
- Institutional compatibility and contribution

Ideally, for each of the above performance variables, there should be multiple inputs – including faculty members' self-evaluation. Without a doubt, evaluation inescapably includes your personal observations and judgment. Make no pretense or apology about that reality. At the same time, when

---

5. L. Gregory Jones and Stephanie Paulsell, eds., *The Scope of Our Art: The Vocation of the Theological Teacher* (Grand Rapids, MI: Eerdmans, 2002). See especially L. Gregory Jones, "Negotiating the Tensions of Vocation," 209–224.

6. I developed and employed this overall rubric during my academic leadership tenure (1988–1998; 2000–2006) at Columbia International University.

faculty evaluation fails to require or credit rigorous self-evaluation, do not be surprised if both its perception and its product are diminished. Moreover, you will doubtless recognize the benefit of self-evaluation as a means of shaping a faculty member's personal awareness of and commitment to a growth and improvement agenda. You will encourage this effect when you make it clear to your colleagues, in writing and in practice, that the purpose of faculty evaluation is primarily *formative* (i.e. for the purpose of improvement and growth) rather than *summative* (i.e. for purposes of promotion, retention, status).

Modeling

The most powerful means of coaching available to you is modeling. Neglect of growth in all dimensions – including one's own scholarly career – constitutes an occupational hazard for educational leaders at all levels and in all contexts. Such neglect is perhaps more acute among global theological educators, due to the essentially bi-vocational (even tri-vocational?) nature of their roles and the economic constraints upon their institutions. Add to this the constant drag of administrators' inefficiency caused by lack of professional training for their educational leadership and administration responsibilities. All these factors make it extremely difficult for educational leaders to advance their own scholarly and professional careers. Often, personal scholarship and professional growth are among the first casualties of an educational leadership assignment. Yet, while circumspection and curtailment of your ambitions in these areas may be required, you should resist the tendency toward passivity that leads to stagnation.

If you fail to maintain the posture of a learner in every sphere of your endeavors, do not be surprised that no amount of cajoling or other ways of incentivizing your colleagues' professional growth will fail miserably. Allow the sentiments of Leonard Sweet's "A Learned to Learner Litany"[7] to permeate the disposition you model to your colleagues:

- I once was a learned professor. Now I'm a learner.
- When I was learned, life was a quiz show. Now that I'm a learner, life is a discovery channel.

---

7. Leonard Sweet, "A Learned to Learner Litany of Transformation," accessed 2009, http://leonardsweet.com/. No longer available at that location.

- When I was learned, it was a question of how much I knew. Now that I'm a learner, it's a question of how much I'm being stretched.
- When I was learned, knowledge was everything. Now that I'm a learner, kindness is everything.
- When I was learned, I used to point my finger and pontificate. Now that I'm a learner, I slap my forehead all the time.
- When I was learned, I was frightened of new ideas. Now that I'm a learner, I'm just as frightened of old ideas.
- When I was learned, I loved to talk. Now that I'm a learner, I prefer to listen because that is when I'm learning.
- When I was learned, I had something to teach everybody. Now that I'm a learner, everybody has something to teach me.
- When I was learned, I thought that all knowledge was a form of power. Now that I'm a learner, I suspect much knowledge is a form of weakness.
- When I was learned, from the high ground of hindsight I instructed the past about where it went wrong. Now that I'm a learner, the past instructs me about how I can right the future.
- When I was learned, the power and mystery were in the big words. Now that I'm a learner, the power and mystery are in the small, simple words.

Resources

A final means available to you in the quest to coach your colleagues toward professional and scholarly career advancement is resource allocation. Peter Drucker's business executive insight is also applicable to educational leaders: effective leaders focus more on resource allocation than on solving problems.[8] You may believe you have few resources to allocate, or that you are powerless to allocate resources, but that is not the case. Resources consist not only of funds but also – and of equal or greater importance – of time and connections. You may have little to allocate in terms of funds, but you can nevertheless allocate meaningful resources toward the career development of your faculty by

8. Peter F. Drucker, "Managing for Business Effectiveness," *Harvard Business Review* (May 1963), accessed 4 October 2015, https://hbr.org/1963/05/managing-for-business-effectiveness/ar/1.

(1) connecting your faculty members to persons and entities that are eager and able to invest in them; and (2) allowing them time to pursue such connections. Some of my greatest professional growth has come through opportunities to share individually and in the community of professional peers. Do all you can to encourage, make introductions, and make allowances for these connections.

When it comes to allocating financial resources toward faculty development, I admit you likely have an uphill battle. While you may face actual scarcity, you are more likely confronted with lack of imagination and failure to grasp that funds spent on professional development represent an investment, not an expense. Secular corporations understand this. They invest, on average, 5–10 percent of their operating budget on employee training and development. Why do we not do the same? Because we do not believe the resources are available, and we do not believe they will pay dividends. But they are available, and they will pay dividends!

If you have not already done so, start by taking inventory of all current faculty career and professional development investments your institution makes annually. Such investments would include payment or subsidy for academic book purchases; journal subscriptions; conference registration and travel allowances (both time and funds); professional/scholarly organization membership dues; sabbatical/study leave; and loans or grants for advanced study. While you are at it, don't forget allocations of time and opportunity to build and expand professional connections. Just keeping track of such investments will have its own effect. You measure what you value, and you value what you measure. Once you have, however roughly, quantified your present resource allocation on behalf of faculty professional growth and career development, set a modest goal to increase it, and track those increases year by year. A percentage allocation goal is one you can achieve regardless of your institution's financial scale.

When I started this practice at my former institution some years ago, I was chagrined to learn that the total annual institutional investment in professional and scholarly development amounted to less than one-half of 1 percent of our operating budget. It was an amount of which you may well be envious, but it was a paltry token of our purported convictions regarding the importance of faculty development. Now that we had at least a rough measure of annual professional development investment, however, we set a goal to double our annual investment to 1 percent, and we worked hard over a period of several years in order to achieve it. Not surprisingly, we met challenge and resistance when budget reconciliation crunch time came around. In the end, few truly believe professional development is an investment. But you must insist and persist. Otherwise, coaching faculty is unlikely to amount to more than mere lip service.

Career Development

With a better understanding of *coaching*, including the critical difference between coaching and training, we now turn to the task of defining and describing *career development*. I urge that as you do so, you adjust your perspective from individual to collective, and from uniformity to uniqueness.

From Individual to Collective

Faculty is a collective noun. Thus, your vision for faculty development should not be merely an individual but a collective one. A mature, fully formed faculty is like a lush garden in full flower, featuring variety and beauty in every conceivable aspect.

In a 1993 faculty workshop I hosted at Columbia International University, Robert Clinton of Fuller Theological Seminary introduced me to a most instructive conceptual framework in support of this idea. Clinton asserts that "A faculty needs a faculty profile which best facilitates its corporate mission or God-given prophetic mandate."[9] What is a faculty profile? Clinton continues, "A faculty profile is the weighted description . . . of a faculty in terms of major faculty functions and specialized functions needed by the school to fulfill its mandate or carry out its corporate purpose."[10]

Accordingly, a collective vision for faculty development recognizes and affirms "gifts that differ" (Rom 12:6). Clinton offers the following taxonomy[11] of faculty profiles:

9. J. Robert Clinton, "Faculty Profile," unpublished lecture notes presented at Columbia Bible College and Seminary faculty retreat, 23–26 August 1993.
10. Clinton, "Faculty Profile."
11. Clinton.

- *Academic Faculty*: Those who give credibility to the school in the outside academic world. They write technical texts or conceptual texts which are at the forefront of thinking in the field. They publish for the academic world.
- *Researchers*: Those who focus on developing new ideation or fresh applications of biblical and theological thinking with respect to contemporary realities and developments in the church and world.
- *Effective Life-Changing Teachers*: Those whose classroom activities and course designs have particular impact upon students in terms of life-changing perspectives, challenges, and concepts.
- *Publicity Faculty*: Faculty with inclination and skill for writing and speaking on a popular level. They can simplify concepts, and make them palatable for people on the front lines of ministry and church engagement.
- *Ministry Faculty*: Faculty who demonstrate via off-campus ministry the reality and relevance of the concepts communicated and commended on campus. They significantly and consistently affect stakeholder churches, organizations, and individuals through their forays into external ministry.
- *Recruiters*: Faculty members who are particularly effective in attracting students to the school.
- *Public Communicators*: Those who can motivate and instill values in campus constituents; they consistently move people informationally, affectively, and volitionally.
- *Organizational Faculty*: Faculty members who understand the faculty profile and faculty needs, and can facilitate a supportive environment such that each faculty member consistently and effectively carries out the role for which he or she is distinctively suited.
- *Networkers*: Faculty who connect outwardly toward organizations, resources, and people who have the potential to significantly advance the institution's overall effectiveness.

I think it best to regard Clinton's taxonomy as merely suggestive, not exhaustive. Moreover, the profiles Clinton posits need not be viewed as discrete. One person may possess attributes and inclinations that correspond to two or more of the "profiles." Nevertheless, this framework should be useful in further disabusing you of the notion that there exists a singular vision for *career development*, or a uniform notion of an optimally developed, superior faculty member. Clinton recommends that educational leaders devote deep thought and conversation to developing an ideal faculty profile, a configuration and composition of individual contributions that offers the best prospects for advancing the institutional mission. He wisely advises that faculty recruitment efforts should then seek to advance conformity to the profile rather than, as is more customary, seek merely to fill vacancies.

The tendency for institutions – especially for institutions craving and clawing for greater credibility in the realm of academe – is to privilege the "academic faculty" profile and press all faculty members to conform to it. According to this "academic faculty" category definition, *career development* is synonymous with contributions to, and advancement within, one's academic guild. I submit that such an exclusive view of faculty career development is bound to frustrate – even alienate – some faculty members, confine the institution's spheres of impact, and contribute to mission drift.

From Uniformity to Uniqueness

From the above discussion, you likely have anticipated the present one. Conformity, uniformity, is not the object of faculty career development coaching. While fully developed faculty careers may share similar characteristics, you should aim to employ the skills and dispositions of inquiry and to supply resources in order to see that each person on your faculty reaches full potential. Fully formed faculty members' professional and career maturity will be distinct from that of peers. It is as fitting in the academic arena as it is in the spiritual realm: true development does not find its fullest expression in conformity, but in diversity. Gifts differ (Rom 12; 1 Cor 12); callings are as unique as individuals (John 15:16; Eph 3:10). Having said this, I nevertheless also believe there are categories of development that pertain to all faculty members. Let us examine a few.

Self-Understanding

Self-awareness is the soil in which personal growth occurs.[12] The following statement has been attributed to John Calvin: "Our wisdom consists almost entirely of two parts, our knowledge of God and our knowledge of ourselves; it is impossible to distinguish which determines which."[13] You have the responsibility to position the mirror and pose the questions that lead your colleagues to deeper self-understanding. Capacity is the enemy of humility. Exceedingly gifted individuals, as would be most of your faculty, need coaching that helps them cultivate humble self-awareness. There is a vast difference between exercising acquired skills, however proficiently, and engaging in what you are passionate about. While faculty members should embrace their obligation as members of a team to employ their skills in service of the larger cause, the most fruitful, fulfilling service – energizing service that can be sustained – flows from circumstances in which there is a high correspondence between faculty members' daily activities, and their core gifts and passions.[14] At the early stages of personal and career maturity, many faculty members lack discernment relative to their core gifts and passions, the areas in which they have the potential to make their greatest contribution. As an educational leader and mentor, your probing questions and encouraging guidance should aim to foster such self-understanding among your colleagues, and release and resource the professional development that corresponds to it.[15]

Scholarly Currency

Knowledge has a shelf life. Faculty members should be encouraged and enabled to stay current with advances in knowledge and contours of scholarly dialogue within their disciplinary fields. A course syllabus that has remained unchanged for five years is a telltale sign that a colleague is coasting. Your review of syllabi

---

12. Reggie McNeal, *Practicing Greatness: 7 Disciplines of Extraordinary Spiritual Leaders* (San Francisco: Jossey-Bass, 2006).

13. John Calvin, *The Institutes of the Christian Religion*, edited by John Murray, from the 1845 translation by Henry Beveridge (Mitchellville, MD: Fig, 2012). (ASIN: B006US2R6G.)

14. Steve Moore, *Who Is My Neighbor? Being a Good Samaritan in a Connected World* (Colorado Springs, CO: NavPress, 2011).

15. Judith Viorst, *Necessary Losses: The Loves, Illusions, Dependencies and Impossible Expectations That All of Us Have to Give Up in Order to Grow* (New York: Random House, 1987).

should include a check for evidence that faculty members are updating their resource and reading lists. In your coaching conversations, you frequently should inquire what your faculty colleagues are learning in their fields. Such inquiry should also probe how conversant and engaged faculty are in current research and dialogue about contemporary and contextual issues, not only in the academic community, but also in the contexts in which your present and future graduates will exercise ministry leadership. When knowledge or skill deficits are acknowledged or perceived, you must allocate available time, connections, and funding resources in order that disciplinary currency may be maintained.

Interdisciplinary Conversations and Contributions

One of the endemic weaknesses of contemporary scholarship is the degree of sub-specialization most faculty members experience in their academic preparation.[16] This is true in many fields, but it is increasingly pervasive in biblical and theological studies.[17] Academic silos serve neither you nor your students well. Compartmentalization is the enemy of ministry effectiveness. One rather urgent current example is the failure of behavioral science experts to recognize the echoes of Gnosticism in the categories and unchallenged scientific orthodoxies that underlie entrenched opposition to a biblical view of sexuality.[18] Biblical and theological studies obsessed with the arcane are as dangerous as social science studies devoid of biblical and theological grounding and insight.[19] And both appear increasingly rampant across Christian higher education's faculty landscape. Your coaching should persistently probe and prompt your colleagues to be proactive in engaging in interdisciplinary conversation. Your graduates do not exercise their ministries within the artificial categories represented by most of our curricula. You need relentlessly

---

16. Edward Farley, *Theologia: The Fragmentation and Unity of Theological Education* (Philadelphia: Fortress, 1983), 40–41.

17. Daniel O. Aleshire, *Earthen Vessels: Hopeful Reflections on the Work of Theological Schools* (Grand Rapids, MI: Eerdmans, 2008), 17.

18. Russell Moore, "What Should the Church Say to Bruce Jenner?," *Russell Moore* (blog), 24 April 2015, accessed 2 October 2015, https://www.russellmoore.com/2015/04/24/what-should-the-church-say-to-bruce-jenner/.

19. John H. Coe and Todd W. Hall, eds., *Psychology in the Spirit: Contours of a Transformational Psychology* (Downers Grove, IL: IVP Academic, 2010).

to coach your colleagues to reach and teach across the artificial divides of knowledge domains.

Teaching and Learning

Effectiveness for theological school faculty members will require threefold proficiency: (1) proficiency in one's academic/professional discipline; (2) proficiency in biblical/theological knowledge and integration (more about that in the following section); and (3) proficiency in learning and teaching principles and practices. The typical faculty member possesses only the first of these, namely, proficiency in one's academic/professional discipline. In practice, too many faculty members equate listening with learning. Although they may deny that their responsibility extends merely to the transfer of information, their actual methods too often leave upon their students the burdens of learning, and of acquiring and exercising the skills necessary for deep biblical and theological reflection. Through your coaching questions and promptings, you must seek to persuade your colleagues how essential are the latter two proficiencies named above. Through your guidance and resource allocations (remember, resources are not limited to funds; they include time and connections), you must provide the encouragement, incentives, and support colleagues need in order to develop the threefold proficiency that is so vital to the truly transformational educational outcomes to which you together aspire.

Biblical Integration

In cases where a faculty member's primary academic discipline is not Bible or theology (note: the earlier section regarding *interdisciplinary conversations and contributions* more directly pertains to Bible/theology faculty), your coaching should emphasize the importance of achieving a high and ever-increasing level of commitment to, and proficiency in, biblical integration.[20] It would be ideal if the academic preparation of each member of your faculty included formal biblical/theological study. However, if, as is more likely, some of your colleagues lack such educational preparation, you should make it a priority

---

20. J. C. Moreland, "A Call to Integration and the Christian Worldview Integration Series," in Coe and Hall, *Psychology in the Spirit*, 11–32.

for them to acquire it. Integration is impossible when, in reality, faculty members possess only one of the subject area ingredients. When a person lacks substantive biblical/theological preparation, it follows that substantive and sound integration is unlikely to occur. The biblical/theological knowledge deficit of many otherwise sincerely godly and spiritually vital faculty members cannot equip them to integrate above the level of superficial sentiment to sound and substantive integration of thinking and living. It seems to me that true integration requires faculty members to develop command of at least the following aspects of their scholarly or professional disciplines:

- *Epistemology*: What are the prevailing orthodoxies among scholars and practitioners related to this discipline with regard to what can be known, and what constitutes appropriate means of testing and validating truth claims within this field of study?[21]
- *Disciplinary belief core consensus*: What key ideas, theories, vocabulary, definitions, and conclusions are embraced by virtually the entire community of scholars and students of this discipline?[22]
- *Competing beliefs/theories*: What are the major competing theories and beliefs (i.e. "schools of thought") various segments of disciplinary scholars adhere to and advocate?[23]
- *Theoretical foundations of key methodological approaches*: What theoretical grounding underlies major methodologies of research and practice in this field? How would you critique these biblically and theologically?[24]

---

21. Coe and Hall, *Psychology in the Spirit*. See especially chapter 4, "Foundations and Contours of a Transformational Psychology," 74–104, for an example of biblical and theological critique of consensus disciplinary epistemology.

22. John Swinton, *Dementia: Living in the Memories of God* (Grand Rapids, MI: Eerdmans, 2012). See especially chapter 2, "Redescribing Dementia: Starting from the Right Place," 27–28, for an example of the kind of core consensus, definitions, and vocabulary critique I am commending.

23. For an example of such competing beliefs and theories analysis, see Stan Jones, *Modern Psychotherapies: A Comprehensive Christian Appraisal*, 2nd ed. (Downers Grove, IL: IVP Academic, 2011).

24. Coe and Hall, *Psychology in the Spirit*. See especially chapter 3, "Ways of Seeing Psychology and Christianity," 57–73, for an example of a mature grasp of theoretical foundations of key methodological approaches. For a similar, though less comprehensive example, see Eric Johnson and Stan Jones, *Psychology and Christianity: Four Views* (Downers Grove, IL: IVP Academic, 2000).

The above categories and questions should be high on the list of coaching conversation topics.

Conclusion

Coaching faculty members in their career development requires an understanding of the difference between coaching and training. This difference can be seen in the contrasting object (individual rather than institutional) and the contrasting means (inquiry rather than instruction) of the endeavor. It involves the development of a collective vision for the composition and shape of your faculty, and the cultivation of individual potential rather than the imposition of conformity to a uniform ideal. Coaching is what military experts call a force multiplier.[25] Make it a priority, and develop proficiency in your exercise of it as an educational leader.

Reflection and Action Points

1. Create a chart similar to the one below, listing each of your faculty members in the left-hand column. In the right-hand column, designate the nature of each faculty member's contribution to your faculty's collective strength. Note that some faculty members may contribute strongly in more than a single category. Feel free also to name additional categories appropriate to your context that may not be included among those offered in this chapter.

Faculty Member Name	Primary Role

---

25. Oren Harari, *The Leadership Secrets of Colin Powell* (New York: McGraw-Hill, 2003), 215–216.

- *Academic Faculty*: Those who give credibility to the school in the outside academic world. They write technical texts or conceptual texts which are at the forefront of thinking in the field. They publish for the academic world.
- *Researchers*: Those who focus on developing new ideation or fresh applications of biblical and theological thinking with respect to contemporary realities and developments in the church and world.
- *Effective Life-Changing Teachers*: Those whose classroom activities and course designs have particular impact upon students in terms of life-changing perspectives, challenges, and concepts.
- *Publicity Faculty*: Faculty with inclination and skill for writing and speaking on a popular level. They can simplify concepts, and make them palatable for people on the front lines of ministry and church engagement.
- *Ministry Faculty*: Faculty who demonstrate via off-campus ministry the reality and relevance of the concepts communicated and commended on campus. They significantly and consistently affect stakeholder churches, organizations, and individuals through their forays into external ministry.
- *Recruiters*: Faculty members who are particularly effective in attracting students to the school.
- *Public Communicators*: Those who can motivate and instill values in campus constituents; they consistently move people informationally, affectively, and volitionally.
- *Organizational Faculty*: Faculty members who understand the faculty profile and faculty needs, and can facilitate a supportive environment such that each faculty member consistently and effectively carries out the role for which he or she is distinctively suited.
- *Networkers*: Faculty who connect outwardly toward organizations, resources, and people who have the potential to significantly advance the institution's overall effectiveness.

(a) Based on the roster you have developed above, work with your institution's leadership team to create a pie chart or Venn diagram that illustrates your faculty's current collective profile in proportional terms.

(b) Create a pie chart or Venn diagram that illustrates the collective faculty profile you believe ideally corresponds to your institutional mission and vision. Compare your actual present profile with the ideal, and craft a long-term faculty recruitment and development plan that moves you from the present actual profile to the ideal one.

2. Review your overall operating expenditures for the past five years.

(a) Identify any and every expenditure related to faculty development. Such expenditures might include, but are not limited to, academic book purchases; journal subscriptions; conference registration and travel allowances (both time and funds); professional/scholarly organization membership dues; sabbatical/ study leave; and loans or grants for advanced study.

(b) Total your professional development expenditures for each year, then calculate and chart your overall annual percentage investment trend for faculty development.

(c) Set a realistic five-year goal to increase your institution's annual investment in faculty development. Monitor your progress, and adjust your goals annually.

3. Ask all of your faculty members to submit a biblical integration assessment of themselves based upon the four criteria presented in this chapter: epistemology; disciplinary belief core consensus; competing theories/beliefs; and theoretical foundations of key methodological approaches. Invite them to rate themselves with regard to their grasp of these basic integrative components, and develop a remediation/improvement plan complete with action steps and timelines.

Resources for Further Study

Burge, G. M. *Mapping Your Academic Career: Charting the Course of a Professor's Life.* Grand Rapids, MI: IVP Academic, 2005.
From his vantage point as a career Christian college faculty member, Burge offers practical guidance on faculty career development, but primarily oriented to scholarly guild professional development, growth, and advancement.

The Coaching Source, http://thecoachingsource.com/.
This contains a rich array of teaching, training, and assessment material related to the topic of coaching. The site's primary context and target audience is the

world of business and commerce rather than higher education. Many concepts and resources, however, are nevertheless quite relevant and transferable to the realm of Christian higher theological education.

Bobby Clinton, http://bobbyclinton.com/?s=mentoring.
J. Robert Clinton is a leading research scholar/theorist on the subject of Leadership Emergence. Virtually all of Clinton's research and teaching materials, published and unpublished – which include extensive writings on the subject of mentoring – can be accessed via this website.

My Passion Profile, http://mypassionprofile.com/.
This is an online assessment tool designed to help individuals gain a model and framework for self-understanding of their core passions. Steve Moore's book (see below) provides deeper explanation and links to this assessment profile. Personal life and career alignment based upon such self-understanding leverages deep fruitfulness and fulfillment.

Moore, Steve. *Who Is My Neighbor? Being a Good Samaritan in a Connected World.* Colorado Springs, CO: Navpress, 2011.

Palmer, Parker. *The Courage to Teach: Exploring the Inner Landscape of a Teacher's Life.* San Francisco: Jossey-Bass, 2007.

The Professional and Organizational Development Network in Higher Education (POD Network), http://podnetwork.org/.
The POD Network comprises hundreds of higher education professionals working in the field of faculty and instructional development. It is the most prolific producer of shared research and resources in all areas of faculty development. POD Network's peer reviewed annual journal, *To Improve the Academy*, has thirty-five volumes to date. Most POD Network resources are accessible exclusively to members, though the website offers some useful downloadable resources for free. If you are serious about faculty development, you should not be ignorant of the POD Network and its resources.

Simon, Caroline J. *Mentoring for Mission: Nurturing New Faculty at Church-Related Colleges.* Grand Rapids, MI: Eerdmans, 2003.

9

Developing the Faculty as Mentors: Cultivating a Developmental Culture to Meet a Critically Missing Element in Evangelical Higher Education

Ron Watters

The mentoring of students attending evangelical academic institutions must be strengthened significantly to better fulfill the Great Commission given by Jesus. Rick Woods with Mission Frontiers has observed:

> One of the most troubling obstacles to world evangelization facing us today [is] the failure of the Church . . . to equip most followers of Jesus to reproduce their faith in the lives of others. The vast majority of Bible-believing followers of Jesus are not regularly sharing their faith nor investing their lives in helping to bring others to maturity in Christ. And those who are concerned about this [do not] seem to know what to do about it. . . . In short, we

are largely failing to develop mature followers of Jesus who are able to make disciples who can make disciples.[1]

Since this critical deficiency exists in evangelical churches worldwide, and since the professional leaders of these churches are usually trained in evangelical educational institutions, there is a problem in the way those leaders are being trained as spiritual multipliers at them since alumni, no matter how good they are in meeting other ministry needs, are seriously failing to meet this foundational aspect of the Great Commission. The solution involves providing a discipleship model during their educational programs that they can incorporate into their ministries during their studies and after graduation. This chapter will refer to this model in the institutional context as "mentoring." It can, however, only exist in the programs students complete if faculty members know how to effectively mentor these students, and are personally committed to doing so, and if the institutions where they serve value such mentoring enough to include it as a crucial element in their philosophy of education, and in the job descriptions of the faculty and staff.

One chapter cannot provide a comprehensive guide for solving this problem. However, it can and will present an image of what more effective mentoring involves for students, faculty members, and school leaders who want to move forward toward a solution; and it will list resources to help them do so.

The Importance of Mentoring in the Evangelical Academic Environment

"Mentoring" might be most simply defined as one person influencing the life of another person. Given this definition, it has always been an aspect of formal education simply because teachers are people of significant influence (for good or bad) in the lives of their students. Even lectures with purely one-way communication are a form of this kind of mentoring and have an important role to play in the educational context. However, there is a broader definition and a more formal role that mentoring should have in education that

---

1. Rick Wood, "A Discipleship Revolution: The Key to Discipling All Peoples," *Mission Frontiers* (Jan–Feb 2011), https://www.missionfrontiers.org/issue/article/a-discipleship-revolution.

is not met in the classroom context alone. It involves a deeper, more personal relationship between faculty members and students.

Because most students worldwide must attend elementary-level classes, and often also secondary-level ones, schools at these levels continue to exist whether the relationship between students and teachers is positive or negative. However, higher educational institutions provide entirely optional training and thrive only when enough students choose to enroll in them. A faculty member's good reputation draws more students, which helps keep the doors open and the faculty employed; but a poor reputation encourages potential students to go elsewhere.

Howard Hendricks had a troubled home life and developed a bad reputation in his early elementary school years. However, a new teacher at the beginning of his sixth-grade year took a personal interest in him and helped him know someone cared about him. He subsequently became one of the foremost evangelical educators in the United States of America in the last half of the twentieth century, with a reputation as an effective classroom teacher and, even more so, as an effective mentor. This dual role provides the best of both spheres of influence; it is the type of role to which faculty members should aspire, and it can make the difference in student selection between institutions of otherwise equal academic status.[2]

True, not everyone has Hendricks's personality, nor will every faculty member be as effective as he was. However, the type of personal mentoring that is the focus of this chapter can be developed by faculty members of differing classroom ability and personality types. In addition, it is necessary that they do so because it significantly aids in the transformation of student lives, which is the function of education, by providing a mechanism that integrates the cognitive, affective, and psychomotor areas of personal development; and it meets the relational element, so much a part of modern student expectations, as seen in the rise of social networking.

---

2. Karen Giesen and Sandra Glahn, "The Life of Howard G. 'Prof' Hendricks," *DTS Voice*, Dallas Theological Seminary, 20 February 2013, accessed 26 June 2015, https://voice.dts.edu/article/howard-hendricks-prof/. My personal contacts testify that his reputation in both roles was a significant factor for many students, including themselves, deciding to attend that school rather than others.

Moreover, this type of mentoring will help faculty be more effective in the classroom with the adjustments that are increasingly required as education globally moves into the future. Before the information age, instructors could focus primarily on content transfer as their primary form of instruction. However, information is now abundant and easily accessible for anyone with a relatively functional Internet connection, especially with advances in smartphone technology and rapidly spreading connectivity. Since it can be acquired easily elsewhere, classroom time needs to shift toward helping students learn to process and use that information, which means less time lecturing and more time interacting with students. The skills required to mentor them in small-group and one-on-one settings have direct application to better interaction with them in the classroom and during distance-education online sessions.

The Biblical Basis for Mentoring

The type of mentoring envisioned in this chapter is very comprehensive in that it calls each mentor to assume several roles in relating to a student, including being an academic advisor, crisis care-giver, spiritual guide, and vocational coach. Based on the problem explained in the opening comments, it also requires helping students have a vision for and becoming spiritually reproductive. Even if a student is studying business administration or engineering, evangelical institutions are usually founded to help students make a positive spiritual impact on people and society. The motivation for this impact is usually, or should be, obedience institutionally and personally to Jesus's Great Commission (Matt 28:18–20 ESV). The main verb in it is "make disciples." A disciple in the first century was not primarily an academic learner (a pupil, student), but more of an apprentice learning the vocation of the master. The eleven people given this command by Jesus and identified as his "disciples" (v. 16) were people who had made a significant commitment to be with him, were learning to be like him, and were participating in his work of advancing the kingdom of God. As Jesus was about to return to heaven, he entrusted the work he had started to them. Declaring his universal authority as the reason and motivation for accomplishing it (the "therefore" in v. 19

refers to the content in v. 18), he gave them the responsibility of enlisting and training others globally to associate with him, and to help fulfill this work, too.

Three supporting verbs describe the broad elements Jesus gave them for the process of making disciples: "Go . . . baptizing . . . teaching [to obey]." The third term calls them to help others understand and obey his teachings, which focus primarily on godly character and actions perhaps best summarized as loving God with every aspect of one's being, loving others as one's self, and being people of the kind of grace and truth he modeled (Matt 22:37–40; John 1:14, 17 ESV). By teaching *all* that he commanded, they would need to include teaching the Great Commission to others, resulting in those they discipled being called themselves to make Christlike, multiplying disciples, who would also be called to make Christlike, multiplying disciples – the process repeated from one spiritual generation to the next across the globe until Jesus returns.

Similarly, Paul calls Timothy to carry on his mission by asking him to find "faithful men, who will be able to teach others also" (2 Tim 2:2 ESV). Paul is not simply calling for transfer of doctrinal truth. In verse 2, he does tell Timothy to transfer to others what he has "heard" from him; however, it is clear from Paul's writings that he was interested in people both believing correct spiritual truth (the first part of his epistles) and, based on that truth, behaving in a way consistent with it. He is, therefore, calling for the transfer of orthodoxy (right belief) and orthopraxy (right behavior), though the modern use of these two distinct terms is alien to a proper understanding of Scripture, where the concept of orthodoxy incorporates both aspects that should never be separated in a disciple's life.

Both passages, then, involve producing four generations with the same spiritual DNA:

Generation	Matt 28:19	2 Tim 2:2
1st (spiritual parent)	Jesus	Paul
2nd (spiritual child)	The eleven disciples	Timothy
3rd (spiritual grandchild)	Those baptized and taught to obey	Faithful people
4th (spiritual great-grandchild)	Others when those above also obey the command of Matt 28:19 taught to them	Others

There is educational wisdom in this multi-generation perspective: the quality of development done with the second generation is not confirmed until the third generation effectively develops the fourth generation. Weakness in the fourth generation confirms the need for more attention by the person at the top of this reproductive chain in mentoring those in the second generation who have been deficient in what they have done with the third generation. Unfortunately, mentors often look only at those they directly influence and not the succeeding generations under them to learn what type of long-term impact they have had down the line, and the adjustments needed to mentor the second generation more effectively.

The goal in this process is both quantitative and qualitative. It *is* to increase the number of multiplying disciples involved (quantity reproduction), but *also* they should be Christlike disciples (quality reproduction). Focusing on quantity reproduction to the detriment of quality reproduction results in many believers who are not properly Christlike, as seen in one megachurch pastor's confession that his church had grown in numbers without producing disciples even in the midst of excellent Bible teaching and various helpful church programs.[3] On the other hand, focusing on quality without quantity makes Christ's mandate of reaching the nations unnecessarily slow as the world's population continues to grow dramatically. Only a balance of both quality and quantity will provide the expanding network of committed, spiritually mature, kingdom-oriented leaders needed to impact the church and various key segments of society sufficiently to hasten Christ's return (2 Pet 3:9–12).

The difference between the terms "discipling" and "disciple-making" has been described as the former focusing on a person's spiritual growth, while the latter is the essence of the Great Commission that incorporates the former, but goes beyond it.[4] This is an unfair distinction because the meaning of either term depends entirely on the context in which it is used; they can be synonyms with either meaning. The key point, however, is this: mentoring

---

3. Robby Gallaty, *Growing Up: How to Be a Disciple Who Makes Disciples* (Bloomington, IN: CrossBooks, 2013), 9; citing "Willow Creek Repents?" *Christianity Today*, October 2007, accessed 29 March 2013. *Christianity Today* article found at: https://www.christianitytoday.com/pastors/2007/october-online-only/willow-creek-repents.html.

4. "What Is Disciple-Making?," Sonlife, accessed 9 July 2015, http://www.sonlife.com/strategy/what-is-disciple-making/.

people toward spiritual growth without also helping them become effective, multi-generational spiritual-multipliers does not fulfill the Great Commission as Christ intended it. Multitudes of believers around the world are attending Bible studies without becoming people with the vision and ability to make Christlike, multiplying disciples because those leading them do not instill this vision in them and equip them with the skill to do so.[5] This results in a lot of effort without sustainable, ongoing discipleship, as in the story of a mission organization required to leave a certain country and only then realizing that their missionaries left behind numerous Christians but no real disciples to continue fulfilling the Great Commission after their departure.[6]

The Need for an Institution's Commitment to Mentoring

If surveyed, most institutions would probably say they value mentoring that involves spiritual development and reproduction like that described in the previous section. However, how many of these institutions have a vision for it and a commitment to it that involves faculty selection and development, curriculum revision, and resource acquisition and allocation? Personal experience over several decades, both as a student at an esteemed evangelical institution and through interaction with those who graduated from other esteemed ones, has revealed a clear lack of such mentoring in evangelical academia. After God used various means to draw his attention to the priority of mentoring multiplying disciples in his ministry, one pastor candidly told me recently that he now believes his formal training at two of the better-known evangelical institutions in the United States was in the secondary aspects of ministry (preaching, teaching, counseling, marrying, burying, etc.), rather than in the primary one of making spiritually mature, multiplying disciples that he now sees as the essence of the Great Commission. He understands that he needed these other areas of training, for they are important in his work, too; however, he regrets that the institutions he attended did not emphasize spiritual reproduction more and have better faculty mentoring models to train him in

5. Herb Hodges, *Tally Ho the Fox! The Foundation for Building World-Visionary, World-Impacting, Reproducing Disciples*, 2nd ed. (Augusta, GA: Manhattan Source, 2001), 109.
6. Hodges, *Tally Ho the Fox!*, 78.

it, so he could envision and develop a church-based multi-generation plan and effectively mentor others as multiplying disciples earlier in his ministry.

This does not mean evangelical institutions are devoid of significant mentoring by some faculty mentors; however, it does seem to be the exception rather than the rule. During one of my graduate programs, I heard students talking about a respected professor who took a student with him on a speaking trip and gave five minutes of his speaking time for that student to share his testimony with the congregation. This faculty member understood some critical aspects of effective mentoring: he wanted to spend individual time with the student apart from that experience in their group context, he wanted some of that time to occur off-campus, and he wanted some of it to include shared ministry experiences when the student could observe him and he could observe the student. Unfortunately, this was all at the initiative of the professor, and not an official component of the curriculum or job description for faculty members at that institution, because it was not the common experience of the other students attending there who were involved in the discussion. Those few hours together with this faculty member were likely more meaningful for that student than what he experienced in regular classroom settings. Moreover, from the students' discussion of his trip, it is what they also wanted but lacked in their relationships with faculty members. Mentoring outside of the classroom, then, cannot simply be defined as student participation in an advisee group that results primarily in Christian fellowship among students and between a faculty member and students. Instead, effective mentoring moves beyond this into a more significant relationship that models the type students should have with people in their ministries to truly build Christlike, multiplying disciples.

Some official personal mentoring established by institutions does take place in fieldwork situations; but it often does not involve faculty members *regularly* overseeing and/or working alongside students off-campus. Instead, it can mean nothing more than a student being assigned to an overworked off-campus ministry professional who may not spend much time, if any, actually mentoring and assessing the student based on substantial observation and interaction in ministry situations. Even if such mentors do have time and a desire to do it, how can they do it well if they did not have a mentor who modeled it for them, and trained them in effective mentoring (which points out the need to provide mentoring for mentors, too)? Ineffective mentors may pass students on their requirements out of guilt at their own inadequacy in mentoring rather than from an accurate assessment of the students' knowledge, character, and abilities.

Official personal mentoring also occurs when students write theses or dissertations; however, this is usually mentoring with the single goal of helping the student produce the required piece of literature. It may not involve more holistic mentoring on issues of character development that are actually also relevant to the process, including how the research and writing load may be negatively affecting the student's family and field ministry.

The comments above describe a common situation that exists as the result of educational philosophy being influenced both by modernism, with its emphasis on knowledge, and the Information Age, with its emphasis on content. By stressing intellectual ability over physical skills, the master–apprentice relationship, so much a part of pre-modern society, has been greatly minimized in modern Western society except when training people for manual vocations (e.g. auto mechanics) or as physicians (e.g. during their internship and residency requirements). As modernism and Western education spread globally, they replaced mentoring that was so much a part of traditional societies. The rise and influence in the West of postmodernism, with its emphasis on subjective experience and personal relationships, is correcting this imbalance and may be behind the greater role mentoring is being given in society, and the rise of Life Coaching as a new profession.[7] Unfortunately, evangelicalism seems slower at correcting this imbalance in its educational institutions. Overemphasis on the cognitive area of personal development is detrimental to the affective and psychomotor areas also needed for the kind of healthy spirituality Christ commissioned when making his disciples. Mentoring provides a specific context for more holistic, integrated student development with its strong emphasis on affective and psychomotor development, in addition to the usually stronger emphasis on the cognitive development found in the higher education classroom (except in specific courses such as "Spiritual Disciplines" or "Evangelism and Discipleship").

7. Web searches using the terms "mentoring" and "coaching" return numerous sites and information (including some annotated bibliographies) that reveal a rising interest in mentoring (esp. related to business, education, and psychology) beginning near the end of the twentieth century.

Furthermore, providing mentoring as part of evangelical higher education is an increasingly critical need in light of the family and moral breakdown occurring in societies globally. Institutions must give extra attention to a student's character development as more who matriculate come from dysfunctional homes and are affected negatively by them. Moreover, as the gospel penetrates non-Christian cultures, and the West is increasingly less Christian in its worldview, more students will come with non-biblical perspectives that need additional attention before graduation. The classroom and purely academic-focused mentoring do not adequately address these personal needs, nor do they develop the weak interpersonal skills that may exist in students with significant relational challenges who need stronger skills to succeed in ministry to others, whether as ministry professionals or within secular professions. Effective mentoring provides the relationships and model they must experience to help them be the kind of people Jesus wants them to be as his disciples.

What, then, does it take for faculty members at evangelical educational institutions to mentor students effectively?

Inclusion in the Institution's Guiding Principles

Businessman, author, and motivational speaker Zig Ziglar is famously quoted as saying, "If you aim at nothing you will hit it every time."[8] For faculty members to become effective mentors, mentoring must first be a significant aspect of the institution's guiding principles, which are usually delineated in its vision, mission, and core values. Unless a vision and commitment to mentoring are clearly stated in the principles that provide institutional direction, mentoring will be left to the individual faculty members as optional, and without the formal support of the institution's leadership. Any effective mentoring that then occurs is the unusual experience of certain students instead of the common experience for all of them. The rise and growth of many evangelical parachurch organizations that focus on discipleship has occurred, in part, because churches have not adequately fulfilled this need. Indeed, they cannot do so if institutions

---

8. Tom Ziglar, "If You Aim at Nothing . . .," *Ziglar* (blog), accessed 27 July 2015, http://www.ziglar.com/quotes/zig-ziglar/if-you-aim-nothing.

training their spiritual leaders have had a publish-or-perish mentality for their faculty members, without an equally strong mentor-or-perish mentality. There is nothing wrong with evangelicals being scholars, and applauded for such accomplishments; it is entirely appropriate within the context of higher education. However, they are faculty members of *evangelical* institutions where mentoring should be, at least, equal in importance. The imbalance in favor of scholarship has resulted in graduates seen as ineffective and irrelevant in important aspects of ministry by their constituents.[9] Conversely, mentoring without adequate academics has the potential to turn out very good spiritual multipliers who may repeat the problems of the past, which could have been avoided if they had the critical knowledge necessary for greater wisdom as leaders in the Christian community. The goal should be to have scholars who are practitioners and practitioners who are scholars. A proper inclusion of both in the institution's guiding principles will help fulfill the Great Commission as the church moves into the future.

While completing my master of divinity studies, I was attending a weekly meeting of students affiliated with my mission organization on campus when a person accidentally interrupted it. After asking who we were and apologizing for the interruption, he left, only to immediately return and introduce himself as a leader in a significant evangelical denomination. He then told us we were the very types of people he wanted most in his group – people who were academically trained at seminary, but who knew how to reach and disciple others because of our parachurch training and involvement. While I appreciated the affirmation that our organization was doing something well, I was saddened that he did not view the institution's training as effective as our organization's training in developing mentors who could produce multiplying disciples, though its academic programs were established to develop competent pastors, church planters, and missionaries, in addition to faculty members for

---

9. Based on an extensive study of theological institutions worldwide by Overseas Council International, Manfred Kohl identifies the problems with current theological education, and the disconnection and tension between theological educators and their constituencies. He observes, "It seems, therefore, that both theological institutions and churches tend to live more and more in isolation from each other, to the detriment of both in terms of effectiveness." Manfred Waldemar Kohl, "Theological Education: What Needs to Be Changed," *Torch Trinity Journal* 12, no. 1 (2009): 149–162.

other evangelical educational institutions training these types of workers in other locations.

Overcoming this problem requires an institution to make sure the key principles guiding it include a mentoring aspect that is both clearly stated and regularly reviewed to monitor institutional progress toward it. The institution where I was on the faculty for several decades, and with which I still have a development role, was started and continues to exist, in large part, because of faculty members frustrated by the lack of effective mentoring they encountered during their graduate studies at numerous well-known evangelical institutions. To help guarantee that this institution provides a solution to that problem, aspects of Great Commission mentoring are intentionally included in statements of its guiding principles.[10] These statements are regularly revisited by leaders and faculty members to determine whether they need rewording for better clarity, and whether the institution with its various offices and departments is deviating from them in the midst of many good opportunities and activities. Discussions include determining how such mentoring needs to be strengthened along with the other principles that guide the institution. This has resulted in ownership of, and accountability for, mentoring as part of the common DNA within every aspect of the institution and every person officially associated with it – faculty members, employed staff, and students – and greater effectiveness by them in helping fulfill the Great Commission in ministry settings off-campus, which has resulted in constituents having greater confidence in the institution shown by significantly funding it.

Inclusion in Program Curricula

With mentoring established as part of the institution's guiding principles, the second step is incorporating it into each program's curriculum. Doing so gives better assurance it will occur, be effective, and be reinforced as part of the institution's DNA. Without inclusion in each program, students should not be faulted for wondering about its true importance in fulfilling

---

10. International Graduate School of Leadership, "Mission & Vision," accessed 6 July 2015, http://www.igsl.asia/about/mission-vision-values/; and "Core Values," same source and access date, http://www.igsl.asia/about/core-values/.

the Great Commission, or for devaluing it in various ministry contexts upon graduation. They are simply accepting the value modeled broadly for them by the institution. For example, if mentoring is included in professional degree programs but not in research programs, students may think it unnecessary for scholars. If they then become faculty members or researchers, they may not value mentoring in institutional contexts but only in pastoral ones, to the detriment of the students studying where they teach, who will not know how to make disciples in churches after they graduate. (This mentality may be the source of the problem mentioned at the beginning of this chapter.)

When incorporating mentoring into a program, it is best to have related cognitive, affective, and psychomotor development outcome goals appropriate for that type of program (though diverse programs can and do share many of the same goals). The primary focus of these goals should be a student's spirituality and character development through helping integrate all aspects of the curriculum into his or her worldview and vocational calling, which should include a commitment and ability to make Christlike multiplying disciples as a way of life, even if that vocation will involve secular employment.

Cognitive development goals in the mentoring curriculum should reinforce classroom material so that it is not missed, forgotten, or given delayed application until after graduation by students. They should also include exposure to critical content related to the primary mentoring focus but not covered by the particular program's classroom-related curriculum. It is important, however, that mentoring to achieve these goals not become content-heavy, small classroom sessions, or private one-on-one tutoring (though there may be times when these are also needed in addition to the type of mentoring in view here). Rather, achieving them within the mentoring curriculum should revolve around building deeper, more meaningful relationships with students to address critical areas of personal growth less likely to be effectively addressed with them in the classroom context.

Character issues play a significant role in the stories of the Old Testament, and receive significantly more emphasis than gifting ability as qualifications for spiritual leadership in the New Testament (1 Tim 3:2–12; Titus 1:6–9 ESV). Therefore, affective development goals related to mentoring should include helping a student grow to love God more, and to keep that love first place in the midst of the heavy academic demands, since students who put academics first while undertaking their programs are more likely also to put vocation first upon graduation from them. It will also require helping students deal with various sins, especially in their private lives (e.g. viewing pornography), and learn to walk in the Spirit when under the pressure of extreme or unusual circumstances. In addition, it should involve helping a student develop an increasing commitment to the Great Commission by participating sufficiently in a multiplication-oriented ministry in the midst of academic pressures to minimize it. Finally, it should include helping a student be a better team player and servant-steward leader in the lives of others, rather than secretly wanting a higher degree primarily as a symbol of power or authority over others.[11]

Psychomotor development mentoring curriculum objectives should include those helping a student succeed in life that are not covered in classes, either because they are unrelated to the type of courses the student is required to take or because it is impossible for some reason for the student to take those types of courses. These could include helping a student with interpersonal communication skills to have better relationships with people, or with personal and family budgeting to have as much financial success as possible with God's provision. It should also include helping each student practice various leadership and mentoring skills through giving them opportunities to direct mentoring-group activities, engage other students and the mentor in areas where they want personal development, and participate in making multiplying disciples in a specific ministry setting. This will require the mentor to be with the student in those settings often enough to observe with some regularity and depth the student's progress and needs, and to work with him or her to become more successful.

Including faculty mentoring with a clear primary focus and related developmental goals in a program's curriculum has additional institutional and personal benefits. It provides an important mechanism by which each student's

---

11. Servant leadership is well known in the church, and has become increasingly popular in the secular business world. However, my colleague Steve Hobson sees *servant-steward* leadership as the type modeled by Jesus. The servanthood aspect calls leaders to have the best interests of others in mind instead of their own, perhaps selfish, ones (Phil 2:3–8). On the other hand, the stewardship aspect holds leaders accountable for also fulfilling the responsibilities with which they have been entrusted (John 17:4). Wisely balancing in a dynamic tension these two aspects avoids an unhealthy, unbiblical lifestyle that does not do justice to Jesus's type of leadership, which his disciples are also called to model.

growth and maturity can be evaluated personally through regular, consistent, and interpersonal interaction, making it possible for earlier correction or temporary suspension where needed, or dismissal where required. It allows the faculty mentor to act as a more effective intermediary should an issue arise between a student being mentored and other students, or with instructors, or school officials. It gives faculty members better insight in answering questions on reference forms when a student is applying for a job or further studies. It also sets the ground for a potential confidential, long-term relationship between a faculty member and a mentored alumnus, whereby they can continue to influence one another significantly and be used by God in each other's ongoing process of sanctification.

Inclusion in the Institution's Resource Allocations

Mentoring cannot go from being a concept to a reality without the institution's leaders proving a commitment to it through adequate allocation of the following resources.

Allocation of Time

This area considers both formal and informal elements in faculty and student workloads. Allocating formal mentoring time will involve determining how much minimal time to give to regular, designated mentoring activities, and when they will occur. Some institutions may choose to set a certain time when classes cannot occur, so mentors and students throughout the institution can be in their mentoring groups. Other institutions may choose simply to designate the amount of time required for formal mentoring in both groups and with individuals, leaving the actual time when it occurs to the people involved in each situation. Some of these formal times will be regular meetings at the same location, probably on campus. Other formal times may take them off campus for participation together in sporting and other leisure activities, extended times of prayer, and spiritual retreats, or having meetings in one another's homes, so they can experience their relationships and observe one another in non-academic settings.

For mentoring to be effective, mentors cannot simply attend the scheduled meetings and spontaneously float through them, hoping the Holy Spirit does something that is effective. Instead, they need time to prepare the agenda and the logistics needed to be with students, and to think through adjustments and future meetings with them. Therefore, as with classroom teaching, formal mentoring time should include what faculty members need both to prepare for meeting with students and to debrief themselves when meetings end. Finally, formal mentoring time should also include required events and activities to train mentors in being more effective.

Apart from the formal element, mentor workload should include an additional buffer for informal mentoring time needed to visit sick or distressed students, or be with them when other unexpected events arise in their lives in which the mentor should be involved. This will model to students the commandment of loving others more than oneself, since they know that mentors are busy people, and will impress upon them the need to ingrain it into their own lives.

Providing adequate time is important because the greatest hindrance to effective mentoring is busyness. Busy people with good motives and adequate ability are still busy people. Faculty members and students with too many time-consuming high priorities must try to find the time to do them all, which usually results in doing many things below what is expected or required. Institutional leaders must find a balance of responsibilities that allows for effective mentoring. Without this, it will not occur as established in the institution's guiding principles. The significant investment of time needed for effective mentoring may be another major reason why it is weak in so many institutions. Even Jesus as the eternal Son of God had no more time on earth for his earthly activities than the 168 hours a week available to every other human being. Providing the time required for faculty members to mentor effectively will require hard decisions by institutional leaders in collaboration with faculty members and student leaders on the best way to secure it. It may mean requiring students to make a greater time commitment to achieve graduation than at schools that do not include effective mentoring in program curricula. It will probably mean academic leaders setting maximum homework limits for each credit hour related to certain types of class assignments (e.g. maximum time allowed for technical reading vs. non-technical reading, and/or writing research papers vs. writing reflection papers) to avoid academic overload interfering with mentoring. Teaching faculty will need to honor these limits by being more selective in their assignments, with priority given to quality over quantity in their work, and to equipping students with the tools to be life-long learners (since so much content is accessible to them after graduation) rather than, as in the past, giving them so much content while they are at the institution. If faculty members cannot make these adjustments without the concern that academic quality will suffer, it will probably be difficult to find the necessary time for effective mentoring to become a reality at the institution.

Allocation of Facilities

The use of facilities for regular mentoring will depend on the size of the mentoring group. An ideal mentoring group size for teaching faculty members and institutional leaders is probably six to eight students. On the one hand, covering their other responsibilities plus having time for the heavy relational component required in effective mentoring may be difficult for these mentors to achieve with more than eight students. Unless the mentor has additional time for mentoring usually unavailable for teaching faculty members, regular one-on-one time between mentor and student will likely be minimized or deleted, except the little needed if the mentor is also the student's academic advisor. On the other hand, group dynamics may also be affected negatively with fewer than six students since there may not be good representation among the students of personality types, background differences, and/or of each academic year with its distinct perspective on the student experience to promote the type of co-mentoring possible with such diversity.

Facility use will not be difficult where academic advising groups of this size are already established since the location can be retained – the groups now functioning more holistically with the mentor also the academic advisor. Group locations only need to be adjusted if the length and frequency of mentoring meetings go beyond what has been given for advisee meetings and a conflict is created with other uses for the same location. Unfortunately, academic advisee groups may be much larger than what is optimal for mentoring, based on the size of the student body needed to generate income for the institution. Breaking these groups into the size optimal for mentoring will require additional use of facilities, and may conflict with other uses. This will require greater facilities coordination than in the past, or providing facilities previously not used by the institution. It may mean that the space needed to hold mentoring groups should be designed into faculty offices as part of architectural plans when renovating old structures or building new ones. Multiple groups could use the same larger room; however, this will likely hinder transparency among group members because confidentiality within the group will be compromised when people in other groups can hear what is shared.

Allocation of Personnel

The first type of personnel needed to support mentoring is the mentors themselves. They do not need to come only from the teaching faculty. The small group size mentioned above as ideal is hardly achievable by normal institutions with a fifteen-, thirty-, or higher-to-one ratio between students and teaching faculty members. In them, even with all teaching faculty members mentoring, additional mentors are needed who can be secured in a number of ways. One way is by using the Registrar, Head Librarian, and other staff members who have faculty status but do not normally work so closely with a designated group of students. Other personnel resources might be qualified employees, adjunct faculty members (either those who are instructors or those specifically enlisted as mentors), and area pastors and lay leaders who are effective mentors. Students may prefer institutional leaders and teaching faculty members; however, the criteria for effective mentoring are the maturity and skills needed for it, not a mentor's institutional position. The value of the relationship will increase as the student experiences the ability of the mentor. One caution: the farther down potential mentors are on the list above, the less likely they are to fulfill their mentoring responsibilities. As mentioned above, busy people with good intentions are still busy people. Mentors are more likely to fulfill their mentoring responsibilities when these are part of their institutional job descriptions, with salary connected to completing their specified mentoring responsibilities and positive reviews in how well they completed them. The institution is less likely to achieve its mentoring goals through an unpaid volunteer or person funded by an honorarium unless that individual has a strong personal commitment to, vision for, and history of mentoring students consistently apart from other regular employment responsibilities not connected to the institution.

Personnel allocation also involves designating a mentoring steward and providing support people for the steward to keep the institution moving forward in this area of its guiding principles, so it does not get de-emphasized or sidetracked in the midst of all the things the institution and the people in it are trying to do. This team, especially the steward, should understand the type of mentoring envisioned by the institution, and have the commitment and skills necessary to provide the resources (training, material, ideas, etc.) mentors need. Of course, they should access outside resources to help as required when they cannot provide them internally; but they are responsible to identify the needs and determine how to meet those needs. This team should also collaborate with the alumni relations office to understand the ongoing impact of discipleship chains in various alumni ministry settings, so mentors can correct past weaknesses to improve how they work with current students.

Allocation of Funding

Allocating funding requires establishing line items in the fiscal budget, and the acquisition of funds to cover them. Funding might be needed to supply student scholarships as the designated student-to-mentor ratio lowers because it will mean less student-sourced income for the institution. Funding might be needed as salary or honorariums for adjunct faculty, pastors, and other external mentors; or to pay for utilities and custodial services related to on-campus mentoring facilities use. In addition, line items and related funding (either full or subsidized) should provide for off-campus activities (such as group spiritual retreats and group ministry activities) required as part of the formal curriculum and schedule. Finally, funding should provide for training mentors. This may involve bringing trainers from outside the institution to lead and facilitate seminars and workshops for current and potential mentors, or sending faculty members to training events. Costs for external trainers, fees, facilities, materials, housing, food, and transportation for training activities should all be considered for inclusion in this area of the budget.

Inclusion in the Faculty Development Plan

Mentoring is ultimately accomplished by persons, not academic programs or institutions.[12] Therefore, the institution must develop its mentors.

---

12. Hodges, *Tally Ho the Fox!*, 70.

The Picture of an Effective Mentor

Mentors need to be what they want the students to become. Ezra was committed to studying the law (his cognitive development), applying it to his life (his affective development), and teaching it to others (his psychomotor development) (Ezra 7:10). The order shows his commitment to apply in his own life what he learned from his studies before helping others know and apply it in their lives. Students are always watching, listening, and making mental notes about faculty members. How mentors behave may leave as much of an impression as, and perhaps more than, any content taught or skills developed by them. Are mentors appropriately transparent in their own challenges to be Christlike, multiplying disciples, so students see them as people in the process of sanctification (though hopefully more mature than the students), just like every other believer, rather than as people who are unwilling to admit their weaknesses and who project an air of perfection because of their academic credentials or positions in the institution? Such humility by well-educated people is a powerful leadership model for students.

Mentors should also model on the faculty team the types of relationships students should build and have with others. Are relationships between institutional leaders and faculty members, and between faculty members, warm and encouraging even when disagreements arise, or are they distant and tense? Do they all see themselves on the same team, or are there territorial defenses against a perceived internal enemy? Do they increasingly appreciate one another, with their relationships moving closer toward friendships; or is there an unsupportive, perhaps uneasy, tolerance of one another, and/or unhealthy competition between faculty members? If problems exist, institutional leaders must work toward improving the institutional relationship environment, so it is a healthy model for the students.[13] In his book *The Five Dysfunctions of a Team*, Patrick Lencioni identifies and explains how to correct major team problems (which also applies within institutional relationships). It starts by creating a safe environment with an atmosphere of trust in which people are willing to reveal their weaknesses and become more vulnerable to one another, which then makes them more likely to accept and engage in the type of healthy conflict

---

13. A good relational environment will also likely encourage faculty retention when salaries are less than desirable.

necessary to move them forward with greater commitment, accountability, and unity towards common goals.[14] Creating the right institutional environment best begins at the top of any organization. Institutional leaders need to model appropriate transparency and relationships with the members of the faculty, and work with them to overcome the challenges of personal and institutional imbalances that affect the entire institutional team – faculty, staff, and students.[15]

Mentors must also be with students, not just available for students. Howard Hendricks is famously quoted saying, "More is caught than taught,"[16] which emphasizes the importance of modeling and participation in learning over content transfer alone. Robert Coleman, author of *Master Plan of Evangelism*, exemplified this. As a faculty member where I studied, he both made himself available to students beyond what was expected in his job description, and was with them in ways that clearly helped students catch Christ's principles of discipleship. He made himself available in his normal faculty duties as an instructor and academic advisor, but also invited students to join him in his early morning devotions. In addition, he invited students to go with him weekly to do ministry. He did not confine his relationship with them either to the academic area of his life or to the campus. They were able to observe outside the classroom and off-campus whether he lived by the principles he taught; and he was able to help them learn to experience and value those principles, as well. This does not mean students are a mentor's disciples in some cultish sense; rather, they are Christ's disciples whom mentors have the privilege of developing. Mentors, therefore, need to maintain a healthy perspective on what is best for each student, including humbly allowing or encouraging a change to another mentor if that is most beneficial for a student (though maintaining a single mentor throughout a program of study until graduation is usually preferable to provide depth of relationship and continuity in mentoring).

---

14. Patrick Lencioni, *The Five Dysfunctions of a Team: A Leadership Fable* (San Francisco: Jossey-Bass, 2002).

15. Tim Irwin, *Impact: Great Leadership Changes Everything* (Dallas: BenBella, 2014); and Kevin Leman and William Pentak, *The Way of the Shepherd* (Grand Rapids, MI: Zondervan, 2004).

16. I am not sure whether this was in the same message I heard years ago and referenced previously in this chapter, or in a different taped message (there were several I heard from him around the same time in my life). Other people on various websites also ascribe it to him with the same words, though, like me here, without an accurate reference.

Some might object that requiring all faculty members to mentor does not take into consideration various faculty personality types. Some faculty members are more introverted and may be more insecure in mentoring situations than in research and classroom settings. However, even extroverts can have difficulty as effective mentors if they have weak listening skills. Excuses abound, and discernment is needed to determine whether faculty resistance to mentoring is the result of placing excessive value on scholarship to the detriment of mentoring, of not having been mentored well and, therefore, not knowing what to do as a mentor, and/or not valuing mentoring because it was never a significant, positive personal experience. The Great Commission, with the mentoring it requires, was given to all believers, not just those with certain personality types, talents, spiritual gifts, or specific vocational callings. This will require some faculty members to take steps of faith outside their normal comfort zones and beyond their past professional perspectives to fulfill an area of personal responsibility to which God has indeed called them simply as his disciples.

Although there are many more things to include in the picture of an effective mentor which space will not allow, it is important to have mentors who know the difference between mentoring and coaching. Both are needed, but they have very distinct uses. Mentoring (in this distinction of terms) involves more directive guidance on certain topics or issues – often with significant verbal explanation by the mentor. Coaching comes in two types. The first type guides a student's skill development in various vocational and ministry settings (as is accomplished by various athletic coaches) through explaining the skill, modeling it, and letting the student practice it under the guidance and correction of the coach. The second type involves the coach asking appropriate questions to help a student process, and to discover the answer to a problem or the best way to address a situation.[17] Mentors must know how to do all three, and discern which is best for students in specific development situations.

---

17. See Keith Webb's *The COACH Model for Christian Leaders: Powerful Leadership Skills for Solving Problems, Reaching Goals, and Developing Others* ([n.p.]: Active Results LLC, 2012) for a detailed explanation of the second coaching type.

Securing Mentors That Resemble the Picture

Institutions have three options for providing the mentors envisioned: (1) training current personnel to mentor effectively and regularly measuring their success at it; (2) replacing those not willing to become effective mentors (perhaps through attrition); and (3) evaluating potential personnel as successful mentors before they are accepted by the institution to fill this role.

Based on Hendricks's "More is caught than taught" principle, the best method of training a mentor is with an effective mentor for an apprenticeship period as a co-mentor. After an appropriate time of observation, the apprentice co-mentor is given responsibilities he or she understands and can successfully fulfill with the students. Behind the scenes, the lead faculty mentor observes, and works with the co-mentor in areas of weakness that must be improved before the apprenticeship is over. Thus, the apprentice mentor experiences the same type of interpersonal faculty-to-faculty environment involving more directive mentoring, and the two types of coaching he or she is expected to have in his or her faculty-to-student relationships. Along the way, apprentice mentors can also attend training seminars, read required materials, and utilize other resources provided by the mentoring stewardship team (mentioned above) for personal development.

Furthermore, all mentors (whether at the apprentice stage or not) should be part of a small group affiliated with the institution where they build co-mentoring relationships with one another, and share their struggles and personal concerns as colleagues more deeply and transparently than is appropriate at times with students.[18] These should be groups of probably four to six mentors who relate relatively well to one another. Putting people together with those of different ages and from different academic departments and, where possible, from different cultures and/or subcultures will provide opportunities for integration and understanding of diverse personal perspectives. Genders are best not mixed, so sexual accountability issues can be discussed more freely, and groups can take retreats or other trips together without the potential

---

18. This chapter is not about faculty members mentoring other faculty members in additional responsibilities related to their professional development and advancement, though many of the principles related to the type of mentoring covered here apply to those other areas of mentoring as well. Literature on mentoring related to those other responsibilities can be easily found online (e.g. through "academic mentoring" and "faculty mentoring in higher education" web searches).

complications a mixed-gender group creates. These groups will be a place for mentors to improve their interpersonal skills and to participate in the type of environment they should create for students.

Understanding the need to include mentoring in the institution's curriculum, resources, and faculty development plan reveals in very concrete ways why it is important to include it in the institution's guiding principles. Without it stated as part of the vision, mission, and core values, the institution is unlikely to take the significant steps necessary to include it in program curricula and faculty development with the related resources needed for it.

Conclusion

Training effective mentors is not an option for evangelical academic institutions; it is the essence of their calling in helping make Christlike, multiplying disciples. It pulls together the academic, character, and field ministry aspects of development in a very personal and communal way within the otherwise larger, less personal institutional setting. It brings faculty members and students in touch on a level not usually achieved by classroom and advising relationships alone; and it brings faculty co-mentors in touch with one another in a personal way not otherwise achieved in other faculty settings. Mentors will not be perfect models for the students or one another, nor will groups always be as successful as ideally intended; however, mentoring provides the missing element needed within institutions and beyond them to become more successful in helping fulfill the Great Commission as Christ envisioned it.

A committed Christian acquaintance recently asked me what I was covering in writing this chapter. After I gave her a brief overview, she told me her pastor of several years had previously been a seminary professor for several decades before coming to her city. She had enjoyed and benefited greatly from the biblical and other knowledge in the sermons he preached and the study small-group lessons he taught. Then she said, "Sadly, he never taught us to reproduce spiritually. Would you?" This chapter has sought to stimulate and guide effective mentoring, so no believer wanting to help fulfill the Great Commission as Christ intended it will be disappointed in this way by those who have graduated from *evangelical* educational institutions or who are on their faculties.

Reflection and Action Points

Below are activities to help you personally or institutionally move toward more successful mentoring.

1. In what ways do you agree or disagree with the definition of the Great Commission given in this chapter? In what ways do you agree or disagree with the main thesis of this chapter, that this type of discipleship is a critical need not being accomplished adequately by the church today because students are not mentored efficiently in it at most evangelical educational institutions? Support your answers with examples from your broader and more local geographical setting and at your institution.

2. Reflect on your own spiritual and educational journey. What role has the type of mentoring described in this chapter played in your own life (was it absent, minimal, or extensive)? If you were mentored, what was the mentoring context – parachurch-, church-, or educational-program-based? How effectively did mentors in each context disciple you, especially in having a vision for and making Christlike, multiplying disciples through four generations? What did you appreciate, and why? What were your mentors' strengths? What were their weaknesses? How could you have benefited from better mentoring at various stages in your journey? How could you benefit now from more effective mentoring of this type (what are some current needs you have for which a mentor would be helpful or necessary)?

3. How high on your list of personal priorities is being this type of mentor to others? Why or why not? Breen wisely advises in his book on discipleship that people not assume reading it will give them the ability to disciple others. He knows reading transfers a set of concepts but not life experiences. Before people start their own groups, he encourages them to be part of a good mentoring environment before mentoring others.[19] If mentoring Christlike, multiplying disciples is a personal high priority, and if you have not experienced being

---

19. Mike Breen, *Building a Discipling Culture*, 2nd ed. (Pawleys Island, SC: 3DM, 2011), 167.

mentored as described in this chapter, what steps will you take to find and participate in a mentoring relationship to become more effective?[20]

4. Make a list of the positive effects the type of mentoring described in this chapter should provide for individuals (students and faculty members), the institution where you serve, and the churches where your faculty members, students, and alumni serve. Explain each effect based on your own reflection and ideas to expand what was stated in the chapter.

5. What type of mentoring occurs at your institution? Evaluate the priority of the type of mentoring described in this chapter in your institution based on its guiding principles. What needs change in these principles to make this type of mentoring more of a priority? What changes also need to occur in program curricula, resources, faculty development, alumni assessment, and ongoing relationships to strengthen mentoring at your institution?

6. Make a list of individual-related hindrances (students, faculty members, and other mentors), field ministry-related hindrances (churches, vocational settings, constituents, etc.), and educational institution-related hindrances to mentoring this way in your situation. List action steps needed to overcome each hindrance, prioritize the steps according to which is needed first to last, and develop a plan to put each step into action.

Resources for Further Study[21]

Breen, Mike. *Building a Discipling Culture.* 2nd edition. Pawleys Island, SC: 3DM, 2011.
    A clear vision and helpful principles for developing a multiplying disciple mentality in any church or organization; the included discipleship system is only a suggestion for which others may easily be substituted.

---

20. If no local solution exists for your personal development as this type of mentor, contact the author at ronw@ilc.global. Put "IPAL Faculty Mentoring Chapter Action Points" on the email subject line. If you are in a sensitive location, suggest in the message your preferred alternate contact method(s).

21. I appreciate the suggestions given by various colleagues and friends for inclusion in this section.

Coleman, Robert E. *The Master Plan of Evangelism*. Grand Rapids, MI: Revell, 2006.
A classic with reprints continuing from the early 1960s; the title is misleading as it is really about Jesus's way of making disciples.

Eims, LeRoy. *The Lost Art of Disciple Making*. Forward by Robert E. Coleman. Grand Rapids, MI: Zondervan, 1978.
Another classic with foundational insights on making multiplying disciples.

Gallaty, Robby. *Growing Up: How to Be a Disciple Who Makes Disciples*. Bloomington, IN: CrossBooks, 2013.
A more modern publication than the classic Coleman and Eims texts, with many insights that build upon or supplement theirs. It contains key questions for reflection on becoming a better mentor who wants to make multiplying disciples, and an appendix of helpful, more recently published resources.

Hodges, Herb. *Tally Ho the Fox! The Foundation for Building World-Visionary, World-Impacting, Reproducing Disciples*. 2nd edition. Augusta, GA: Manhattan Source, 2001.
Significant insights in discipleship from a pastor with a burden for it and experience of training others in it.

House, Paul R. *Bonhoeffer's Seminary Vision: A Case for Costly Discipleship and Life Together*. Wheaton, IL: Crossway, 2015.
A look into Bonhoeffer's philosophy of education that emphasized relationships.

Hull, Bill [Robert W.]. *The Complete Book of Discipleship: On Being and Making Followers of Christ*. Navigators Reference Library. Colorado Springs, CO: NavPress, 2006.
Gives theological, historical, and various practical insights related to discipleship and making disciples.

Irwin, Tim. *Impact: Great Leadership Changes Everything*. Dallas: BenBella, 2014.
Insights from an organizational psychologist and management consultant into issues of personal character that mentors need to have themselves and develop in those who will be leaders.

Kohl, Manfred Waldemar. "Theological Education: What Needs to Be Changed." *Torch Trinity Journal* 12, no. 1 (2009): 149–162.
A critical reflection by a knowledgeable educator on theological education globally.

Leman, Kevin, and William Pentak. *The Way of the Shepherd*. Grand Rapids, MI: Zondervan, 2004.

A brief, easy read from two corporate leadership consultants that reflects on how to lead and mentor workers to bring out their potential for the benefit of the organization.

Lencioni, Patrick. *The Five Dysfunctions of a Team: A Leadership Fable*. San Francisco: Jossey-Bass, 2002.

Analyzes why teams do not work well together, and how to correct that problem; the insights are applicable to small groups, faculty relationships, and institutional leadership.

MacDonald, Gordon. "Going Deep: Cultivating People of Spiritual Depth Is a Pastor's Top Priority." *Christianity Today*, 27 June 2011. Accessed 9 July 2015. http://www.christianitytoday.com/le/2011/spring/goingdeep.html.

Calls pastors to the primary ministry responsibility of making reproducing disciples.

McCallum, Dennis, and Jessica Lowery. *Organic Discipleship: Mentoring Others into Spiritual Maturity and Leadership*. Revised edition. Columbus, OH: New Paradigm, 2012.

Contains a number of practical topics in mentoring not covered in most other resources.

Scott, Marty. "Annotated Bibliography." Mentoring/Coaching course, Spring 2013. Dallas Theological Seminary. Accessed 9 July 2015. http://www.dts.edu/download/academic/sfl/DTS-mentoring-bibliography.pdf.

Some resources I was going to provide in my resource list are included in this document with more extensive comments.

Spader, Dann. *4 Chair Discipling: Growing a Movement of Disciple-Makers*. Chicago: Moody, 2014.

Provides insights with Scripture and a discipleship focus in four areas: engaging non-believers, building believers in their faith, equipping believers for service, and expanding the kingdom through these people making additional disciples.

Stanley, Andy. *The Next Generation Leader*. Sisters, OR: Multnomah, 2003.

Focuses on leadership involving coaching and character development that applies to mentoring.

Webb, Keith. *The COACH Model for Christian Leaders: Powerful Leadership Skills for Solving Problems, Reaching Goals, and Developing Others.* [n.p.]: Active Results LLC, 2012.

A professional coach provides an orientation to the art of asking critical questions as a highly undervalued skill in mentoring.

Woods, Rick. "A Discipleship Revolution: The Key to Discipling All Peoples." *Mission Frontiers* (Jan–Feb 2011). Accessed 15 June 2015. https://www.missionfrontiers. org/issue/article/a-discipleship-revolution.

The entire issue, entitled "A Discipleship Revolution," has several relevant articles and is available at https://www.missionfrontiers.org/issue/archive/discipleship-revolution.

10

Developing Academic Leaders from among the Faculty

Orbelina Eguizabal

Joseph had been approached several times by the dean of his seminary, asking him to serve as chair of his department, but he always found the nicest responses to avoid committing to such a responsibility with the excuse that he had other responsibilities that prevented him from considering it. Circumstances in his department changed and somebody needed to take charge of the department administration. Now, it was not an option; it was a real need, and Joseph was asked to take the position. By the time I listened to his story, it had been several years since he started to lead his colleagues in his department, and they were happy with his leadership. Although Joseph keeps most of his teaching load, he enjoys his administrative responsibilities and shares very enthusiastically about his experiences. He says he has learned by doing.

Joseph's case is probably not new to you, and it is most likely you have already started to identify with him. Faculty serving in Christian and non-Christian institutions of higher education are well trained in their fields, and they do well applying their knowledge and training in their areas of expertise and do not want to bother with academic administration challenges. What is more, in recent years, accreditation demands have set the tone for instruction and research, making them a priority in many institutions that continue to develop short-term and ongoing training programs to help their faculty excel in instruction and research to meet the demands of the consumers of education. "Yet, few of them have received training on university services, not to mention learning and practicing academic administration."[1] Thus, in this chapter I consider some aspects related to the need for, and practices in, developing their own academic leaders in institutions of higher education in general, as well as in Christian higher education institutions, including schools of theology and evangelical seminaries.

The purpose of the chapter does not allow an exhaustive discussion of the many programs that already exist, mainly in Western contexts, to develop Academic leaders. Therefore, I intend to encourage current academic leaders to consider how to develop their own faculty members and help them to be ready to undertake academic leadership positions in their institutions.

Academic Leadership: Aspiration or Calling?

As is well known, a majority of institutions of higher education are facing the challenges of the global academic meltdown that has visibly taken its toll on higher education in the last decade. Some institutions sooner than others have begun to experience a decrease in their student enrollment, financial cutbacks, and governmental pressures. They are therefore taking drastic measures to deal with the impact of the financial constraints. The merging of departments, closing down of programs, course delivery changes, curriculum changes, laying-off of adjunct faculty and staff, making arrangements with full-time faculty members to reduce their teaching loads in order to reduce their salaries, and arranging early retirement have, among other things, become the day-to-day topics of discussion and decision-making in many institutions. Leading in this period is challenging and painful, as Bolman and Gallos express it well: "Leading in a time of shrinking budgets, program cuts, furloughs, and staff layoffs is debilitating. Many higher education leaders are

---

1. Sheying Chen, "The Pursuit of Excellence in Academic Administration," in *Academic Administration: A Quest for Better Management and Leadership in Higher Education*, ed. Sheying Chen (New York: Nova Science, 2009), 10.

struggling with levels of pain, pressure, and uncertainty beyond anything they ever imagined."[2] In light of these challenges, why would a faculty member who is being successful in his or her teaching and research, and attaining significant publishing achievements, want to take over an academic leadership position? According to the authors, it requires a significant amount of faith in the mission and a passion about one's calling.[3] On the other hand, the reality is that, "whether we lead the parade or work in the shadows, we are needed to move our institutions forward and to make the case for higher education."[4] Yet institutions of higher education "looking to recruit leaders from within the faculty ranks will face more and more difficulty."[5] For that reason, it is critical to ask the question: What would make a faculty member aspire to an academic leadership position?

When the former dean at the seminary where I serve communicated his plans to begin his retirement process, the university started the search process to find the person who was going to succeed him. A search committee was established and various persons submitted applications for the position. Surprisingly, one of the most promising candidates for the position emerged from the faculty, a prominent New Testament scholar who at the time had been serving in the institution for about twenty-five years. The search process ended by selecting him to take the position of dean of the school. But why would a faculty member who was successful in teaching, research, and publishing aspire to such a position? What made him want to become the dean? When he was appointed to the position, he shared about what had made him consider becoming the dean of our school of theology. Some of the reasons he shared with us align with what literature highlights as reasons to aspire to academic leadership positions. For example, Buller, who has done extensive work on academic leadership, argues that,

---

2. Lee G. Bolman and Joan V. Gallos, *Reframing Academic Leadership* (San Francisco: John Wiley & Sons, 2011), 221.

3. Bolman and Gallos, *Reframing Academic Leadership*, 221.

4. Bolman and Gallos, 221.

5. Dennis M. Barden and Janel Curry, "Faculty Members Can Lead, but Will They?" *The Chronicle of Higher Education* (8 April 2013): 1, accessed 16 August 2017, http://www.chronicle.com/article/Faculty-Members-Can-Lead-but/138343.

After having demonstrated success in teaching, scholarship, and service, some faculty members begin to consider the possibility of seeking an administrative assignment. It could be that after having chaired several committees, designed a few new courses, and solved a number of problems, the faculty member thinks that administrative work might be interesting or perhaps that he or she has a talent for it. It could also be that after seeing a chair, dean, or president make several mistakes or prove to be ineffective in some capacity, the faculty member thinks, "Well, even I could do better than that. Perhaps there is a need for someone with my perspective and experience in administration." Or it could be that after having achieved most of the goals that the person has set as a college professor, he or she begins to wonder, "What is next? Where can I find the next level of challenge?"[6]

Buller's comments highlight a sense of capacity to carry on academic administrative responsibilities when faculty members consider taking on or feel inclined to take on an academic leadership position. Among other reasons for faculty aspiring to academic leadership positions, here I consider two that are critical, especially in the context of theological education.

Response to a Calling

The term *calling* is used in many different ways to serve the purpose of the person using it. In most literature, "calling" and "vocation" are interchangeable. When it relates to academic leadership, we find that most sources, whether written from a Christian perspective or not, refer to calling or vocation as a leading component due to the demands that academic leaders must fulfill in their institutions. For instance, Elizabeth Hoffman, reflecting on her long career in senior academic leadership, states, "Serving as an academic administrator is a calling as strong as being a world-class scholar, a social worker, or a minister. . . . The time you spend with the 'smartest people in the room' –

---

6. Jeffrey L. Buller, *The Essential College Professor: A Practical Guide to an Academic Career* (San Francisco: John Wiley & Sons, 2010), 382.

faculty, staff, students, alumni, donors, and community members – is one of the great joys of the job."[7]

Similar to academic administrators in other institutions of higher education, academic leaders in theological seminaries or institutions of Christian higher education in Western and non-Western contexts need to serve in the midst of tough times. They face the day-to-day internal institutional demands permeated with endless difficulties along with the external pressures of higher education. It thus requires that they have a clear understanding of why they are in the position in which they are serving or are moving in to serve; as Deininger expresses it, "Knowing God's call to academic leadership provides strength and endurance in times of difficulties."[8] It must be more than an aspiration prompted by wrong motivations; faculty aspiring to an academic leadership position need to distinguish between pursuing an aspiration and following a calling. Aleshire, Campbell and Mannoia provide an example of this, speaking of the call to seminary presidency: "They should take this work only with a deep sense of calling, but that calling is like Samuel's. It is not a 'calling' to which one aspires; it is a calling that one experiences in the context of a board or religious superior's summons to this work."[9] They add, "Religious work that is bound on the one hand by deep satisfactions and on the other by persistent difficulties is best accomplished with a deep sense of calling, of vocation."[10] It can be said, then, that the response of Christian academic leaders to their calling surpasses that of their counterparts in non-Christian institutions, in the sense that they are responding in obedience to God's calling, which comes after our first calling to faith in God to be disciples of Jesus. Graham expresses it thus: "Any vocation to a particular work, place, or role

---

7. Elizabeth Hoffman, "What Have We Learned about Academic Leadership?," in *Academic Leadership in Higher Education: From the Top Down and the Bottom Up*, eds. Robert J. Sternberg, Elizabeth Davis, April C. Mason, Robert V. Smith, Jeffrey S. Vitter, and Michele Wheatly (Lanham, MD: Rowman & Littlefield, 2015), 12.

8. Fritz Deininger, "President and Dean as Partners in Theological Education," in *Leadership in Theological Education, Volume 1: Foundations for Academic Leadership*, eds. Fritz Deininger and Orbelina Eguizabal (Carlisle: Langham Global Library, 2017), 116.

9. Daniel Aleshire, Cynthia Campbell, and Kevin Mannoia, "The President's Vocation and Leadership," in *A Handbook for Seminary Presidents*, eds. G. D. Lewis and Lovett H. Weems Jr. (Grand Rapids, MI: Eerdmans, 2006), 3.

10. Aleshire, Campbell and Mannoia, "President's Vocation and Leadership," 4.

is based on that foundation of discipleship."[11] In light of this, one can agree with Deininger's conclusion that "Viewing the appointment into leadership positions as God's appointment articulates it rightly and not as a burden (1 Tim 1:12). This understanding can lead to a greater sense of accountability before God on the part of the leader and the constituency of the institution."[12]

Viewing the calling to academic leadership from this perspective in our institutions of theological education will help all of us to humbly submit to Jesus' discipleship and respond to the everyday challenges with a servant heart and attitude. It will also help us to be willing to move our institutions to a higher level, but most of all, to see our faculty, students, and staff as Christ's disciples called to serve and transform our communities and, therefore, our societies.

Support of the Institution's Mission and Vision

Another important aspect related to calling is a strong desire or commitment to support the mission and vision of the institution. This is critical because when the institution faces difficult times and academic leaders and administrators need to make hard decisions, an evaluation of how those decisions reinforce the mission and vision of the institution will help in moving forward, although not everybody may understand it.

Coll and Weiss, speaking on how to build and enhance good leaders in higher education, point out that "a good leader is an individual who can establish values-oriented vision and mission that promotes the success of others and their institution."[13] Arthur concurs, claiming, "The personal influence of a leader of a Christian University is the key to the kind of tone established and the direction given to that higher education institution."[14] He adds, "Indeed, the power in the vision for an institution is not usually captured by its mission

11. Stephen R. Graham, "The Vocation of the Academic Dean," in *C(H)AOS Theory: Reflections of Chief Academic Officers in Theological Education*, eds. Kathleen D. Billman and Bruce C. Birch (Grand Rapids, MI: Eerdmans, 2011), 63.

12. Deininger, "President and Dean as Partners," 117.

13. Jose Coll and Eugenia L. Weiss, "Rethinking Leadership Development in Higher Education," The EvoLLLution, 7 January 2016, accessed 17 August 2017, https://evolllution.com/managing-institution/operations_efficiency/rethinking-leadership-development-in-higher-education/.

14. James Arthur, "Great Expectations: Vision and Leadership in Christian Higher Education," in *Leadership in Christian Higher Education*, eds. Michael Wright and James Arthur (Exeter: Imprint Academic, 2010), 6.

statement, but it certainly can [be] by its leaders on the basis of their vision and principles, producing a leadership that is underpinned by the motivations and passion behind their actions, thoughts and words."[15]

Patterson-Randles, reflecting on her experience as a Chief Executive Officer (CEO) and on the opportunity that CEOs have to impact education at a higher level, claims, "Without vision an administrator is merely a manager of endless details."[16] Therefore, academic leaders at all levels need to have a clear vision for their department, division, school, college, or the entire university which needs to be aligned with and supportive of the institution's mission. In some cases, they are the ones who need to articulate the vision or bring their own vision to the institution; such is the case for presidents, who are expected to present their vision to the board of trustees and all the external and internal constituents of the institution. Similarly, the provost needs to have a vision for the entire academic area. An essential function of the dean is to define the vision for the school, which he or she can create either in collaboration with faculty serving in the school or on his or her own; however, the dean cannot impose it on faculty. One critical point with this is that academic leaders who seek commitment to the institution's vision and mission need themselves to be committed to it first.

The Academic Leadership Structure

Understanding the academic leadership structure is also very important when considering any leadership development program or plan. The structure varies according to the institution's size, geographic context, and type, such as university, stand-alone seminary, Bible college, or fully-online degree-granting institution. These factors also determine the terms used to refer to the academic leaders. In spite of the differences in what the leaders are called, most authors identify two main levels to refer to the educational institutions' leadership: middle, and upper/senior level leadership. It is not my intention here to provide an exhaustive discussion of the full leadership structures of

---

15. Arthur, "Great Expectations," 6.
16. Sandra R. Patterson-Randles, "Chief Executive in Academic Administration: High Expectations and Leadership Lessons," in Chen, *Academic Administration*, 35–36.

academic institutions, but simply a brief description of the levels and more common titles or positions.

Middle-Level Leadership

Middle-level leadership varies from serving as director of a program, center, or institute, to department chair and associate or assistant dean. In most cases, these positions are filled by faculty members from the institution on a voluntary basis, or by reducing a percentage of their teaching load. According to Black, "academic leadership roles (such as Deans or Heads of School) are unusual and commonly have complications such as transitory nature of role-holders (for example on a 3-year rotating basis, much like a secondment)."[17]

Department Chair

Gmelch and Miskin, in their book *Department Chair: Leadership Skills*, argue, "The department chair position is the most critical role in the university, and the most unique management position. . . . 80 percent of the university decisions are made at the department level."[18] Usually, the position is filled by a faculty member who is given the administrative position in his or her department based on his or her reputation as a teacher and researcher. The functions and responsibilities of department chairs vary with each institution; however, institutions expect department chairs to perform certain responsibilities and tasks such as "organizing and supervising curriculum, distributing teaching/ research loads, supervising department funds, recommending promotions and salaries, and so on."[19] Based on popular literature on the main roles of department chairs, Gmelch and Miskin also identify the four main roles that contribute to the success of the departments in which they serve. These include "faculty developer, manager, leader and researcher."[20] Each of these roles carries its own responsibilities and department chairs juggle many responsibilities

---

17. Simon A. Black, "Qualities of Effective Leadership in Higher Education," *Open Journal of Leadership* 4, no. 2 (June 2015): 54–66, accessed 24 November 2017, http://dx.doi.org/10.4236/ojl.2015.42006. Published online in Scientific Research, http://www.scirp.org/journal/ojl.

18. Walter H. Gmelch and Val D. Miskin, *Department Chair: Leadership Skills*, 2nd ed. (Madison, WI: Atwood, 2011), 5.

19. Gmelch and Miskin, *Department Chair*, 9–10.

20. Gmelch and Miskin, 10–11.

on a daily basis, but the development of faculty serving in their department is a critical one. Another critical function in their leadership is to provide direction and vision for their departments. At the end of the chapter I suggest some resources for further study and understanding of the critical functions and roles of the department chair.

Associate or Assistant Dean

The roles and authority of the associate or assistant dean vary in scope in educational institutions. Large institutions are able to define them more clearly; however, it becomes ambiguous at times. In institutions of theological education, the associate dean plays a variety of roles. The work that associate deans are expected to do in theological seminaries in the Majority World resembles that described in Stone and Coussons-Read's statement:

> Frequently, the charge of the job is to ensure smooth day-to-day running of the school and attending to various details that enable the dean to concentrate on the larger issues of strategic planning, fund-raising, and the role of the school within that larger university and community context. In other words, associate deans may enforce policy, ensure classes are offered, aid faculty in making it through the tenure process, settle fights between chairs and their faculty, negotiate conflicts between departments, and address student complaints about the faculty and student disciplinary issues, to name just a few specifics.[21]

The associate or assistant dean position does not exist in an institution until the need arises. Thus, when that happens, faculty members with very limited experience, or no training at all for the specific roles they play, take charge of academic administration. Stone and Coussons-Read argue, "In many institutions, associate dean is one of the first 'real' administrative positions faculty may take that exposes them to the real inner workings of a school or university."[22] Some institutions appoint assistant deans instead of associate

---

21. Tammy Stone and Mary Coussons-Read, *Leading from the Middle: A Case-Study Approach to Academic Leadership for Associate Deans* (Lanham, MD: Rowman & Littlefield, 2011), 1.
22. Stone and Coussons-Read, *Leading from the Middle*, 9.

deans; however, the functions and responsibilities are very similar, and in either case, they are called to work in close relationship with the dean. Therefore, faculty interested in academic leadership in their institutions need to keep in mind Stone and Coussons-Read's claim, "Being an associate dean can be a critical, formative, and incredibly valuable step in your career."[23]

Academic Dean

The role of the academic dean varies among institutions. For instance, "In small colleges, the dean is usually the chief academic officer and may also have the title of vice president of academic affairs or provost. In larger universities, the dean is the head of a college and, along with the deans of other colleges, reports to the provost."[24] In the Majority World, with the exception of some schools of theology that function under the big university umbrella, most institutions of theological education are stand-alone Bible colleges or seminaries with a person serving in the deanship. Although some authors place the position of academic dean within the senior leadership category, by its nature the deanship is still considered a middle management position, because deans "carry administrative responsibilities and at the same time they are very much involved with faculty and academic affairs."[25] Administrative roles of academic deans include, according to Bryan, "daily administrative matters, monitoring and enforcing academic policies, meetings, reports, program staffing, oversight of course offerings and curriculum development, new course development, leading faculty meetings, promoting faculty development, research and publishing, mediation, building trust and collegiality among faculty and other unmentioned and unwritten responsibilities as they occur."[26]

Bryan adds, "In addition, some deans are responsible for oversight for accreditation, budgets, faculty evaluation, faculty promotion and tenure,

23. Stone and Coussons-Read, 9.

24. Marc M. Roy, "Preparing for a Successful Career in Academic Leadership: Understanding Your Role," in *The Resource Handbook for Academic Deans*, ed. Laura L. Behling, 3rd ed. (San Francisco: Jossey-Bass, 2014), 3–4.

25. Deininger, "President and Dean as Partners," 130.

26. Linda W. Bryan, "The Vocational Call and Multiple Occupations of a CAO," in Billman and Birch, *C(H)AOS Theory*, 81.

academic advising, faculty hiring, and fundraising."[27] Therefore, "Deans are first and foremost academic leaders working with faculty members to shape the curriculum and provide educational opportunities that are consistent with the college's mission and values."[28] The dean's role creates tensions at times, because, while faculty have an important role in curricular decisions, the dean is still responsible to lead them and ensure that the school's mission, vision, and strategic plan guide those decisions.[29] However, in spite of the tensions that the position conveys, "The office is filled with opportunities, personal growth, development as an academic leader, academic achievement in creating a learning community, assisting faculty and staff to succeed, and for training students for ministry. Yet these opportunities are accompanied by challenges and frustrations."[30] The roles and functions of the academic dean have been amply addressed in volume 1 of this series, *Foundations for Academic Leadership*. The authors also suggest several resources for further study.

Upper/Senior-Level Leadership

The two main senior-level leadership positions in most institutions of higher education are the provost or Chief Academic Officer (CAO) and the president or chancellor. However, this varies according to the context.

Provost

The position of provost is defined in the context of large institutions with various schools, and in some cases with a liberal arts or Bible college as a significant portion of the university body. Due to the scope of the provost's responsibilities, some institutions use the title Chief Academic Officer (CAO), referring to the fact that the provost's main function is to lead and manage the "overall academic quality of a college or university."[31] In some contexts, the provost or CAO functions as the vice president or vice chancellor for academic affairs. The CAO, as pointed out by Atnip, "is the administrator with institution-

---

27. Bryan, "Vocational Call," 81.
28. Roy, "Preparing," 4.
29. Roy, 4.
30. Deininger, "President and Dean as Partners," 130–131.
31. Gilbert W. Atnip, "Role of the Chief Academic Officer," in Chen, *Academic Administration*, 39.

wide responsibility for the core academic functions of a college or university."[32] Atnip adds, "Typically all of the academic, degree-granting units (schools and colleges) report to the CAO, along with many of the academic support units such as the library, the teaching–learning center, and the registrar."[33] Yet the CAO's responsibilities are not limited to the ones highlighted here. Some institutions have information technology and admissions, and sometimes other areas related to faculty research, reporting directly to the provost.

An important aspect that distinguishes the CAO from other academic administrators in the institution, such as deans and department chairs, "is that he or she must both lead and manage from an *institutional, long-term perspective*."[34] The provost, therefore, is responsible for the long-term welfare of the institution. In that sense, there may be times when decisions made at the provost office may not be received with excitement by some academic administrators and faculty, but in the end, one of the main goals of an effective CAO is getting the institution to flourish. Lambert's summary of the CAO's functions provides a picture of the position:

> The CAO is an interpreter and shaper of campus culture, a leader who challenges the status quo by nudging seemingly intractable problems toward resolution, a champion of academic life and the campus intellectual environment, and a solver of dozens of non-routine problems in academic life, which, if left unresolved, would lead to chaos. It is one of the most difficult, demanding leadership positions in academe, but one that has strong potential to guide an institution toward a clearer mission, an improved environment for teaching and learning, and a healthy climate for positive change.[35]

In order to provide long-term welfare for the institution, the provost needs to be in full support of the institution's mission and to be able to operationalize it through an achievable vision for the institution.

---

32. Atnip, "Role of the Chief Academic Officer," 39.
33. Atnip, 39.
34. Atnip, 39.
35. Leo M. Lambert, "Chief Academic Officers," in *Field Guide to Academic Leadership*, ed. Robert M. Diamond (San Francisco: Jossey-Bass, 2002), 434.

President or Chancellor

The president is the person who leads the entire academic institution and reports directly to a board of trustees. The American Council on Education (ACE) report in 2012 stated that, "Since the 2001 survey, the areas in which presidents spend the most time have remained unchanged. Presidents cited fundraising, budgets, community relations, and strategic planning as the areas that occupy most of their time." Moreover, the report highlights five top areas in which presidents currently spend most of their time, including budget/financial management, fundraising, managing a senior-level team, governing board relations, enrollment management.[36]

Presidents serve as Chief Executive Officer (CEO) in the institution. They serve many constituents externally as well as internally, including students who, according to the ACE 2012 study report, "continue to be the group presidents say provides the greatest reward, followed by administrative and faculty colleagues. Interestingly, presidents also cite faculty as one of their greatest challenges."[37]

Developing Academic Leaders

The need to develop leaders in schools and institutions of higher education has remained a constant for decades. In addition, with the proliferation of technology and the demands and challenges of the twenty-first century, the need to have more teachers and faculty members who can serve either in full leadership positions or alongside the institution's leaders has increased. In his book *Learning to Lead*, Davis argues, "An important challenge for colleges and universities today is the cultivation of leadership in all corners of the organization, so that collectively the resources of the institution can be marshalled to address the issues spawned by the new era."[38] The

---

36. Bryan J. Cook, "The American College President Study: Key Findings and Takeaways," *American Council on Education* (Spring Supplement 2012), accessed 28 November 2017, http://www.acenet.edu/the-presidency/columns-and-features/Pages/The-American-College-President-Study.aspx.

37. Cook, "American College President Study."

38. James R. Davis, *Learning to Lead: A Handbook for Postsecondary Administrators* (Westport, CT: American Council on Education and Praeger Publishers, 2003), xiii.

development of academic leaders, then, can be undertaken with two goals in mind: (1) developing those who are already serving in leadership positions in the institution to help them become more effective in their work, and (2) discovering emergent leaders with leadership potential and aspirations to academic leadership. Since the majority of academic administrators begin their careers as faculty members, specialized in a specific discipline in their teaching and research, this chapter focuses on both current academic administrators who need to continue growing to become more effective in leading and managing their specific units, and those who aspire to serve in academic leadership positions. Developing academic leaders is critical for the flourishing of any academic institution; hence, it is important to consider the following questions and challenges.

Who Should Do It?

With the exception of a small group of graduate students and some faculty who are already serving in their institutions, most cannot afford to attend doctoral programs offered by Western universities or other institutions located outside of the Majority World to attain specific training to serve in leadership positions in Christian higher education institutions or seminaries. What is more, not all institutions of higher education across the globe have access to training centers or development programs. Therefore, the training of new and future academic leaders becomes the task of each institution. Educational institutions are those primarily called to "invest in developing leadership programs that prepare young or early-stage faculty to become leaders, as well as to become purposeful contributors to the broader university strategic goals."[39] Coll and Weiss support this perspective: "we believe that leadership development must begin early and from within the institution, leaving the more advanced programs for senior-level faculty and administrators."[40]

Previous chapters in this book have already highlighted that faculty development is a fundamental task among the many roles and responsibilities of academic leaders and administrators. Most literature addressing the roles and functions of the department chair, associate dean, dean, and provost

---

39. Coll and Weiss, "Rethinking Leadership Development."
40. Coll and Weiss.

amply discusses their responsibilities in developing their faculty. Fortunately, they do not need to do that alone. Nowadays, there are many organizations which, aware of how faculty with no training or with minimum experience in academic leadership are appointed to academic leadership positions at different levels, have created programs to provide in-service training. Institutions can benefit and get their faculty trained through campus-based institutes, academies, seminars or workshops, networks, and regional associations, to mention just a few. Nevertheless, institutions need to be intentional and include these resources as part of their faculty or academic leaders' development plans, allowing them flexibility to arrange their schedules, and providing them with resources to participate in the in-house training programs as well as with financial support, when needed, to attend some seminars and conferences outside campus.

Some Challenges in Developing Academic Leaders Internally

While most authors agree that institutions need to develop their academic leaders internally, certain institutional aspects create challenges to accomplishing it. From their interactions with senior leadership, trustees, and search committee members in academic institutions, Barden and Curry highlight some of the institutional aspects that become challenges in building leaders from among the faculty.[41] I discuss here only a few, namely, institutional/faculty culture, decision-making structures, influx of outsiders, and limited resources.

Institutional and Faculty Culture

In chapter 3 of this volume, Paul Sywulka addresses key aspects of institutional culture. Yet finding a culture that is conducive to the development of faculty to academic administration is not always easy, because "academic culture tends to be suspicious of faculty members who desire administrative responsibility."[42] In addition, and reinforced by the institutional culture, faculty culture is sometimes unfavorable toward those aspiring to academic leadership in their institution. Therefore, "Faculty members who have the personality, acumen, and drive to lead are seldom, if ever, exposed to issues at the strategic level,

---

41. Barden and Curry, "Faculty Members Can Lead, but Will They?," 1.
42. Barden and Curry, 2.

leaving them largely unprepared for campus leadership when the opportunity presents itself."[43] What is more, those who are able to attain a leadership position will face the challenges that, depending on the leadership level to which they are appointed, will come with the position due to some of the academic administrators' responsibilities. Such challenges include faculty perceptions of desire for power, faculty evaluation, handling the budget, managing change, communicating, and implementing institutional policies.

A clear example of these challenges is Anne's experience in her institution. When she got a letter from her institution's board of trustees inviting her to take charge of the deanship after having served as the associate dean for two years, she was hesitant about accepting it because she anticipated the challenges it would bring due to the culture in her institution. While she had the support of the other academic leaders and the majority of faculty members, some fellow faculty members were suspicious of her leadership, due to their personal interests and the fact that she was the first woman to move into academic leadership at that level. Those who resisted her leadership expressed their resistance in their reactions and attitudes, and in conversations with other fellow faculty members and academic administrators. Although Anne tried to be innovative and implemented some new practices in the deanship, those manifestations of faculty culture inevitably affected her relationships in one way or another, especially with those who opposed her leadership. As a faculty member, Anne had experienced some of the challenges of her institution's culture and some issues among her colleagues; but her new appointment brought her new issues to face. This is just one of the many situations that exist among faculty in institutions of higher education, from which their counterparts in institutions of Christian higher education are not exempt.

Decision-Making Structures

Faculty governance or its equivalent in other contexts is increasingly being encouraged, and institutions of higher education, some more than others, are creating opportunities for faculty to participate in decision-making. Faculty are allowed to make decisions on various important aspects of the institution, especially those related to curriculum; however, a major issue concerns

---

43. Barden and Curry, 1.

limited or no access at all to budget or financial aspects: "their decisions are too frequently disconnected from costs and fiscal realities. This sort of disconnection can lead some professors to avoid or be outright hostile to the business side of the institution."[44] This lack of opportunity to participate in budget matters can lower not only faculty morale, but also their desire to participate in the leading of the institution.

Influx of Outsiders

Raising academic leaders from within the faculty has been a common practice in institutions of theological education in Majority World contexts. Many of these institutions have also benefited from the presence of missionary personnel and have heavily relied on them to lead the institution. However, more recently, with institutions changing from stand-alone seminaries to government-chartered universities, institutions are recruiting key leaders from outside academe for key leadership positions in the institution. This change has helped to meet the need for a broad perspective in certain areas of academic disciplines and administration. Nonetheless, it also raises some concerns, as, increasingly, models and practices from the corporate world are adopted to manage and lead such institutions.

Another challenge has to do with the values and vision of these new leaders. Such institutions need to make sure that their new hires are aligned with the mission and vision of the institution.

Limited Resources

Facing the challenge of scarce resources is not new for most institutions of Christian higher education and seminaries in the Majority World. However, the complex changes and demands that higher education faces every day require academic leaders to deal with "allocating scarce resources, directing complex change initiatives, and making influential decisions at a rapid pace."[45] Added to this, "New regulatory requirements have intensified administrative burdens

---

44. Barden and Curry, 1.

45. EAB, "Developing Academic Leaders: Executive Summary," accessed 20 August 2017, https://www.eab.com/research-and-insights/academic-affairs-forum/studies/2011/developing-academic-leaders.

on leaders at all levels; increasingly rapid news cycles and the rise of social media technologies have raised the stakes on leadership missteps. What is being asked of leaders, as well as the context in which leaders are operating, is more complicated than ever before."[46]

Institutional leaders, therefore, need to keep up with resources available internally as well as externally to support faculty already serving in administrative positions and those who are aspiring to administrative responsibilities.

Academic Leadership Capacity

As institutions of Christian higher education continue to grow and new programs are created to meet the demands of the consumers of education, the need for new capable academic leaders increases. Continuous improvement and innovation are critical to successful academic leadership, which, according to Fullan and Scott, in their book *Turnaround Leadership for Higher Education*, calls for attributes such as

> being able to work productively, calmly, persuasively, and deftly with diversity and uncertainty; a willingness to take responsibility and make hard decisions; a capacity to inspire others to action through sound decision making, integrity, and enthusiasm; an ability to diagnose and figure out what is really going on in a complex situation; and a capacity to see the big picture, to identify and set down what ultimately proves to have been a successful new direction, and to engage and support people in making it happen in a way that is both tactical and responsive.[47]

The authors argue that leadership capability involves "reading and responding to a rapidly external environment . . . Capability sets the limits for both the development of competencies and their appropriate deployment, and it entails

---

46. EAB, "Developing Academic Leaders."

47. Michael Fullan and Geoff Scott, *Turnaround Leadership for Higher Education* (San Francisco: Jossey-Bass, 2009), 113.

having the emotional and cognitive capacity to figure out when and when not to draw upon specific competencies."[48]

In light of the array of challenges faced by institutions of higher education nationally and internationally, the development of leadership capacity requires specific competencies or skills that work in the contexts where academic leaders implement them. It also requires some specific attributes. Related to this, Mary Henkel, based on two previous empirical studies of higher education reforms in three European countries (UK, Norway, and Sweden), argues that academic leaders, more specifically deans and heads of department, face conflicting demands in three areas: "those of academic and administrative work; the flow of external demands or crises competing with strategic responsibilities; and the desire to nurture individuals against the need to change their departments."[49]

Space is too limited to focus on the specific skills needed for each academic leadership position (readers can explore them in the resources for further study recommended at the end of the chapter). Thus, I focus on the capacity needed at all leadership levels. For instance, Gmelch and Miskin suggest three spheres of influence that are essential for the development of effective academic leaders: "(1) conceptual understanding of the unique roles and responsibilities encompassed by academic leadership; (2) the skills necessary to achieve results through working with faculty, staff, students, and other administrators; and (3) the practice of reflection in order to learn from past experiences and perfect the art of leadership."[50]

Gmelch and Buller, after many years of work on the roles and functions of academic leaders, argue for a three-dimensional model that integrates the fundamental needs and expectations of academic leaders serving in any institution of higher education. Their model builds upon research by Gmelch and Miskin (2004 & 2011) "to help new department chairs make the transition from faculty to administration."[51] Gmelch and Buller examined the findings from an Academic Leadership Forum that Gmelch and two other colleagues

---

48. Fullan and Scott, *Turnaround Leadership*, 113–114.

49. Mary Henkel, "Emerging Concepts of Academic Leadership and Their Implications for Intra-Institutional Roles and Relationships in Higher Education," *European Journal of Education* 37, no. 1 (2002): 37.

50. Gmelch and Miskin, *Department Chair*, 18–19.

51. Gmelch and Miskin, 9.

used as a strategy for developing academic leaders in Iowa University from 2000 to 2004, and found that, in order to build capacity, any successful leadership development strategy should include three ingredients: "content in the form of conceptual understanding, practice in the form of providing opportunities to apply various skills, and integration in the form of reflecting on the outcomes of their decision."[52] Generalizing from those three ingredients, they describe three essential spheres in which to develop academic leaders:

1. *Habits of the mind*: Developing the conceptual understanding of how academic leadership requires unique roles, concepts, and areas of knowledge.
2. *Habits of practice*: Perfecting the skills needed to achieve the desired results through work with faculty, staff, students, other administrators, and external constituents.
3. *Habits of the heart*: Engaging in reflection to learn from experience and continue making progress in the art of leading.[53]

Gmelch and Buller also suggest three levels of intervention for each leadership development component, namely, personal, institutional, and professional.[54] For each level of intervention, they include specific resources that can be used in ongoing leadership development. Academic leaders committed to building capacity among their current leaders can work together with new and seasoned leaders to design a plan that will help them keep current with higher education challenges.

Some Strategies for Training and Preparing Academic Leaders

In the various chapters of this book, the authors have focused on developing faculty to fulfill the main tasks of teaching and the work that faculty members are expected to do with students. Yet a critical element in faculty development

---

52. Walter H. Gmelch and J. L. Buller, *Building Academic Leadership Capacity: A Guide to Best Practices* (San Francisco: Jossey-Bass, 2015), 45.

53. Gmelch and Buller, *Building Academic Leadership Capacity*, 116.

54. Gmelch and Buller, 119. The authors identify various strategies suitable for each habit and level of intervention. See also Gmelch and Miskin, *Department Chair*, 155–162.

has to do with training them to participate in the administration of their institutions – in other words, preparing leaders to run the institution and provide the direction the institution needs, which is not an easy task due to the complexity of higher education leadership and its multidimensional nature. According to Coll and Weiss, it requires "an exploration through a systemic lens. A perspective that takes into account the intersection of relationships with regard to family, research, students, local communities, athletics, alumni, parents, media, public officials, faculty and global interests."[55]

Strategies for developing faculty to undertake leadership positions at all levels in institutions of Christian higher education and theological schools include committee assignments, short-term training programs, mentoring, coaching, and other approaches that may be unique to the institution's situation and context. However, they also depend on the level to which the emerging leaders are being developed. In some cases, the leaders have already been serving in another administrative position before moving into their current position, but not every institution has a conventional pattern for preparing its academic leaders. For example, Thomas F. George argues that "There is no unique pathway to becoming a president or chancellor. While the most common pathway entails progressing through the academic faculty and administrative ranks, successful presidents and chancellors have come from outside academe, such as from the corporate world, government, and private foundations."[56]

Likewise, Contreras, in a study to fulfill the doctoral requirements for her PhD, investigated the career paths for academic deans in institutions pertaining to the Church of God in Latin America and the Caribbean. She found that in most cases the path was incidental to the position. The results of her study showed that the deans "did not follow a structured path toward their position, that they were recruited or invited to come into the role and that this invitation was seen as an honor and a challenge."[57] The study revealed, too, that

---

55. Coll and Weiss, "Rethinking Leadership Development."

56. Thomas F. George, "Maintaining a Personal Program of Research and Scholarship While Serving as President/Chancellor," in Sternberg et al., *Academic Leadership in Higher Education*, 23.

57. Jenniffer Contreras, "A Phenomenological Study of the Preparation and Career Paths of Academic Deans in Church of God Institutions of Theological Education in Latin America and the Caribbean" (PhD diss., Biola University, 2016), 210–211.

the majority of schools that participated in the study were not intentional in preparing their academic deans for the position. Most deans had as their entry point serving as adjunct faculty, and some of them had served in some type of administrative responsibilities that had got them familiar with the running of their institutions, but it seemed that none of them were intentional in making their careers toward the deanship.[58] Among some of the experiences mentioned by the participants were study abroad, which opened up opportunities to serve in some capacity in the institutions where they were pursuing their degrees. They also mentioned other experiences in higher education that helped them to thrive in their current position, including "teaching assistant, editor of a publishing house, department head, registrar, director of assessment and quality assurance, director of ministry development, student mentor, board member, faculty and public relations director. . . . Three of the participants had founded seminaries."[59] Although these experiences were within the Latin American context, when it comes to pathways to academic leadership one can identify similar experiences in other contexts in the Majority World.

Here I discuss some strategies, which have been found effective in intentional academic leadership training.

Committee Assignments

Involving faculty to serve on different committees is an effective strategy to help them discover and develop leadership skills. Deans and department chairs constantly ask faculty members to take on administrative responsibilities as part of their participation and collaboration in the institution, such as participating on different committees, developing new centers, and developing new programs. Faculty members need to be aware that opportunities to serve on committees start at the departmental level, where they can demonstrate whether they are capable to handle interpersonal relationships appropriately and complete their administrative assignments. On the other hand, department chairs who are committed to the development of academic leaders from among their faculty need to keep in mind that faculty members who are successful in their leadership assignments are more likely to be considered for other

---

58. Contreras, "Phenomenological Study," 211–213.
59. Contreras, 218, 219.

leadership positions. Buller affirms this, saying, "Frequently it is the person who has already demonstrated success while leading one committee who is asked to take on another major assignment, or the person elected president of the faculty senate who is invited to chair the next major administrative search committee."[60] Buller provides some suggestions of specific actions that faculty members should consider as ways to prepare for the next leadership role:

- Volunteer for assignments that are likely to be complex, even contentious . . . chairing grievance hearings, reviews of academic programs outside your area, broad curriculum reforms such as general education revisions, strategic planning bodies, and the like.
- Review suggestions on "The Faculty as a Fundraiser" and participate in at least one significant development activity.
- Run for election to the faculty senate (or the equivalent body at your institution) to gain an even broader range of leadership experience.
- Volunteer to serve as a member of committees for other colleges that require outside representations.[61]

It is important for faculty who aspire to academic leadership in their institutions to be willing to serve in leadership positions on committees and to take advantage of open opportunities in their institutions.

Training Programs

As was mentioned earlier, nowadays there is an array of programs and resources for training academic leaders, especially in North America. Some institutions provide internship and on-the-job opportunities as well as training programs for emerging leaders. Strom, Sanchez, and Downey-Schilling state that among the main methods and strategies used for internal leadership growth are (1) on-the-job training or internships, (2) leadership training programs, and (3) graduate school programs.[62] According to the authors, the first one is more self-directed, while the second one can be carried on within and outside the

---

60. Buller, *Essential College Professor*, 314.

61. Buller, 384–385.

62. Stephen L. Strom, Alex A. Sanchez, and JoAnna Downey-Schilling, "Inside–Outside: Finding Future Community College Leaders," *Community College Enterprise* 17, no. 1 (March 2011): 11, *Academic OneFile*, accessed 8 August 2018, http://link.galegroup.com/apps/doc/A260691278/AONE?u=biola_main&sid=AONE&xid=351853b0.

institution. The last one is offered by graduate schools located across the United States and requires a longer commitment.

The usefulness of internal programs run by the institutions is still under scrutiny. Therefore, institutions tend to rely on existing training programs organized and provided by organizations established for that purpose. For example, in the North American context where I currently serve, the American Council on Education (ACE) provides a training program that is considered by some as "the most effective and comprehensive leadership development program in higher education."[63] It focuses on the training of senior leadership through a Fellows Program, providing a "learning opportunity that results from placement for one academic year at another institution with mentors who are typically the president or chancellor, vice presidents, and other senior administrators."[64] The program "condenses years of on-the-job experience and skills development into a single semester or year, and combines that experience with structured seminars and interactive learning opportunities."[65] Participants in the program are able to observe "firsthand how the institution and its leaders address strategic planning, resource allocation, policy formulation, and other issues. The ACE Fellows Program enables participants to immerse themselves in the culture, policies, and decision-making processes of another institution."[66] The ACE also offers the Institute for new CAOs, which consist of a two-day workshop to Advance to the CAO, workshops for new CEOs, and programs to advance women in leadership. Among other professional organizations that provide training in academic administration are the American Association of Higher Education (AAHE), the American Association of Colleges and Universities (AACU), and the Council of Christian Colleges and Universities.

There are training programs outside the North American context, such as the Institute for Excellence in Christian Leadership Development, offered by Overseas Council (OC) for academic leaders from theological institutions that partner with OC in five different regions across the globe. Another program

---

63. PAID Program, "Developing Academic Leaders," 43, accessed 15 January 2018, http://paid. uci.edu/Developing%20Aca%20Leaders.pdf.

64. Elizabeth A. McDaniel, "Senior Leadership in Higher Education: An Outcomes Approach," *Journal of Leadership and Organization Studies* 9, no. 2 (2002): 80.

65. PAID Program, "Developing Academic Leaders," 43.

66. PAID Program, 44.

is IPAL (ICETE Program for Academic Leaders), which consists of a series of one-week seminars offered by ICETE (International Council for Evangelical Theological Education) through its regional accrediting associations to academic leaders of institutions within each association. Other organizations have developed ongoing training programs to support institutions of theological education by training and preparing their academic leaders.

Mentoring

Mentoring as a development strategy is not a new concept for us. For decades, business and industry have been using mentoring successfully in the development of established and emergent leaders. "Higher education administration is not different; mentorship either formal or informal can be leveraged to provide exposure to aspirant leaders."[67] Academic leaders in institutions of higher education also know the value of having formal and informal mentoring programs to assist students "in discovering and engaging with careers throughout their collegiate experience" and to benefit from "candid and practical advice, establishment of context, and the development of specific skills, often in a risk reduced environment."[68]

Two chapters in this volume discuss fundamental aspects of mentoring. Watters's chapter provides very valuable insights for institutions of Christian higher education regarding their responsibility and commitment to mentor students and to train those who are called to serve as mentors. Ferris, too, addresses the mentoring of faculty as an important component in their professional development as effective teachers. Both chapters will help readers to better understand foundational aspects of how mentoring works.

Mentoring has proved to be effective in the motivation and development of faculty to serve in leadership positions, as Strom, Sanchez, and Downey-Schilling express: "To provide motivation for internal institutional employees to assume administrative and leadership roles, formal mentoring by current administrators and leaders may provide the best encouragement."[69]

---

67. Jennifer P. Bott and Michele Wheatly, "Developing Mentors on the Path to Leadership: A Case Study and Conversation," in Sternberg et al., *Academic Leadership in Higher Education*, 71.

68. Bott and Wheatly, "Developing Mentors," 71.

69. Strom, Sanchez, and Downey-Schilling, "Inside–Outside," 12.

Mentoring has become "one of the most typical forms of development in the academy."[70] Yet not all institutions have established mentoring programs for emerging and new academic leaders or administrators. Thus, faculty new in their administrative positions would benefit by identifying senior leaders who would be willing to commit to a mentoring relationship, keeping in mind that "*Developing a mentoring relationship* is a fluid process, based on needs. Mentors can provide specific help at a singular time . . . or can be a relatively constant source of support, advice and perspective."[71] In this respect, Bott and Wheatly suggest, "*Asking those you respect to assist you with a problem can be a powerful way to begin a mentorship relationship.* Keep in mind, however, that mentoring relationships are additional work for both the mentor and mentee, and establishing expectations of commitment up front will generate greater satisfaction with the relationship over time."[72]

Another important aspect that mentors and protégés need to decide at the beginning of the mentoring relationship is timing. For how long do they want to commit to the mentoring relationship? What are the expectations on both sides? Always keep in mind that a mentoring relationship ". . . is built on mutual respect and requires compatibility between the two individuals involved."[73] Motivation is also critical in a mentoring relationship, since "a faculty mentor in a leadership position may be able to facilitate leadership skills in an appropriately motivated individual."[74] Mentoring is thus a valuable strategy that, if used appropriately, can contribute to the development of the skills of new academic administrators.

Personal Career Development Plans

Deans and department chairs who are intentional on developing emergent academic leaders need to consider including a personal leadership development plan that faculty could follow as part of their career development plan. It would

---

70. PAID Program, "Developing Academic Leaders," 36.

71. Bott and Wheatly, "Developing Mentors," 76.

72. Bott and Wheatly, 76.

73. Donald Jeanmonod, "Developing Leaders among Your Faculty Members," *International Journal of Academic Medicine* (serial online) 2, no. 1 (2016): 83–88, accessed 8 August 2018, http://www.ijam-web.org/text.asp?2016/2/1/83/183327.

74. Jeanmonod, "Developing Leaders," 83–88.

be self-paced, and each prospective academic leader would work on it, but it could be included as part of the annual faculty reviews so that the department chair can support faculty being intentional in pursuing academic leadership positions in the institution. According to Buller, "Seeking leadership positions can be an important part of a faculty member's career plan as well as a major part of one's role as a good academic citizen."[75] Faculty who hope to get involved in academic leadership in their institution or in another institution need to be intentional and plan strategically towards that and develop an integral plan on how they can move to the next leadership level. In this respect, Buller suggests that faculty members take some initial steps: "if you hope someday to be a university president, you may want to develop a strategy that enables you to serve first as a department chair, then as a dean, and then perhaps takes you in a new direction."[76]

Buller's recommendation brings to my mind the case of a colleague in a theological institution located in a Majority World country. At the time we talked, he was serving as the academic dean in his institution and he knew that the president was going to retire in the next few years. His aspiration was to succeed the president, and he was intentional on how to get to that position. Thus, part of his plan was to pursue a doctoral degree in order to qualify for the position. In this particular case, pursuing a doctoral program outside his context was a natural move to get the training he needed to qualify for the presidency in his institution. However, such is not the case for each aspirant to upper-level academic leadership positions, and an intentional development plan would serve the need of being trained.

Buller also advises faculty to examine their motivations in pursuing academic leadership, advising them to do so "only if you truly believe that you have the appropriate temperament for the leadership position you are seeking and would find that position an effective role in which to make a positive difference."[77]

---

75. Buller, *Essential College Professor*, 322.
76. Buller, 321.
77. Buller, 321.

Inclusion of Female Faculty in Academic Leadership

The inclusion of women in academic leadership has gained more acceptance in recent years, and we often see women serving in academic administration in institutions of higher education and in theological institutions as well. Nonetheless, women serving at upper levels of higher education administration, such as deans, provosts, or presidents, remain limited in many institutions, where women serving in such positions are underrepresented compared with men. Studies on the inclusion of women in leadership positions in their institutions reveal the challenges faced by women who aspire to these positions or who are already in an academic administration position. These challenges are either in the way they are treated by male colleagues or in how they feel about serving in those positions.[78] Yet women in academic leadership see these challenges as opportunities to grow and serve.

Women serving in educational institutions are characterized as being high performers and as making an impact on their institutions. Therefore, in a study conducted at her own institution, Augustana College in South Dakota, Hasseler argues, "Since leadership plays such a key role in shaping the mission and daily work of an institution, women and people of color must be engaged in leadership roles at all levels."[79] Based on the findings of her study, Hasseler proposes:

> 1. We need to be more deliberate about nominating, encouraging and appointing women to leadership positions in our institutions. In addition to reviewing hiring and promotion procedures and ensuring that women are in the pool of candidates for leadership positions, we need to look very carefully at the results of these efforts. For example, as I have examined the numbers at Augustana, I have noted that we have good representation

78. Susan S. Hasseler, "Women in Leadership: Obstacles, Opportunities, and Entry Points," *Intersections* 2015, no. 41, Article 8 (2015): 24–30, accessed 1 January 2018, http://digitalcommons.augustana.edu/intersections/vol2015/iss41/8. Also, Canan Bilen-Green, Karen A. Froelich, and Sarah W. Jacobson, "The Prevalence of Women in Academic Leadership Positions, and Potential Impact on Prevalence of Women in the Professorial Ranks," *WEPAN Conference Proceedings* (2008): 1–11, accessed 1 January 2018, https://www.ndsu.edu/fileadmin/forward/documents/WEPAN2.pdf.
79. Hasseler, "Women in Leadership," 26.

of women in the department chair role but not necessarily as council and committee chairs, which are very important roles in the academic division. This is something that needs appropriate review and strategic action.

2. We need to frequently and specifically affirm the leadership gifts of women. Women who have evidenced particular gifting in this area may need to be invited, encouraged, and even persuaded to take on leadership roles since they may not be nominated or nominate themselves. This encouragement needs to be deliberate and ongoing in order to create a climate of support for women in leadership.[80]

Institutions of higher education need to be intentional in promoting women to serve in academic leadership positions, training them and creating opportunities for women to get to positions that traditionally have been occupied by men. For example, during her years serving as provost and chief academic officer at University of West Virginia, Dr Michele Wheatly created a program called Women Leadership Initiatives (WLI), which focused on providing "programs on key issues (like negotiation) to emerging women leaders from across the institution, many of whom have no other women in their immediate work environment."[81] According to Bott and Wheatly, "this program has been successful in empowering women on campus to more confidently seek leadership positions."[82] Another example, yet in the North American context, is the HERS Summer Institutes for Women in Higher Education Administration, sponsored by the Office for Women at Purdue University, Indianapolis. It consists of "residential training opportunities which prepare participants to work with issues currently facing higher education. . . . The institute seeks to improve the status of women in the middle and executive levels of higher education administration."[83]

---

80. Hasseler, 29.

81. Bott and Wheatly, "Developing Mentors," 75.

82. Bott and Wheatly, 75.

83. Indiana University–Purdue University of Indianapolis: Office for Women, "HERS Summer Institutes for Women in Higher Education Administration," accessed 15 January 2018, https://ofw.iupui.edu/Leadership/HERSBryn-Mawr-Summer-Institute-Alumnae.

Women serving as academic leaders in institutions outside the North American context need to find out what is available in their own contexts. Nonetheless, in most cases, training programs such as institutes, seminars, and conferences are offered for both men and women indiscriminately; or at least that reflects my own experience, having served as a faculty member and as an associate dean and academic dean at Central American Theological Seminary in the Latin American context, before I moved to where I currently serve.

Areas of training may vary depending on geographical and institutional contexts. Though women approach their leadership experience differently from men, there are areas in which both men and women would benefit from some training. Training in communication skills, conflict resolution, vision setting, budgeting, assessment, accreditation, performance evaluation, strategic planning, shared governance, campus politics, faculty development, coaching, mentoring, faculty and student diversity, and technological advances in education, among other things, is needed in most institutions. Institutions can offer them through short institutes, training courses, seminars, workshops, and other means to train their own academic leaders.

It must be pointed out that the strategies suggested in this chapter are not the only ones. As academic leaders who serve globally, we need to consider what applies best to our own institutions and contexts.

Conclusion

In this chapter, I have highlighted some aspects that I hope will help academic leaders serving in institutions of Christian higher education and theological seminaries to develop their own academic leaders. As pointed out throughout the chapter, developing academic leaders to serve in higher education is of critical importance. It requires a clear understanding that academic leadership is a calling that requires commitment to the mission and vision of the institution. Seasoned academic leaders serving in higher education institutions need to commit to training those who are new in their positions as well as those aspiring to academic leadership.

Academic leaders need to keep in mind that building leadership capacity will aid in developing the specific skills needed for each leadership level in the institution. They also need to be aware of the challenges and the resources available in their own contexts to develop and support ongoing leadership training programs in their institutions.

Finally, I conclude with Gmelch and Miskin's words: "Development of leadership rests with the individual's own motivation and talent, and with the receptiveness of their organizations to supporting and coaching their skills. In part, leadership is passion, and you cannot teach people to be passionate."[84] Therefore, faculty moving into academic leadership positions need to have a clear understanding of their calling, commitment to the mission and vision of their institutions, and the desire to make a contribution to their academic institutions and higher education in general.

Reflection and Action Points

As we have seen in this chapter, many academic leaders move into leadership positions in their institutions without much or with no training at all in managerial skills and leadership competencies and perspectives for the position. Now that you have read this chapter, you will have the opportunity to propose a plan to develop your own academic leaders.

1. Identify a group of new and potential academic leaders. It may be people who are already serving in academic leadership positions in your institution, or potential leaders among your faculty in whom you would like to invest in order to train them for academic leadership positions.

2. Invite the group to a meeting to identify the areas of most need for training. Think about specific competencies needed for the different leadership levels in which they are serving.

3. Following the three essential domains suggested by Gmelch and Buller for developing academic leaders, think of a strategy that you would like to follow to help the group develop the three habits of academic leadership – habits of the mind (conceptual understanding); habits of practice (skills development); and habits of the heart (reflective practice) – that you want to include in your plan to train them.

---

84. Gmelch and Miskin, *Department Chair*, 22.

4. Now think of the levels of intervention and include specific actions for each one:

- *Personal*: What they should be able to do at the personal level to contribute to their development; for example, attend a leadership conference, personal assessments, or journaling.
- *Institutional*: What the institution will provide internally and externally to contribute to their development; for example, seminars, mentoring, or coaching.
- *Professional*: What professional organizations, networks, associations, consortia, etc., will provide for them to obtain the training needed.

5. Now think of the process you would like to follow, based on a matrix that integrates the three components of leadership (point 3 above) and the three levels of intervention (point 4 above), in order to establish an ongoing training plan.

6. Consider and integrate other components that are proper to your context.

7. Identify the resources that are available in your context, but remember that some of the strategies you propose may require training outside your institution and context.

8. Propose when and where you will begin to implement your plan.

9. Propose when and how you will assess the results.

10. Complete your plan and discuss it with the potential and new academic leaders to get their input, and implement it.

Resources for Further Study

Behling, Laura L., ed. *The Resource Handbook for Academic Deans.* 3rd edition. San Francisco: Jossey-Bass, 2014.

Billman, Kathleen D., and Bruce C. Birch, eds. *C(H)AOS Theory: Reflections of Chief Academic Officers in Theological Education.* Grand Rapids, MI: Eerdmans, 2011.

Buller, J. L. *Change Leadership in Higher Education: A Practical Guide to Academic Transformation.* San Francisco: Jossey-Bass, 2014.

————. *The Essential College Professor: A Practical Guide to an Academic Career*. San Francisco: John Wiley & Sons, 2010.

Chen, Sheying, ed. *Academic Administration: A Quest for Better Management and Leadership in Higher Education*. New York: Nova Science, 2009.

Davis, James R. *Learning to Read: A Handbook for Postsecondary Administrators*. Westport, CT: American Council on Education and Praeger Publishers, 2003.

Deininger, Fritz, and Orbelina Eguizabal, eds. *Leadership in Theological Education, Volume 1: Foundations for Academic Leadership*. Carlisle: Langham Global Library, 2017.

Finkelstein, Martin J., Valerie Martin Conley, and Jack H. Schuster. *The Faculty Factor: Reassessing the American Academy in a Turbulent Era*. Baltimore, MD: Johns Hopkins University Press, 2016.

Frame, William V. *The American College Presidency as Vocation: Easing the Burden, Enhancing the Joy*. Abilene, TX: Abilene Christian University Press, 2013.

Fullan, Michael, and Geoff Scott. *Turnaround Leadership for Higher Education*. San Francisco: Jossey-Bass, 2009.

Gmelch, W. H., and J. L. Buller. *Building Academic Leadership Capacity: A Guide to Best Practices*. San Francisco: Jossey-Bass, 2015.

Gmelch, Walter H., and Val D. Miskin. *Department Chair Leadership Skills*. 2nd edition. Madison, WI: Atwood, 2011.

Hendrickson, Robert M., Jason E. Lane, James T. Harris, and Richard H. Dorman. *Academic Leadership and Governance of Higher Education: A Guide for Trustees, Leaders, and Aspiring Leaders of Two- and Four-Year Institutions*. 3rd edition. Sterling, VA: Stylus, 2013.

Henkel, Mary. "Emerging Concepts of Academic Leadership and Their Implications for Intra-Institutional Roles and Relationships in Higher Education." *European Journal of Education* 37, no. 1 (2002): 29–41.

Huber, Stephan Gerhard. "School Development and School Leader Development: New Learning Opportunities for School Leaders and Their Schools." In *International Handbook of the Preparation and Development of School Leaders*, edited by Jacky Lumby, Gary Crow, and Petros Pashiardis, 163–175. New York: Routledge, 2008.

Ruben, Brent D., Richard De Lisi, and Ralph A. Gigliotti. *A Guide for Leaders in Higher Education: Core Concepts, Competencies, and Tools*. Sterling, VA: Stylus, 2017.

Sternberg, Robert J., Elizabeth Davis, April C. Mason, Robert V. Smith, Jeffrey S. Vitter, and Michele Wheatly, eds. *Academic Leadership in Higher Education: From the Top Down and the Bottom Up*. Lanham, MD: Rowman & Littlefield, 2015.

Van Velsor, Ellen, Cynthia D. McCauley, and Marian N. Ruderman, eds. *The Center for Creative Leadership Handbook of Leadership Development*. 3rd edition. San Francisco: Jossey-Bass, 2010.

Wright, Michael, and James Arthur, eds. *Leadership in Christian Higher Education*. Exeter: Imprint Academic, 2010.

Bibliography

Adams, David. "Putting Heart and Soul into Research: An Inquiry into Becoming 'Scholar-Practitioner-Saint.'" *Transformation* 25, no. 2 and 3 (April/July 2008): 144–157.

Aleshire, Daniel O. *Earthen Vessels: Hopeful Reflections on the Work of Theological Schools*. Grand Rapids, MI: Eerdmans, 2008.

Aleshire, Daniel, Cynthia Campbell, and Kevin Mannoia. "The President's Vocation and Leadership." In *A Handbook for Seminary Presidents*, edited by G. D. Lewis and Lovett H. Weems Jr., 1–17. Grand Rapids, MI: Eerdmans, 2006.

Amirtham, Samuel, and Robin Pryor. *Invitation to the Feast of Life: Resources for Spiritual Formation in Theological Education*. Geneva: World Council of Churches, 1989.

Armitage, Andy, ed. *Teaching and Training in Post-Compulsory Education*. Maidenhead: McGraw-Hill, 2003.

Arthur, James. "Great Expectations: Vision and Leadership in Christian Higher Education." In *Leadership in Christian Higher Education*, edited by Michael Wright and James Arthur, 3–32. Exeter: Imprint Academic, 2010.

Atnip, Gilbert W. "Role of the Chief Academic Officer." In *Academic Administration: A Quest for Better Management and Leadership in Higher Education*, edited by Sheying Chen, 39–52. New York: Nova Science, 2009.

Austin, Ann E., and Mary Deane Sorcinelli. "The Future of Faculty Development: Where Are We Going?" *New Directions for Teaching and Learning* 133 (Spring 2013): 85–97.

Baldwin, C., and A. Linnea. *The Circle Way: A Leader in Every Chair*. San Francisco: Berrett-Koehler, 2010.

Banks, Robert J. *Reenvisioning Theological Education: Exploring a Missional Alternative to Current Models*. Grand Rapids, MI: Eerdmans, 1999.

Barden, Dennis M., and Janel Curry. "Faculty Members Can Lead, but Will They?" *The Chronicle of Higher Education* (8 April 2013): 1. Accessed 16 August 2017. http://www.chronicle.com/article/Faculty-Members-Can-Lead-but/138343.

Barfoot, Scott, and David Fletcher, eds. *Crisis Leadership*. Austin: XPastor, 2014.

Battle, Michael. "Teaching and Learning as Ceaseless Prayer." In Jones and Paulsell, *The Scope of Our Art*, 155–170.

Bergquist, William, and Kenneth Pawlak. *Engaging the Six Cultures of the Academy.* San Francisco: Jossey-Bass, 2008.

Berryman-Fink, C. "Can We Agree to Disagree? Faculty–Faculty Conflict." In Holton, *Mending the Cracks,* 141–163. A synopsis prepared by Sharon Pearson, FDR Graduate Assistant, is at http://ombudsfac.unm.edu/Article_Summaries/Can_We_Agree_to_Disagree.pdf. Accessed 7 August 2017.

Bilen-Green, Canan, Karen A. Froelich, and Sarah W. Jacobson. "The Prevalence of Women in Academic Leadership Positions, and Potential Impact on Prevalence of Women in the Professorial Ranks." *WEPAN Conference Proceedings* (2008): 1–11. Accessed 1 January 2018. https://www.ndsu.edu/fileadmin/forward/documents/WEPAN2.pdf.

Billman, Kathleen D., and Bruce C. Birch, eds. *C(H)AOS Theory: Reflections of Chief Academic Officers in Theological Education.* Grand Rapids, MI: Eerdmans, 2011.

Birnbaum, Robert. *How Colleges Work: The Cybernetics of Academic Organization and Leadership.* San Francisco: Jossey-Bass, 1988.

Black, Simon A. "Qualities of Effective Leadership in Higher Education." *Open Journal of Leadership* 4, no. 2 (June 2015): 54–66. Accessed 24 November 2017. http://dx.doi.org/10.4236/ojl.2015.42006. Published online in Scientific Research. http://www.scirp.org/journal/ojl.

Blumberg, Phyllis. *Developing Learner-Centered Teaching: A Practical Guide for Faculty.* San Francisco: Jossey-Bass, 2009.

Bohm, D., and L. Nichol. *On Dialogue.* New York: Routledge, 1996.

Bolman, Lee G., and Joan V. Gallos. *Reframing Academic Leadership.* San Francisco: John Wiley & Sons, 2011.

Bonhoeffer, Dietrich. *Life Together.* London: SCM, 1954.

Booker, Doug. *Triangles, Compasses and God.* Milwaukee, WI: Drambert, 2015.

Bowers, Paul, ed. *Evangelical Theological Education Today.* 1st edition. Exeter: Paternoster, 1982.

Bott, Jennifer P., and Michele Wheatly. "Developing Mentors on the Path to Leadership: A Case Study and Conversation." In Sternberg at al., *Academic Leadership in Higher Education,* 71–77.

Brandenburg, Sue. "Conducting Effective Faculty Meetings." EdD diss., Edgewood College, 2008.

Breen, Mike. *Building a Discipling Culture.* 2nd edition. Pawleys Island, SC: 3DM, 2011.

Bright, David F., and Mary P. Richards. *The Academic Deanship: Individual Careers and Institutional Roles.* 1st edition. Jossey-Bass Higher and Adult Education series. San Francisco: Jossey-Bass, 2001.

Brookfield, Stephen D. *Becoming a Critically Reflective Teacher.* San Francisco: Jossey-Bass, 1995.

———. *The Skillful Teacher: On Technique, Trust, and Responsiveness in the Classroom.* 3rd edition. San Francisco: Jossey-Bass, 2015.

Brown, Colin, ed. *The New International Dictionary of New Testament Theology.* Vol. 3. Grand Rapids, MI: Zondervan, 1986.

Brown, J., and G. Gerard. *The World Cafe: Shaping Our Futures through Conversations That Matter.* San Francisco: Berrett-Koehler, 2005.

Bryan, Linda W. "The Vocational Call and Multiple Occupations of a CAO." In Billman and Birch, *C(H)AOS Theory,* 75–85.

Buller, Jeffrey L. *The Essential Academic Dean: A Practical Guide to College Leadership.* 1st edition. San Francisco: Jossey-Bass, 2007.

———. *The Essential College Professor: A Practical Guide to an Academic Career.* San Francisco: John Wiley & Sons, 2010.

Calian, Carnegie S. *The Ideal Seminary: Pursuing Excellence in Theological Education.* Louisville, KY: Westminster John Knox, 2002.

Calvin, John. *The Institutes of the Christian Religion.* Edited by John Murray from the 1845 translation by Henry Beveridge. Mitchellville, MD: Fig, 2012.

Cannell, Linda. *Theological Education Matters: Leadership Education for the Church.* Charleston, SC: Booksurge, 2008.

Cariaga-Lo, L., P. W. Dawkins, R. Enger, A. Schotter, and C. Spence. "Supporting the Development of the Professoriate." *Peer Review* 12, no. 3 (Summer 2010): 19–22.

Carroll, Jackson. "The Professional Model of Ministry: Is It Worth Saving?" *Theological Education* 21, no. 2 (Spring 1985): 7–48.

Cedja, B. D., W. B. Bush Jr, and K. L. Rewey. "Profiling the Chief Academic Officers of Christian Colleges and Universities: A Comparative Study." *Christian Higher Education* 1, no. 1 (2002): 3–15.

Cheesman, Graham. "Competing Paradigms in Theological Education Today." *Evangelical Review of Theology* 17, no. 4 (1993): 484–495.

———. "The Lead Climber." *Teaching Theology* (blog). 30 September 2012. Accessed July 2015. http://teachingtheology.org/2012/09/30/the-lead-climber/.

———. "So What Are They Really Thinking?" *The Theological Educator* 5, no. 2 (Feb. 2013). Accessed July 2015. http://thetheologicaleducator.net/2013/02/08/so-what-are-they-really-thinking/.

———. "Spiritual Formation as a Goal of Theological Education." TheologicalEducation. net. Last modified 2011. Accessed July 2015. http://www.theologicaleducation. net/articles/view.htm?id=106.

————. "A True Professional?" *Journal of Theological Education and Mission* 1, no. 1 (Feb. 2010): 57–64.

Chen, Sheying, ed. *Academic Administration: A Quest for Better Management and Leadership in Higher Education.* New York: Nova Science, 2009.

Clinton, Robert J. "Faculty Profile." Unpublished lecture notes. Faculty retreat, Columbia Bible College and Seminary, 23 August 1993.

Coe, John H., and Todd W. Hall, eds. *Psychology in the Spirit: Contours of a Transformational Psychology.* Downers Grove, IL: IVP Academic, 2010.

Colemann, Robert. *The Master Plan of Evangelism.* Foreword by Billy Graham. Grand Rapids, MI: Revell, 2006.

Coll, Jose, and Eugenia L. Weiss. "Rethinking Leadership Development in Higher Education." The EvoLLLution. 7 January 2016. Accessed 17 August 2017. https://evolllution.com/managing-institution/operations_efficiency/rethinking-leadership-development-in-higher-education/.

Contreras, Jenniffer. "A Phenomenological Study of the Preparation and Career Paths of Academic Deans in Church of God Institutions of Theological Education in Latin America and the Caribbean." PhD diss., Biola University, 2016.

Cooley, R. E., and D. L. Tiede. "What Is the Character of Administration and Governance in the Good Theological School?" *Theological Education* 30, no. 2 (1994): 61–69.

Cook, Bryan J. "The American College President Study: Key Findings and Takeaways." *American Council on Education* (Spring Supplement 2012). Accessed 28 November 2017. http://www.acenet.edu/the-presidency/columns-and-features/Pages/The-American-College-President-Study.aspx.

Cranton, Patricia. *Understanding and Promoting Transformative Learning: A Guide for Educators of Adults.* 2nd edition. San Francisco: Jossey-Bass, 2006.

Davis, Barbara Gross. *Tools for Teaching.* 2nd edition. San Francisco: Jossey-Bass, 2009.

Davis, James R. *Learning to Read: A Handbook for Postsecondary Administrators.* Westport, CT: American Council on Education and Praeger Publishers, 2003.

Deininger, Fritz. "President and Dean as Partners in Theological Education." In *Leadership in Theological Education, Volume 1: Foundations for Academic Leadership*, edited by Fritz Deininger and Orbelina Eguizabal, 107–128. Carlisle: Langham Global Library, 2017.

"*Didaskalos.*" In Brown, *New International Dictionary of New Testament Theology*, 765–768.

Douglass, J. D. "Faculty Development: A Shared Responsibility." *Theological Education* (Autumn 1991): 36–42.

Dowling, Elizabeth M., and W. George Scarlett, eds. *Encyclopedia of Religious and Spiritual Development*. Thousand Oaks, CA: Sage, 2005.

Drucker, Peter F. "Managing for Business Effectiveness." *Harvard Business Review* (May 1963). Accessed 4 October 2015. https://hbr.org/1963/05/managing-for-business-effectiveness/ar/1.

EAB. "Developing Academic Leaders: Executive Summary." Accessed 20 August 2017. https://www.eab.com/research-and-insights/academic-affairs-forum/studies/2011/developing-academic-leaders.

Eckel, P. D., B. J. Cook, and J. E. King. *The CAO Census: A National Profile of Chief Academic Officers*. Washington DC: American Council on Education, 2009.

Edgar, Brian. "The Theology of Theological Education." *Evangelical Review of Theology* 29, no. 3 (2005): 208–217.

Edwards, Tilden H., Jr. "Spiritual Formation in Theological Schools: Ferment and Challenge." *Theological Education* 17, no. 1 (1980): 7–52.

Eims, LeRoy. *The Lost Art of Disciple Making*. Foreword by Robert E. Colemen. Grand Rapids, MI: Zondervan, 1978.

Ellinor, L., and G. Gerard. *Dialogue: Rediscover the Transforming Power of Conversation*. Kindle edition. New York: Crossroad, 2014.

Ellis, Donna E., and Leslie Ortquist-Ahrens. "Practical Suggestions for Programs and Activities." In Gillespie et al., *Guide to Faculty Development*, 117–132.

Elmer, Duane. *Cross-Cultural Servanthood: Serving the World in Christlike Humility*. Downers Grove, IL: InterVarsity Press, 2006.

English, R. A. "The Deanship as a Cross-Cultural Experience." *New Directions for Higher Education* 25, no. 2 (1997): 21–29.

Erb, Peter C., ed. *Pietists: Selected Writings*. Classics of Western Spirituality. New York: Paulist, 2003.

Fagin, C. M. "The Leadership Role of a Dean." *New Directions for Higher Education* 25, no. 2 (1997): 95–99.

Farley, Edward. *Theologia: The Fragmentation and Unity of Theological Education*. Philadelphia: Fortress, 1983.

Ferris, Robert W. *Establishing Ministry Training: A Manual for Programme Developers*. Pasadena, CA: William Carey Library, 1995.

———. "The Faculty Is the Curriculum: A Vignette." Unpublished manuscript, n.d.

———. "Leadership Development in Mission Settings." In *Missiology: An Introduction*, edited by Mark J. Terry, 457–470. Nashville: Broadman & Holman, 2015.

———. "Ministry Education for the Global Church." *Evangelical Missions Quarterly* 52, no. 1 (Jan. 2016): 6–13.

———. "Renewal of Theological Education: Commitments, Models and the ICAA Manifesto." *Evangelical Review of Theology* 14, no. 1 (Jan. 1990): 64–75.

———. "The Work of a Dean." *Evangelical Review of Theology* 32, no. 1 (2008): 65–73.

Fink, L. Dee. *Creating Significant Learning Experiences: An Integrated Approach to Designing College Courses*. San Francisco: Jossey-Bass, 2003.

Fullan, Michael, and Geoff Scott. *Turnaround Leadership for Higher Education*. San Francisco: Jossey-Bass, 2009.

Gallaty, Robby. *Growing Up: How to Be a Disciple Who Makes Disciples*. Bloomington, IN: CrossBooks, 2013.

———. "Willow Creek Repents?" *Christianity Today* (Oct. 2007). Accessed 29 March 2013. http://blog.christianitytoday.com/outofur/archives /2007/10/willow_creek_re.htm.

George, Thomas F. "Maintaining a Personal Program of Research and Scholarship While Serving as President/Chancellor." In Sternberg et al, *Academic Leadership in Higher Education*, 23–29.

Giesen, Karen, and Sandra Glahn. "The Life of Howard G. 'Prof' Hendricks." *DTS Voice*. Dallas Theological Seminary. 20 February 2013. Accessed 26 June 2015. https://voice.dts.edu/article/howard-hendricks-prof/.

Gillespie, Kay J., Douglas L. Robertson, and Associates, eds. *A Guide to Faculty Development: Practical Advice, Examples, and Resources*. 2nd edition. Jossey-Bass Higher and Adult Education series. San Francisco: Jossey-Bass, 2010.

Gmelch, W. H., and J. L. Buller. *Building Academic Leadership Capacity: A Guide to Best Practices*. San Francisco: Jossey-Bass, 2015.

Gmelch, W. H., D. Hopkins, and S. Damico. *Seasons of a Dean's Life: Understanding the Role and Building Leadership Capacity*. Sterling, VA: Stylus, 2011.

Gmelch, Walter H., and Val D. Miskin. *Department Chair: Leadership Skills*. 2nd edition. Madison, WI: Atwood, 2011.

Gmelch, W. H., and M. Wolverton. *An Investigation of Dean Leadership*. New Orleans: American Educational Research Association, 2002.

Gmelch, W. H., M. Wolverton, M. L. Wolverton, and J. C. Sarros. "The Academic Dean: An Imperiled Species Searching for Balance." *Research in Higher Education* 40, no. 6 (1999): 717–740.

Gnanakan, Ken, ed. *Biblical Theology in Asia*. Bangalore: Theological Book Trust, 1995.

Gnanakan, Ken, and Sunand Sumithra. "Theology, Theologization and the Theologian." In Gnanakan, *Biblical Theology in Asia*, 39–46.

Graham, Stephan R. "The Vocation of the Academic Dean." In Billman and Birch, *C(H)AOS Theory*, 63–85.

Guenther, Margaret. *Holy Listening: The Art of Spiritual Direction*. London: Darton, Longman & Todd, 1992.

Harari, Oren. *The Leadership Secrets of Colin Powell*. New York: McGraw-Hill, 2003.

Hardy, Steven A. *Excellence in Theological Education: Effective Training for Church Leaders*. Peradeniya, Sri Lanka/Edenvale, South Africa: The Publishing Unit, Lanka Bible College and Seminary; Distributed by SIM, 2007.

Harkness, Allan, ed. *Tending the Seedbeds: Educational Perspectives on Theological Education in Asia*. Quezon City: Asia Theological Association, 2010.

Hartley III, H. V., and E. E. Godin. *A Study of Chief Academic Officers of Independent Colleges and Universities*. Washington DC: Council of Independent Colleges, 2010.

Hasseler, Susan S. "Women in Leadership: Obstacles, Opportunities, and Entry Points." *Intersections* 2015, no. 41, Article 8 (2015): 24–30. Accessed 1 January 2018. http://digitalcommons.augustana.edu/intersections/vol2015/iss41/8.

Henkel, Mary. "Emerging Concepts of Academic Leadership and Their Implications for Intra-Institutional Roles and Relationships in Higher Education." *European Journal of Education* 37, no. 1 (2002): 29–41.

Hitchen, John M. "Confirming the Christian Scholar and Theological Educator's Identity through New Testament Metaphor." *Evangelical Review of Theology* 35, no. 2 (2011): 276–287.

Hodges, Herb. *Tally Ho the Fox! The Foundation for Building World-Visionary, World-Impacting, Reproducing Disciples*. 2nd edition. Augusta, GA: Manhattan Source, 2001.

Hoffman, Elizabeth. "What Have We Learned about Academic Leadership?" In Sternberg et al., *Academic Leadership in Higher Education*, 3–12.

Hofstede, Geert, Gert J. Hofstede, and Michael Minkov. *Cultures and Organizations: Software of the Mind; Intercultural Cooperation and Its Importance for Survival*. 3rd revised edition. New York: McGraw-Hill Education, 2010.

Holton, Susan A., ed. *Mending the Cracks in the Ivory Tower: Strategies for Conflict Management in Higher Education*. Bolton, MA: Anker, 1998.

Horne, Herman. *Jesus the Teacher: Examining His Expertise in Education*. Revised and updated by Angus M. Gunn. Grand Rapids, MI: Kregel, 1998.

Horowitz, Maryanne C., ed. *New Dictionary of the History of Ideas*. Vol. 3. Detroit, MI: Charles Scribner's Sons, 2005.

Hough, J. C. "The Dean's Responsibility for Faculty Research." *Theological Education* (Autumn 1987): 102–114.

House, Paul R. *Bonhoeffer's Seminary Vision: A Case for Costly Discipleship and Life Together*. Wheaton, IL: Crossway, 2015.

Hudnut-Beumler, J. "A New Dean Meets a New Day in Theological Education." *Theological Education* 33 (supplement, 1996): 13–20.

Hull, Bill. *The Complete Book of Discipleship: On Being and Making Followers of Christ.* Navigators Reference Library. Colorado Springs, CO: NavPress, 2006.

Huston, Therese, and Carol L. Weaver. "Peer Coaching: Professional Development for Experienced Faculty." *Innovation in Higher Education* 33, no. 1 (June 2008): 5–6.

Hutchens, D. *Shadows of the Neanderthal: Illuminating the Beliefs That Limit Our Organizations.* Waltham, MA: Pegasus Communications, 1999.

ICETE. "Manifesto on the Renewal of Evangelical Theological Education." *Evangelical Review of Theology* 19, no. 3 (1995): 307–313.

Indiana University–Purdue University of Indianapolis: Office for Women. "HERS Summer Institutes for Women in Higher Education Administration." Accessed 15 January 2018. https://ofw.iupui.edu/Leadership/HERSBryn-Mawr-Summer-Institute-Alumnae.

International Graduate School of Leadership. "Core Values." Accessed 6 July 2015. http://www.igsl.asia/about/core-values/.

———. "Mission & Vision." Accessed 6 July 2015. http://www.igsl.asia/about/mission-vision-values/.

Irwin, Tim. *Impact: Great Leadership Changes Everything.* Dallas: BenBella, 2014.

Isaacs, W. *Dialogue and the Art of Thinking Together: A Pioneering Approach to Communicating in Business and Life.* New York: Currency, 1999.

Jeanmonod, Donald. "Developing Leaders among Your Faculty Members." *International Journal of Academic Medicine* (serial online) 2, no. 1 (2016): 83–88. Accessed 8 August 2018. http://www.ijam-web.org/text.asp?2016/2/1/83/183327.

Johnson, Eric, and Stan Jones. *Psychology and Christianity: Four Views.* Downers Grove, IL: IVP Academic, 2000.

Johnson-Miller, Beverly C. "History of Christian Education." In *Encyclopedia of Religious and Spiritual Development,* edited by Elizabeth M. Dowling and W. George Scarlett. Thousand Oaks, CA: Sage, 2005. Accessed 15 September 2009. http://sage-reference.com/religion/Article_n77.html.

Jones, L. Gregory. "Negotiating the Tensions of Vocation." In Jones and Paulsell, *Scope of Our Art,* 209–224.

Jones, L. G., and Stephanie Paulsell, eds. *The Scope of Our Art: The Vocation of the Theological Teacher.* Grand Rapids, MI: Eerdmans, 2002.

Jones, Stan. *Modern Psychotherapies: A Comprehensive Christian Appraisal.* 2nd edition. Downers Grove, IL: IVP Academic, 2011.

Kane, Thomas, Kerri Kerr, and Robert Pianta. *Designing Teacher Evaluation Systems.* San Francisco: Jossey-Bass, 2014.

Kelsey, David. *Between Athens and Berlin: The Theological Education Debate.* Grand Rapids, MI: Eerdmans, 1993.

———. *To Understand God Truly: What's Theological about a Theological School?* Louisville, KY: Westminster/John Knox, 1992.

Kempis, Thomas à. *The Imitation of Christ.* Harmondsworth: Penguin, 1952.

Kezer, Adriana, and Peter D. Eckel. "The Effect of Institutional Culture on Change Strategies in Higher Education." *The Journal of Higher Education* 73, no. 4 (July–Aug. 2002): 435–460.

Knowles, Malcolm. *The Modern Practice of Adult Education: From Pedagogy to Andragogy.* Revised and updated. Chicago: Follett, 1980. (Out of print, but used copies are available at reasonable cost.)

Kohl, Manfred W. "Theological Education: What Needs to Be Changed." *Torch Trinity Journal* 12, no. 1 (2009): 149–162.

Kohl, Manfred W., and A. N. L. Senanayake, eds. *Educating for Tomorrow: Theological Leadership for the Asian Context.* Bangalore: SAIACS; Indianapolis: Overseas Council International, 2002.

Krahenbuhl, G. S. *Building the Academic Deanship: Strategies for Success.* Westport, CT: American Council on Education/Praeger, 2004.

Lambert, Leo M. "Chief Academic Officers." In *Field Guide to Academic Leadership,* edited by Robert M. Diamond, 425–435. San Francisco: Jossey-Bass, 2002.

Le Cornu, A. "The Shape of Things to Come: Theological Education in the Twenty-First Century." *British Journal of Theological Education* 14, no. 1 (2003): 13–26.

Leman, Kevin, and William Pentak. *The Way of the Shepherd.* Grand Rapids, MI: Zondervan, 2004.

Lencioni, Patrick. *The Advantage: Why Organizational Health Trumps Everything Else in Business.* Kindle edition. San Francisco: Jossey-Bass, 2012.

———. *Death by Meeting: A Leadership Fable.* San Francisco: Jossey-Bass, 2007.

———. *The Five Dysfunctions of a Team: Facilitator's Guide; The Official Guide to Conducting the Five Dysfunctions Workshop.* San Francisco: Pfeiffer, 2007.

———. *The Five Dysfunctions of a Team: A Leadership Fable.* San Francisco: Jossey-Bass, 2002.

———. *Overcoming the Five Dysfunctions of a Team: A Field Guide for Leaders, Managers, and Facilitators.* San Francisco: Jossey-Bass, 2005.

Lindt, G. *Managers, Movers and Missionaries: Who Leads the Graduate School?* Minneapolis: Association of Graduate Schools, 1990.

Lienemann-Perrin, C. *Training for a Relevant Ministry: A Study of the Contribution of the Theological Education Fund.* Geneva: World Council of Churches, 1981.

Lingenfelter, Judith, and Sherwood G. Lingenfelter. *Teaching Cross-Culturally: An Incarnational Model for Learning and Teaching.* 2nd reprint. Grand Rapids, MI: Baker Academic, 2004.

London, H. B. *The Culture of a Community College.* New York: Praeger, 1978.

MacDonald, Gordon. "Going Deep: Cultivating People of Spiritual Depth Is a Pastor's Top Priority." *Christianity Today,* 27 June 2011. Accessed 9 July 2015. http://www.christianitytoday.com/le/2011/spring/goingdeep.html.

Mallard, Kina S. "The Soul of Scholarship." In Zahorski, *Scholarship in the Postmodern Era,* 67–68.

Manes, Juan M. *Gestión Estratrégica para Institutiones Educativas.* 2nd edition. Buenos Aires: Granica, 2004.

Marshall, Kim. *Rethinking Teacher Supervision and Evaluation.* 2nd edition. San Francisco: Jossey-Bass, 2013.

McCallum, Dennis, and Jessica Lowery. *Organic Discipleship: Mentoring Others into Spiritual Maturity and Leadership.* Revised edition. Columbus, OH: New Paradigm, 2012.

McDaniel, Elizabeth A. "Senior Leadership in Higher Education: An Outcomes Approach." *Journal of Leadership and Organization Studies* 9, no. 2 (2002): 80–88.

McLean, Jeanne P. *Leading from the Center: The Emerging Role of the Chief Academic Officer in Theological Schools.* Scholars Press Studies in Theological Education. Atlanta: Scholars Press, 1999.

McNeal, Reggie. *Practicing Greatness: 7 Disciplines of Extraordinary Spiritual Leaders.* San Francisco: Jossey-Bass, 2006.

Meeter, John E., ed. *Benjamin B. Warfield: Selected Shorter Writings.* Vol. 1. Grand Rapids, MI: Puritan & Reformed, 1970.

Moden, G. O., R. I. Miller, and A. M. Williford. *The Role, Scope, and Functions of the Chief Academic Officer.* Kansas City, MO: Association for Institutional Research, 1987.

Montez, J., and M. Wolverton. *The Challenge of the Deanship.* New Orleans: American Educational Research Association, 2000.

Moore, Russell. "What Should the Church Say to Bruce Jenner?" *Russell Moore* (blog), 24 April 2015. Accessed 2 October 2015. https://www.russellmoore.com/2015/04/24/what-should-the-church-say-to-bruce-jenner/.

Moore, Steve. *Who Is My Neighbor? Being a Good Samaritan in a Connected World.* Colorado Springs, CO: NavPress, 2011.

Moreland, J. C. "A Call to Integration and the Christian Worldview Integration Series." In Coe and Hall, *Psychology in the Spirit*, 11–32.

Muehlhoff, T. *I Beg to Differ: Navigating Difficult Conversations with Truth and Love.* Kindle edition. Downers Grove, IL: IVP Books, 2014.

Nederman, Cory J. "Individualism." In *New Dictionary of the History of Ideas*, Vol. 3, edited by Maryanne C. Horowitz, 1114. Detroit: Charles Scribner's Sons, 2005.

Newman, Barclay M. *A Concise Greek–English Dictionary of the New Testament.* London: United Bible Societies, 1971.

Niebuhr, H. Richard, Daniel Day Williams, and James M. Gustafson. *The Advancement of Theological Education.* New York: Harper, 1957.

Nolan, James. *Teacher Supervision and Evaluation.* 3rd edition. San Francisco: Jossey-Bass, 2011.

Nordbeck, E. C. "The Once and Future Dean: Reflections on Being a Chief Academic Officer." *Theological Education* 33 (supplement, 1996): 21–33.

Nouwen, Henri. *Reaching Out: The Three Movements of the Spiritual Life.* Glasgow: William Collins, 1976.

———. *The Way of the Heart.* New York: Ballentine, 1981.

Ouellett, Mathew L. "Overview of Faculty Development." In Gillespie et al., *Guide to Faculty Development*, 3–20.

Owen H. *Open Space Technology: A User's Guide.* San Francisco: Berrett-Koehler, 2008.

Oyco-Bunyi, Joy. *Beyond Accreditation: Value Commitments and Asian Seminaries.* Bangalore: Theological Book Trust, 2001.

Packer, J. I. *Knowing God.* Downers Grove, IL: InterVarsity Press, 1973.

PAID Program. "Developing Academic Leaders." Accessed 15 January 2018. http://paid.uci.edu/Developing%20Aca%20Leaders.pdf.

Palmer, Parker. *The Courage to Teach: Exploring the Inner Landscape of a Teacher's Life.* San Francisco: Jossey-Bass, 1998.

———. *To Know as We Are Known: Education as a Spiritual Journey.* New York: HarperCollins, 1993.

Patterson-Randles, Sandra R. "Chief Executive in Academic Administration: High Expectations and Leadership Lessons." In Chen, *Academic Administration*, 27–37.

Plueddemann, James E. *Leading across Cultures: Effective Ministry and Mission in the Global Church.* Downers Grove, IL: InterVarsity Press, 2009.

Posner, George J., and Alan H. Rudnitsky. *Course Design: A Guide to Curriculum Development for Teachers.* 6th edition. New York: Addison Wesley Longman, 2001.

Preiswerk, Matthias, et al. "Manifesto of Quality Theological Education in Latin America." *Ministerial Formation* 111 (Nov. 2008): 44–51.

Reason, R. D., and W. H. Gmelch. *The Importance of Relationships in Deans' Perceptions of Fit: A Person-Environment Examination.* Chicago: American Educational Research Association, 2003.

Roy, Marc M. "Preparing for a Successful Career in Academic Leadership: Understanding Your Role." In *The Resource Handbook for Academic Deans,* edited by Laura L. Behling, 3–7. 3rd edition. San Francisco: Jossey-Bass, 2014.

Sarkar, Arun K. "Non-Formal Faculty Development in Theological Seminaries: An Adult Educational Approach." In Harkness, *Tending the Seedbeds,* 129–143.

Schön, Donald A. *Educating the Reflective Practitioner.* San Francisco: Jossey-Bass, 1987.

Schuth, Katarina. *Reason for the Hope: The Futures of Catholic Theologates.* Wilmington, DE: Michael Glazier, 1989.

Seldin, P. *Evaluating Faculty Performance: A Practical Guide to Assessing Teaching, Research, and Service.* San Francisco: Jossey-Bass, 2006.

Senge, P. M. *The Fifth Discipline: The Art and Practice of the Learning Organization.* New York: Doubleday/Currency, 1990.

———. *The Fifth Discipline Fieldbook: Strategies and Tools for Building a Learning Organization.* New York: Doubleday/Currency, 1994.

Senge, Peter M., Nelda Cambron-McCabe, Timothy Lucas, Bryan Smith, Janis Dutton, and Art Kleiner. *Schools That Learn: A Fifth Discipline Fieldbook for Educators, Parents, and Everyone Who Cares about Education.* New York: Crown Business, 2012.

Sensing, T. R. "The Role of the Academic Dean." *Restoration Quarterly* 45, no. 1–2 (2003): 5–9.

Shaw, Perry. *Transforming Theological Education: A Practical Handbook for Integrative Learning.* Carlisle: Langham Global Library, 2014.

Shepson, Don. "A Scriptural Model of Relational Christian Formation." *Christian Education Journal* 9, Series 3 (Spring 2012 Supplement): 180–198.

Simpson, Michael K. *Unlocking Potential: 7 Coaching Skills That Transform Individuals, Teams, and Organizations.* Grand Haven, MI: Grand Harbor Press, 2014.

Smith, Gordon T. "Attending to the Collective Vocation." In Jones and Paulsell, *Scope of Our Art,* 240–261.

———. "Spiritual Formation in the Academy: A Unifying Model." *Theological Education* 33, no. 1 (1996): 83–91.

Smith, J. I. "Academic Leadership: Roles, Issues, and Challenges." *Theological Education* 33 (supplement, 1996): 1–12.

Sonlife. "What Is Disciple-Making?" Accessed 9 July 2015. http://www.sonlife.com/strategy/what-is-disciple-making/.

Sorcinelli, Mary Deane, Ann E. Austin, Pamela L. Eddy, and Andrea L. Beach. *Creating the Future of Faculty Development: Learning from the Past, Understanding the Present.* Boston, MA: Anker, 2006.

Spader, Dann. *4 Chair Discipling: Growing a Movement of Disciple-Makers.* Chicago, IL: Moody, 2014.

Spener, Philip J. *Pia Desideria: or Heartfelt Desires for a God-Pleasing Improvement of the True Protestant Church* (1675). In Erb, *Pietists*, 41–43.

Stanfield, R. B., ed. *The Art of Focused Conversation: 100 Ways to Access Group Wisdom in the Workplace.* Gabriola Island, BC: New Society, 2000.

Stanley, Andy. *The Next Generation Leader.* Sisters, OR: Multnomah, 2003.

Sternberg, Robert J., Elizabeth Davis, April C. Mason, Robert V. Smith, Jeffrey S. Vitter, and Michele Wheatly, eds. *Academic Leadership in Higher Education: From the Top Down and the Bottom Up.* Lanham, MD: Rowman & Littlefield, 2015.

Stoffer, Dale. "Faculty Leadership and Development: Lessons from the Anabaptist-Pietist Tradition." In Billman and Birch, *C(H)AOS Theory*, 143–153.

Stone, Tammy, and Mary Coussons-Read. *Leading from the Middle: A Case-Study Approach to Academic Leadership for Associate Deans.* Lanham, MD: Rowman & Littlefield, 2011.

Strom, Stephen L., Alex A. Sanchez, and JoAnna Downey-Schilling. "Inside-Outside: Finding Future Community College Leaders." *Community College Enterprise* 17, no. 1 (March 2011): 9–21. *Academic OneFile*, accessed 8 August 2018. http://link.galegroup.com/apps/doc/A260691278/AONE?u=biola_main&sid=AONE&xid=351853b0.

Stuhlman, Megan W., Bridget K. Hamre, Jason T. Downer, and Robert C. Pianta. "How Classroom Observations Can Support Systematic Improvement in Teacher Effectiveness." Accessed 3 April 2015. http://curry.virginia.edu/uploads/resourceLibrary/CASTL_practioner_Part5_single.pdf.

Sweet, Leonard. "A Learned to Learner Litany of Transformation." Accessed 2009. http://leaonardsweet.com/. No longer available at that location.

Swinton, John. *Dementia: Living in the Memories of God.* Grand Rapids, MI: Eerdmans, 2012.

Terry, Mark J., ed. *Missiology: An Introduction.* Nashville: Broadman & Holman, 2015.

Theall, Michael, and Jennifer L. Franklin. "Assessing Teaching Practices and Effectiveness for Formative Purposes." In Gillespie et al., *Guide to Faculty Development*, 151–168.

Thrall, Bill, Bruce McNicol, and John Lynch. *Truefaced: Trust God and Others with Who You Really Are.* Revised edition. Colorado Springs, CO: NavPress, 2004.

Thrall, Bill, Bruce McNicol, and Ken McElrath. *The Ascent of a Leader: How Ordinary Relationships Develop Extraordinary Character and Influence.* San Francisco: Jossey-Bass, 1999.

———. *Beyond Your Best: Develop Your Relationships, Fulfill Your Destiny.* San Francisco: Jossey-Bass, 2003.

Toulouse, M. G. "A Dozen Qualities of the Good Dean." *Theological Education* 42, no. 2 (2007): 109–126.

Townsend, B. K., and S. Bassoppo-Moyo. "The Effective Community College Academic Administrator: Necessary Competencies and Attitudes." *Community College Review* 25, no. 2 (1997): 41–57.

Tucker, Allan, and Robert A. Bryan. *The Academic Dean: Dove, Dragon, and Diplomat.* 2nd edition. New York: American Council on Education/Macmillan, 1991.

Vella, Jane. *How Do They Know They Know: Evaluating Adult Learning.* San Francisco: Jossey-Bass, 1998.

———. *Learning to Listen, Learning to Teach: The Power of Dialogue in Educating Adults.* Revised edition. San Francisco: Jossey-Bass, 2002.

———. *On Teaching and Learning: Putting the Principles and Practices of Dialogue Education into Action.* San Francisco: Jossey-Bass, 2008.

———. *Taking Learning to Task: Creative Strategies for Teaching Adults.* San Francisco: Jossey-Bass, 2001.

Viorst, Judith. *Necessary Losses: The Loves, Illusions, Dependencies and Impossible Expectations That All of Us Have to Give Up in Order to Grow.* New York: Random House, 1987.

Volf, Miroslav, Carmen Krieg, and Thomas Kucharz, eds. *The Future of Theology: Essays in Honor of Jürgen Moltmann.* Grand Rapids, MI: Eerdmans, 1996.

Waits, J. L. "Developing the Community of Scholars: An Address to New Academic Deans in ATS Schools." *Theological Education* 33 (supplement, 1996): 71–76.

Walvoord, Barbara E. *Teaching and Learning in College Introductory Religion Courses.* Oxford: Blackwell, 2007.

Wanak, Lee C. "Theological Education and the Role of Teachers in the Twenty-First Century: A Look at the Asia Pacific Region." In Kohl and Senanayake, *Educating for Tomorrow,* 160–180.

Warfield, Benjamin B. *The Religious Life of Theological Students.* Phillipsburg, NJ: Puritan & Reformed, 1983.

Warford, Malcolm L., ed. *Practical Wisdom: On Theological Teaching and Learning*. New York: Peter Lang, 2004.

Webb, Graham. *Understanding Staff Development*. Buckingham: Society for Research into Higher Education/Open University Press, 1996.

Webb, Keith. *The COACH Model for Christian Leaders: Powerful Leadership Skills for Solving Problems, Reaching Goals, and Developing Others*. [n.p.]: Active Results LLC, 2012.

Weimer, Maryellen. *Learner-Centered Teaching: Five Key Changes to Practice*. San Francisco: Jossey-Bass, 2002.

———. *Improving Your Classroom Teaching*. Vol. 1 of *Survival Skills for Scholars*. Newbury Park, CA: Sage, 1993.

Wilkinson, Bruce. *The Seven Laws of the Learner*. Textbook edition. Sisters, OR: Multnomah, 1992.

Wolterstorff, N. "The Travail of Theology in Modern Academy." In Volf et al., *The Future of Theology*, 35–46.

Wolverton, M., and W. H. Gmelch. *College Deans: Leading from Within*. Westport, CT: American Council on Education/Oryx, 2002.

Wolverton, M., W. H. Gmelch, J. Montez, and C. T. Nies. "The Changing Nature of the Academic Deanship." *ASHE-ERIC Higher Education Report* 28, no. 1 (2001): 95–108.

Wood, Rick. "A Discipleship Revolution: The Key to Discipling All Peoples." *Mission Frontiers* (Jan.–Feb. 2011). Accessed 15 June 2015. https://www.missionfrontiers.org/issue/article/a-discipleship-revolution.

Wright, Walter. *Relational Leadership: A Biblical Model for Influence and Service*. Exeter: Paternoster, 2000.

Yardley, Anne B. "Scaffolding That Supports Faculty Leadership: The Dean's Constructive Role." In Billman and Birch, *C(H)AOS Theory*, 133–143.

Yates, Wilson. "The Art and Politics of Deaning." *Theological Education* 34, no. 1 (1997): 85–96.

Zahorski, Kenneth J., ed. *Scholarship in the Postmodern Era: New Venues, New Values, New Visions*. San Francisco: Jossey-Bass, 2002.

Zeus, Perry, and Suzanne Skiffington. *The Complete Guide to Coaching at Work*. Roseville, Australia: McGraw-Hill Australia, 2001.

Ziegenhals, Gretchen E. "Faculty Life and Seminary Culture: It's about Time and Money." In Warford, *Practical Wisdom*, 49–66.

Ziegler, Jesse H. "Report of the Task Force on Spiritual Development." *Theological Education* 8, no. 3 (Spring 1972): 153–197.

Ziglar, Tom. "If You Aim at Nothing . . ." *Ziglar* (blog). Accessed 27 July 2015. http://www.ziglar.com/quotes/zig-ziglar/if-you-aim-nothing.

Zuck, Roy B. *Teaching as Jesus Taught.* Grand Rapids, MI: Baker, 1995.

———. *Teaching as Paul Taught.* Grand Rapids, MI: Baker, 1998.

Zull, James E. *The Art of Changing the Brain: Enriching the Practice of Teaching by Exploring the Biology of Learning.* Sterling, VA: Stylus, 2002.

The Contributors

 **Graham Cheesman** (PhD, Queen's University, Belfast) has been a Baptist minister in England, a missionary lecturer in Nigeria for seven years, and then the principal of Belfast Bible College, a constituent college of Queen's University, Belfast, for seventeen years. He was Director of the Centre for Theological Education in Belfast for the five years of its lifetime, and has been a staff member of the European Evangelical Accrediting Association. He is an honorary lecturer of Queen's University, Belfast, teaches in undergraduate and graduate programs, and supervises doctoral students. He is also involved in administering and tutoring postgraduate courses in theological education at London School of Theology. He has traveled widely to teach and promote good theological education and is the author of three books and a number of articles.

 **Leslie J. Crawford** (EdD, Columbia International University) has been serving as academic dean at Adelaide College of Ministries in Australia for over thirty years and is involved in theological education internationally through the International Council for Evangelical Theological Education (ICETE) as a representative of the South Pacific Association of Evangelical Colleges (SPAEC). He is married to Elizabeth and has three married children and one grandson.

 **Fritz Deininger** (ThD in New Testament, University of South Africa; ThM in New Testament Theology, MA in Missiology, Columbia International University; BA Theological Seminary, St Chrischona) serves as Coordinator of the ICETE Programme for Academic Leadership (IPAL). He served as an associate professor of Columbia International University (CIU) and taught some courses at the Academy for World Mission in Germany.

He and his wife, Marianne, served in Thailand from 1981 to 2008 in church planting, leadership training, and theological education. At Bangkok Bible Seminary Fritz gained leadership experience in theological education as academic dean. Areas of interest include leadership development, integrated theological education, spiritual formation, Bible exposition, world religions, world missions, and ethics.

Orbelina Eguizabal (PhD in Educational Studies, Talbot School of Theology) serves as professor of Christian Higher Education in the PhD and EdD programs in Educational Studies and coordinates the Hybrid-distance programs at Talbot School of Theology, Biola University in Southern California. She also serves as a visiting professor in seminaries in Latin American countries. Before joining Biola, Orbelina spent twenty years teaching and serving in administrative roles at Seminario Teológico Centroamericano (Central American Theological Seminary) in Guatemala City, Guatemala. She has been collaborating with ICETE since 2008, through the ICETE Programme for Academic Leaders (IPAL) and the Association of Evangelical Theological Education in LatinAmerica (AETAL), and as a teaching team member for the seminars for Spanish-speaking academic leaders, offered in Mexico, Central, and South America. Orbelina served on the board of the Society of Professors in Christian Education (SPCE) from 2010 to 2015, and has served on the board of trustees at Moody Global Ministries since 2016.

Ralph Enlow serves as president of the Association for Biblical Higher Education (www.abhe.org). Comprising nearly 200 member and affiliate institutions throughout North America, ABHE colleges engage students in ministerial and professional leadership education that is distinctively biblical, transformational, experiential, and missional. Dr Enlow served for twenty-eight years (1976–1998; 2000–2006) as an educational leader at his alma mater, Columbia International University, culminating in a six-year stint as senior vice president and provost. Dr Enlow's extensive involvement in theological higher education includes service as a consultant; institutional self-study director; accreditation team chair; and chair of ABHE's Commission on Accreditation. A founding member of Global Associates for Transformational Education (www.gateglobal.org), he has been involved in international teaching and consulting in Australia, Bulgaria, Czech Republic, Germany, Hungary, India, Lebanon, Philippines, Thailand, and Ukraine. He has served on and chaired the boards of Bible Christian Union; The Evangelical Alliance Mission (TEAM); and the International Council for Evangelical Theological Education (ICETE, www.icete-edu.org). His Vanderbilt University Higher Education Administration doctoral dissertation topic was "Student Outcomes in General Education: A Comparative Analysis of Bible College Quality." His scholarly publications and teaching interests include higher education accreditation, general education, leadership, biblical studies, and Bible college renewal.

Robert W. Ferris (MA, MDiv, PhD) and his wife, Sue, served for twenty-one years with SEND International in the Republic of the Philippines. There he taught theology on the faculty of Febias College of Bible (1969–1977), directed the Philippine Association of Bible and Theological Schools (PABATS, 1980–1985), and was dean of Asian Theological Seminary (1984–1988). Ferris contributed to the development of the ICETE Manifesto (1983) and was a plenary speaker at ICETE consultations in 1984, 1987, 1991, and 1993. As Missionary Scholar in Residence at the Billy Graham Center, Wheaton College, he authored *Renewal in Theological Education* (1990). In 1989, Ferris joined the faculty of Columbia Biblical Seminary and School of Missions, now Columbia International University, where he served as director of Doctoral Studies (1989–2000), interim dean (2002–2003), and associate provost (2004–2007). In retirement he is a Senior Associate with Global Associates for Transformational Education (GATE, www.gateglobal.org). The Ferrises have two children and five grandchildren.

Steve Hardy (DMiss, Trinity Evangelical Divinity School; MDiv in Biblical Studies from Bethel Theological Seminary; and BA in government from Oberlin College) is from the USA. He has served as SIM International's Advocate for Theological Education as well as a senior consultant to ICETE. He worked as a missionary educator in Brazil, Mozambique, and South Africa, and directed the Overseas Council's Institute for Excellence in Theological Education. His writings have focused on issues of educational administration.

Pablo Sywulka was born in Guatemala, where his parents served as missionaries. He did undergraduate studies at Columbia Bible College (BA, 1961) and the University of Guatemala (history, 1962–1963). He received his ThM (1967) and PhD (2001) from Dallas Theological Seminary. He has served at SETECA (Seminario Teológico Centroamericano) in Guatemala as professor, academic dean, and president. He served as General Secretary of the Asociación Evangélica de Educación Teológica en América Latina (AETAL) from 2007 to 2016.

Pieter F. Theron is a South African. After twenty-six years of intercultural ministry in Zambia, the Philippines and Mongolia, he served for one year as professor of Missiology at Simpson University, Redding, USA. Currently he is serving as the lead pastor of South Umpqua Community Church in Tiller, Oregon, USA. Pieter is married to Haniki and they have two daughters, Anri and Sonja. Pieter is a graduate of North-West University and the University of Pretoria. His doctoral dissertation was in missiology, developing a model for program development for training missionaries based on the educational philosophy of Paulo Freire. He also completed studies in cultural anthropology with the University of South Africa, and in educational management with the University of Bath, UK.

He has served in various educational leadership capacities: faculty member, dean of students, academic dean, president, and board member. He has been involved in various aspects, settings, levels, and formats of education: teaching, administration, accreditation, governance, program/curriculum development, strategic planning, organizational development, recruitment, international schooling, undergraduate, graduate and postgraduate, formal and non-formal education.

 **Ron Watters** (PhD, Trinity International University) is on the President's Team of the International Leadership Consortium (ILC), which is composed of affiliated educational institutions globally. For nearly four decades he has worked in Christian leadership development, mostly in Asia. Thirty of those years were with the International Graduate School of Leadership in the Philippines, where he served primarily as the Dean of Academic Affairs. Throughout his life, he has mentored believers with the goal of developing them into spiritual multipliers. He also works with organizations on the strategic alignment and development of their personnel and systems with their stated mission, vision, and core values.

ICETE  International Council for Evangelical Theological Education
strengthening evangelical theological education through international cooperation

ICETE is a global community, sponsored by nine regional networks of theological schools, to enable international interaction and collaboration among all those engaged in strengthening and developing evangelical theological education and Christian leadership development worldwide.

The purpose of ICETE is:

1. To promote the enhancement of evangelical theological education worldwide.
2. To serve as a forum for interaction, partnership and collaboration among those involved in evangelical theological education and leadership development, for mutual assistance, stimulation and enrichment.
3. To provide networking and support services for regional associations of evangelical theological schools worldwide.
4. To facilitate among these bodies the advancement of their services to evangelical theological education within their regions.

Sponsoring associations include:

Africa: Association for Christian Theological Education in Africa (ACTEA)

Asia: Asia Theological Association (ATA)

Caribbean: Caribbean Evangelical Theological Association (CETA)

Europe: European Evangelical Accrediting Association (EEAA)

Euro-Asia: Euro-Asian Accrediting Association (E-AAA)

Latin America: Association for Evangelical Theological Education in Latin America (AETAL)

Middle East and North Africa: Middle East Association for Theological Education (MEATE)

North America: Association for Biblical Higher Education (ABHE)

South Pacific: South Pacific Association of Evangelical Colleges (SPAEC)

www.icete-edu.org

 **Langham** PARTNERSHIP

Langham Literature, with its publishing work, is a ministry of Langham Partnership.

Langham Partnership is a global fellowship working in pursuit of the vision God entrusted to its founder John Stott –

> *to facilitate the growth of the church in maturity and Christ-likeness through raising the standards of biblical preaching and teaching.*

Our vision is to see churches in the majority world equipped for mission and growing to maturity in Christ through the ministry of pastors and leaders who believe, teach and live by the Word of God.

Our mission is to strengthen the ministry of the Word of God through:
- nurturing national movements for biblical preaching
- fostering the creation and distribution of evangelical literature
- enhancing evangelical theological education

especially in countries where churches are under-resourced.

Our ministry

Langham Preaching partners with national leaders to nurture indigenous biblical preaching movements for pastors and lay preachers all around the world. With the support of a team of trainers from many countries, a multi-level programme of seminars provides practical training, and is followed by a programme for training local facilitators. Local preachers' groups and national and regional networks ensure continuity and ongoing development, seeking to build vigorous movements committed to Bible exposition.

Langham Literature provides majority world preachers, scholars and seminary libraries with evangelical books and electronic resources through publishing and distribution, grants and discounts. The programme also fosters the creation of indigenous evangelical books in many languages, through writer's grants, strengthening local evangelical publishing houses, and investment in major regional literature projects, such as one volume Bible commentaries like the *Africa Bible Commentary* and the *South Asia Bible Commentary*.

Langham Scholars provides financial support for evangelical doctoral students from the majority world so that, when they return home, they may train pastors and other Christian leaders with sound, biblical and theological teaching. This programme equips those who equip others. Langham Scholars also works in partnership with majority world seminaries in strengthening evangelical theological education. A growing number of Langham Scholars study in high quality doctoral programmes in the majority world itself. As well as teaching the next generation of pastors, graduated Langham Scholars exercise significant influence through their writing and leadership.

To learn more about Langham Partnership and the work we do visit **langham.org**

Printed in April 2023
by Rotomail Italia S.p.A., Vignate (MI) - Italy